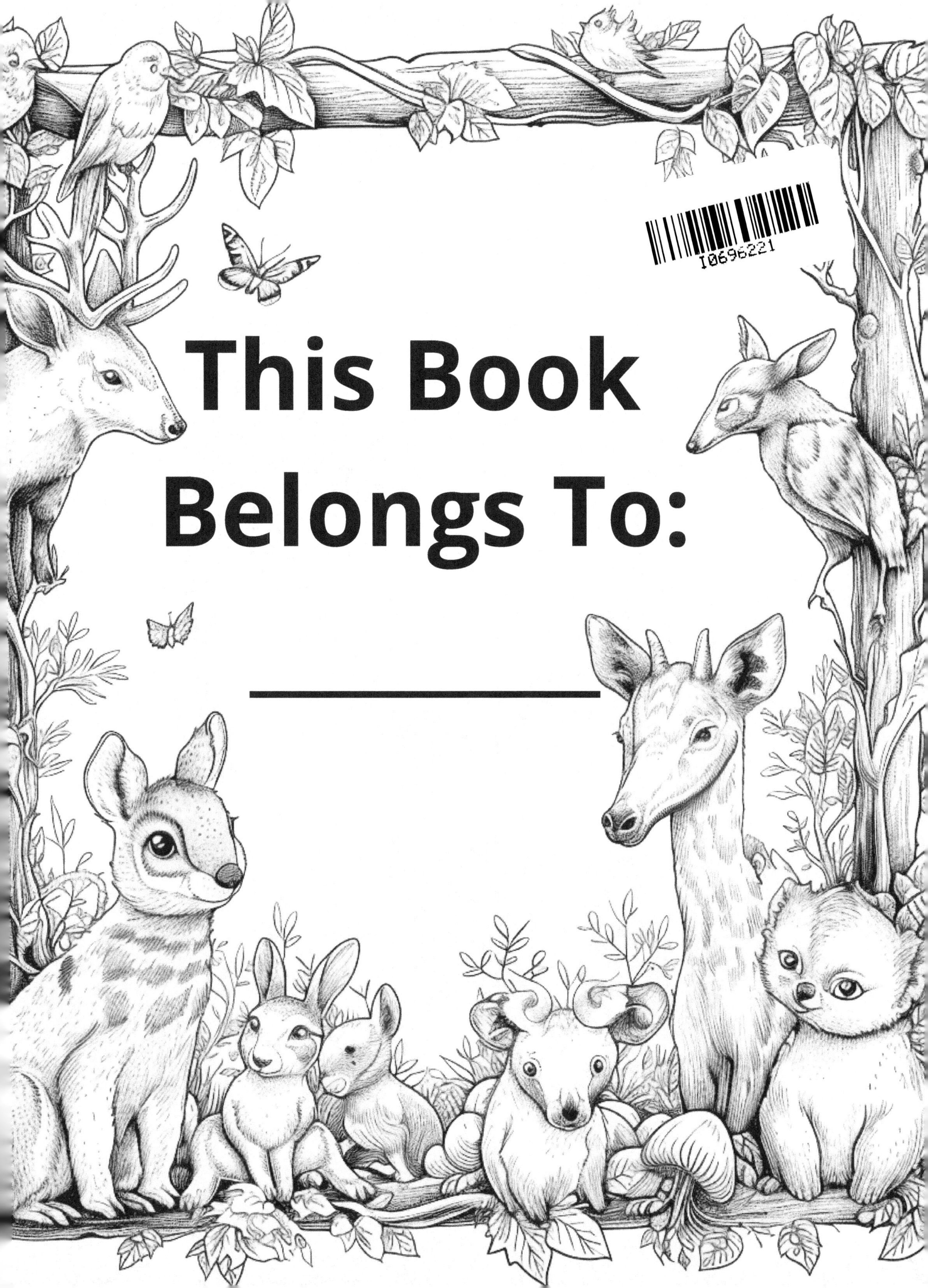
This Book
Belongs To:

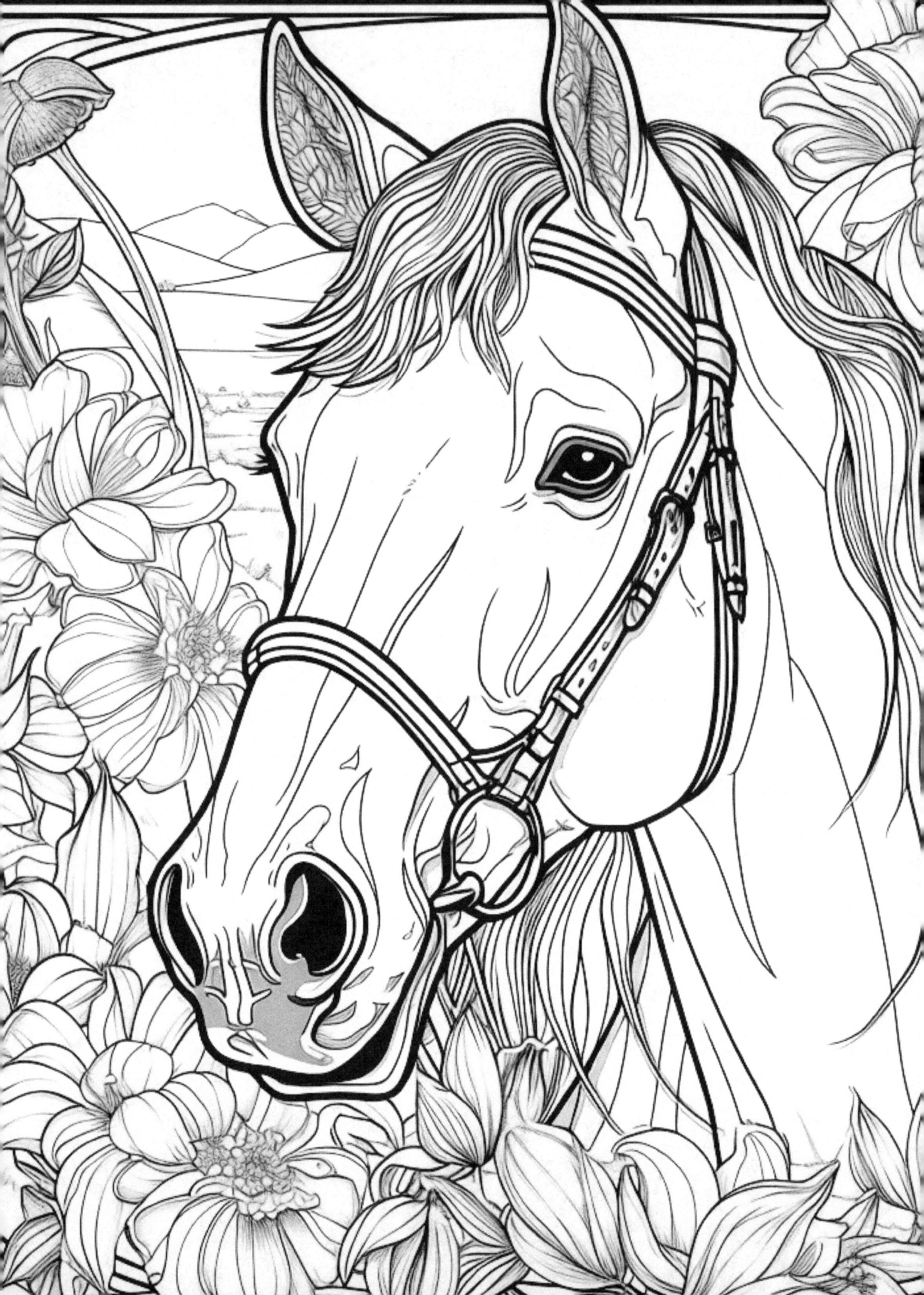

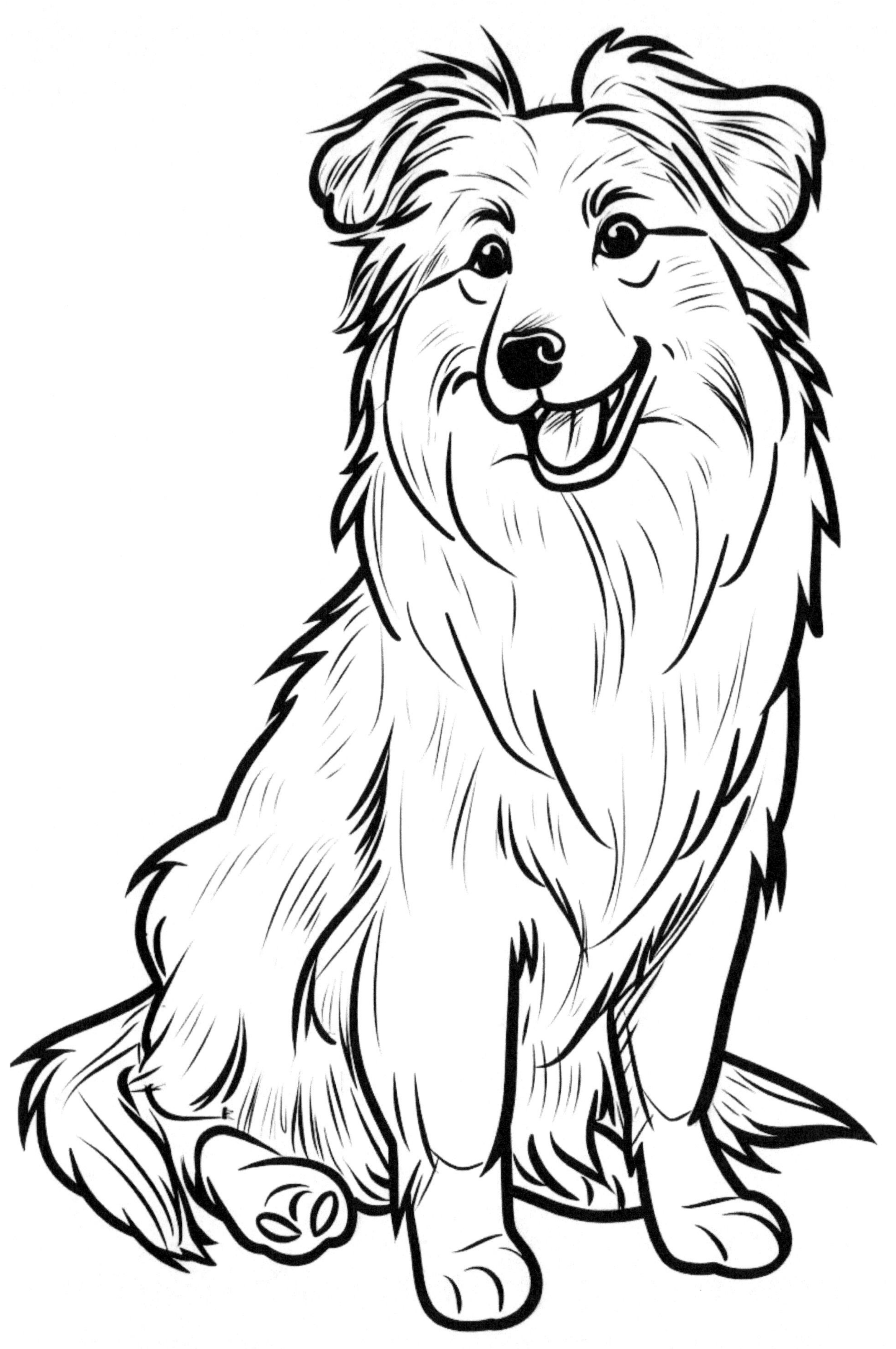

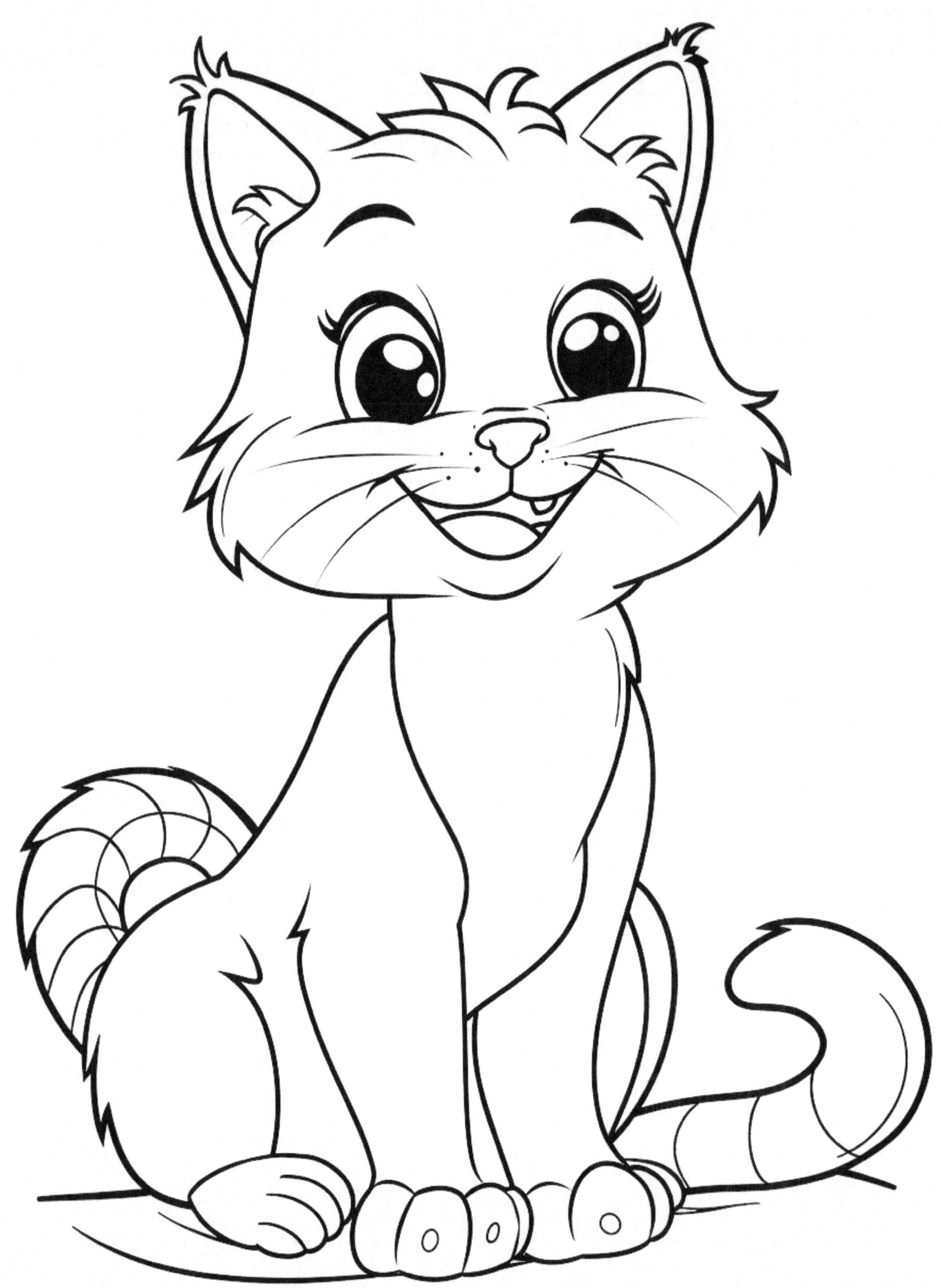

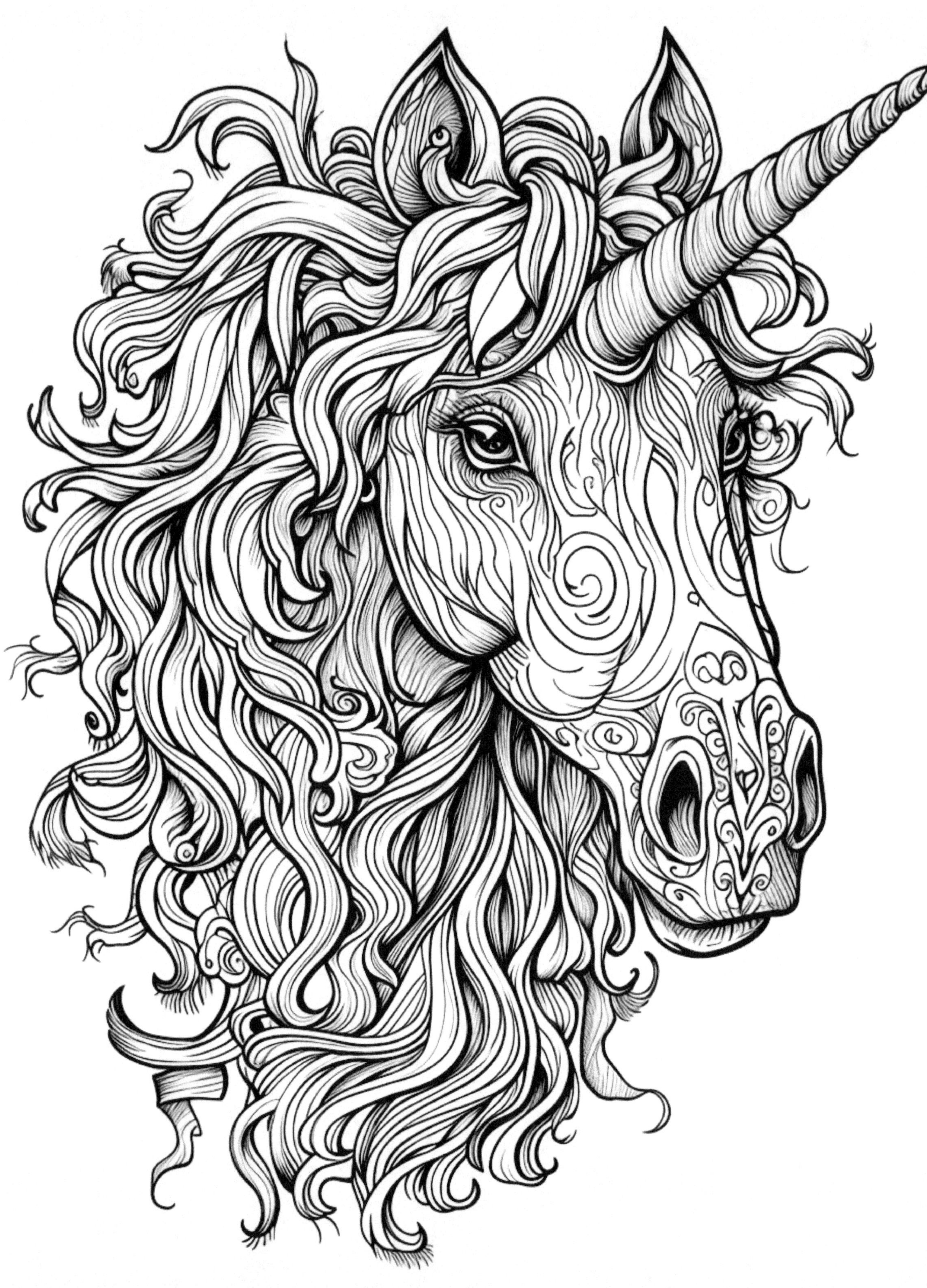

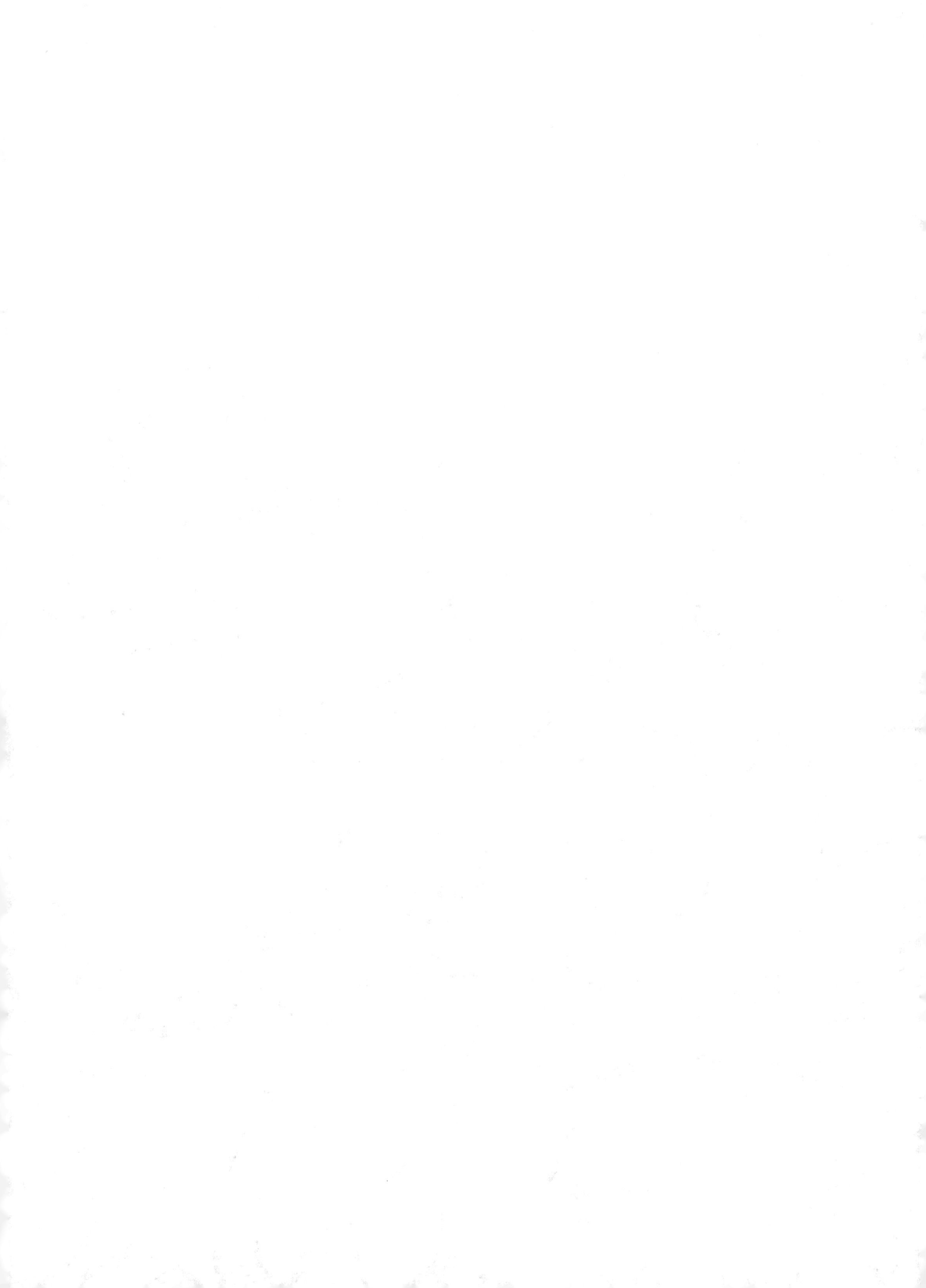

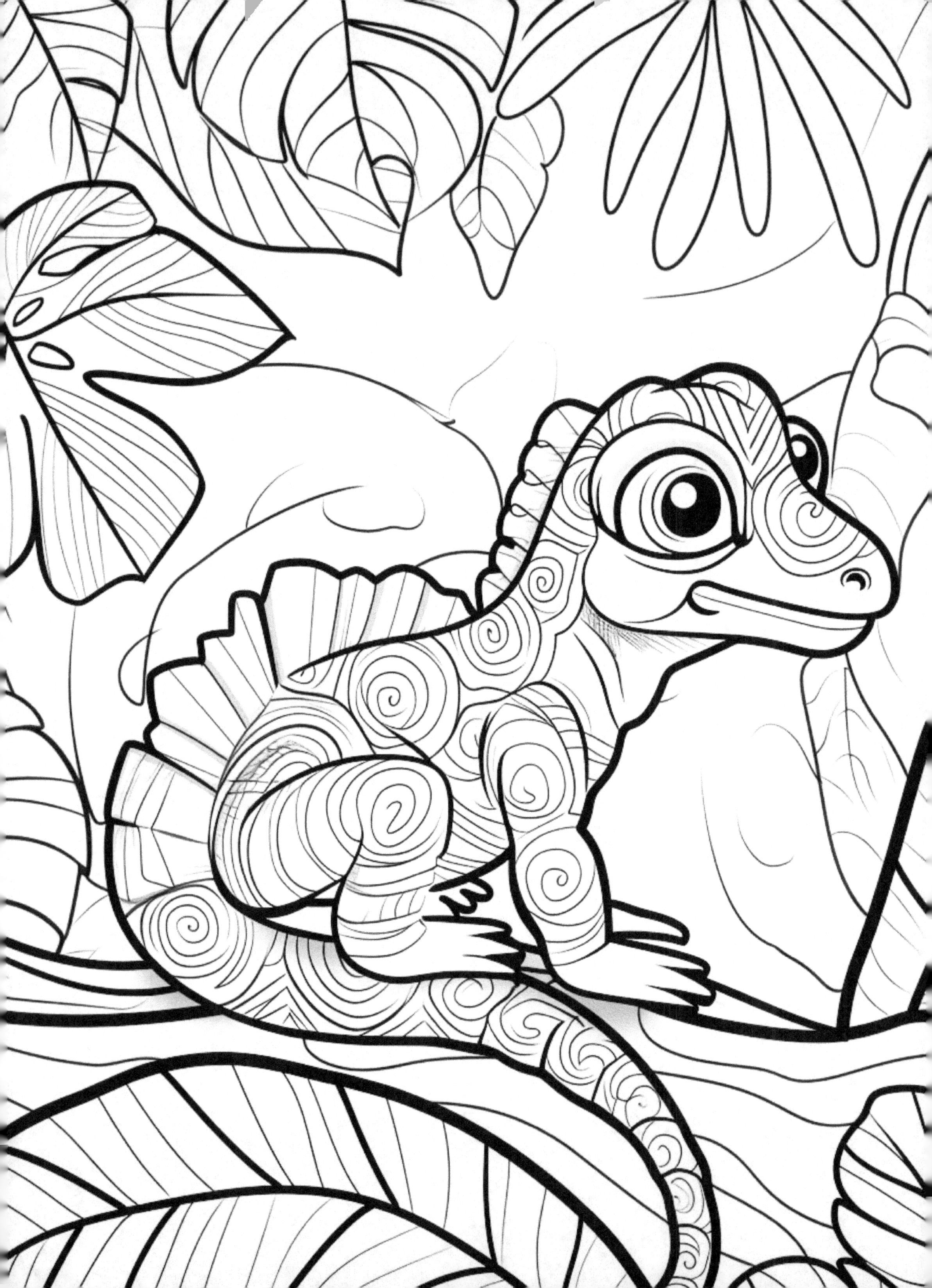

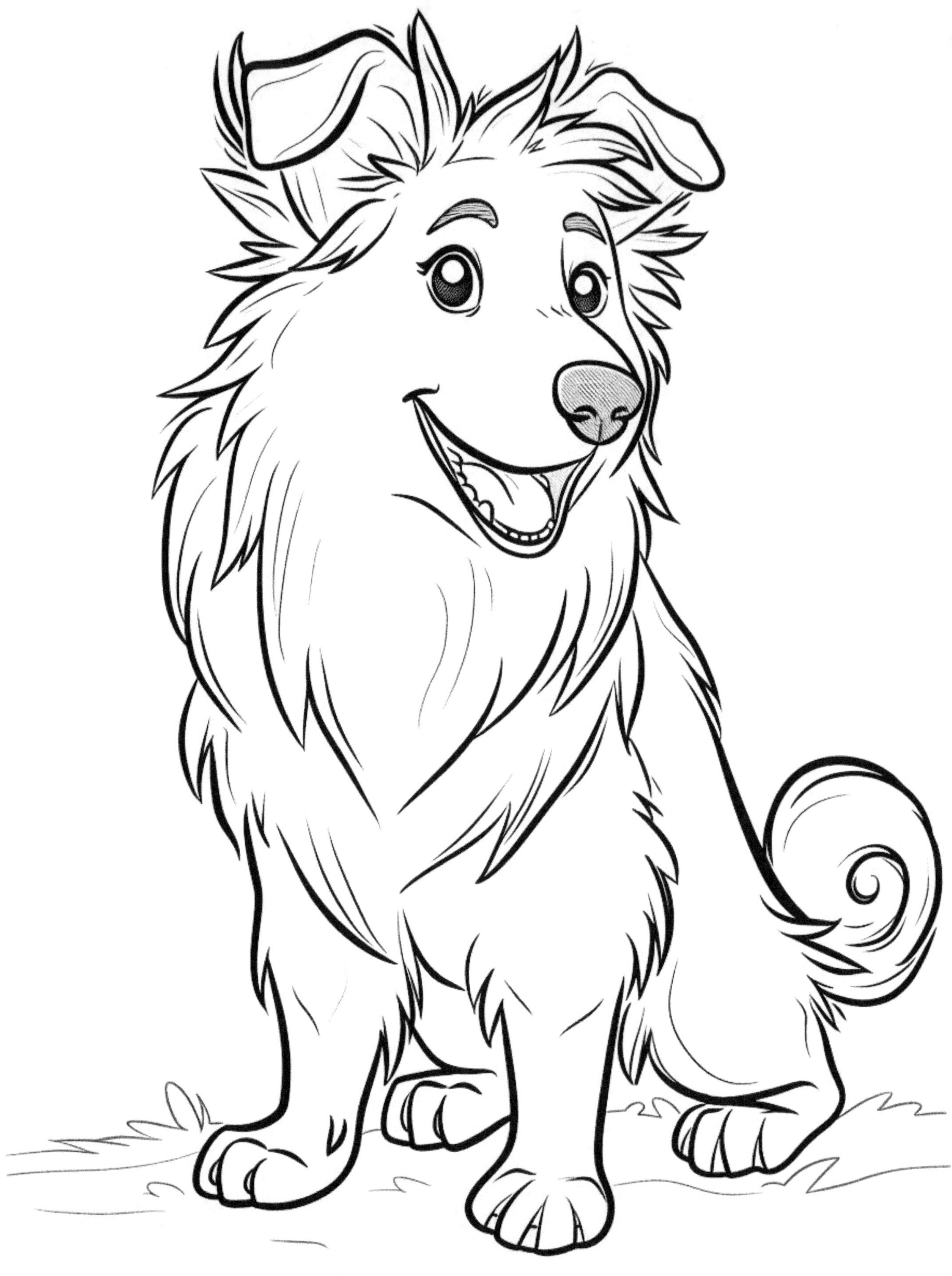

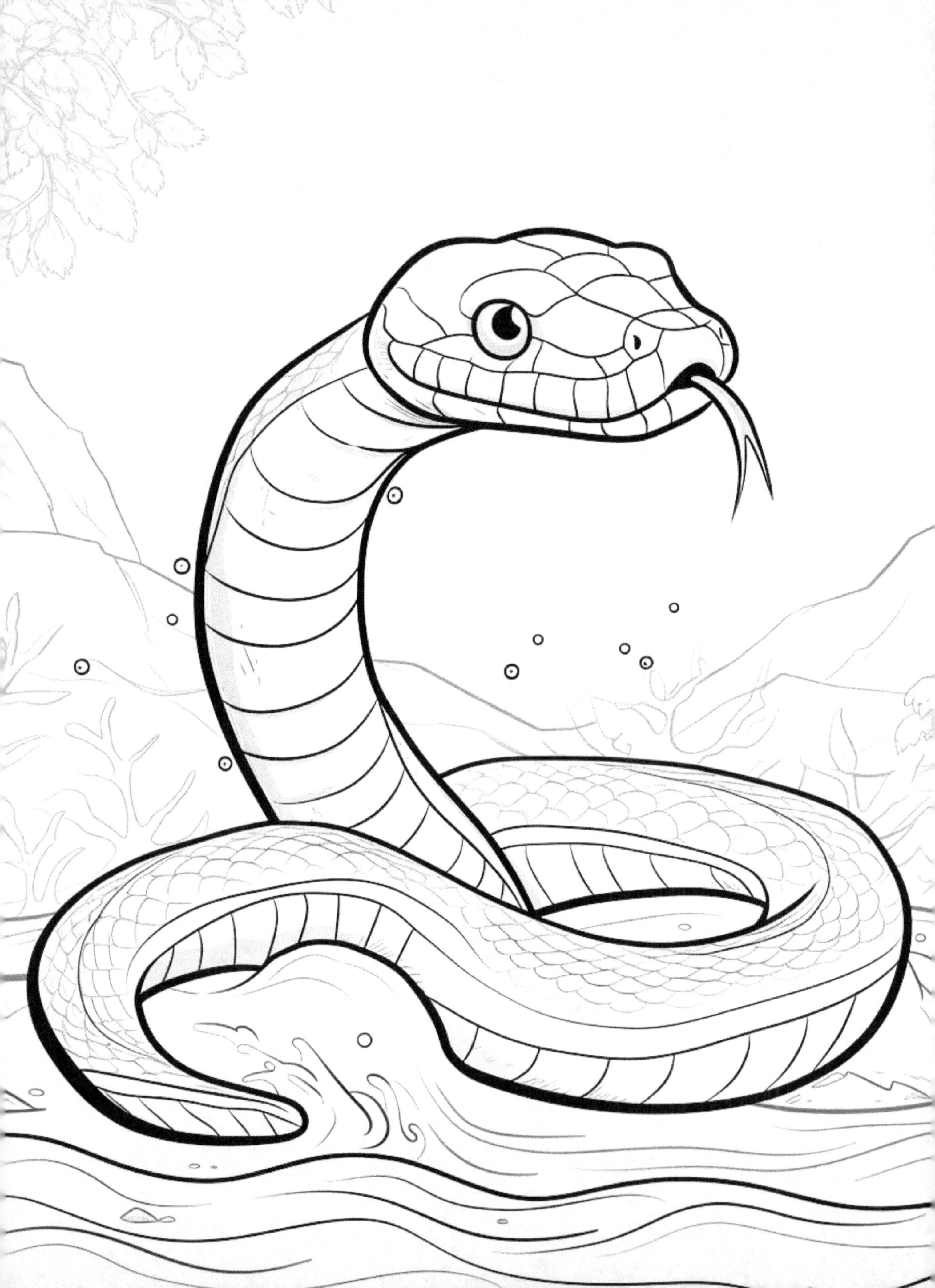

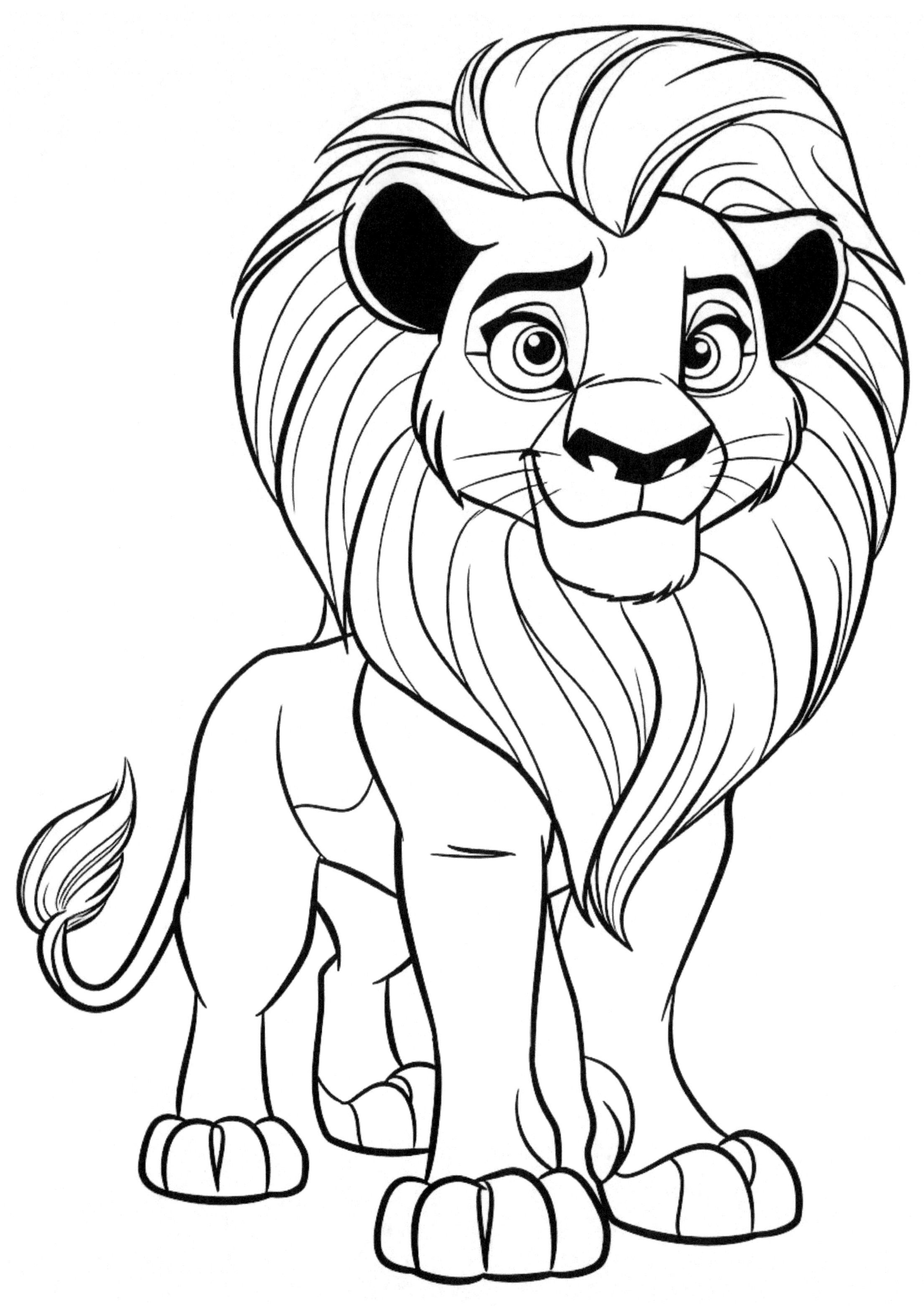

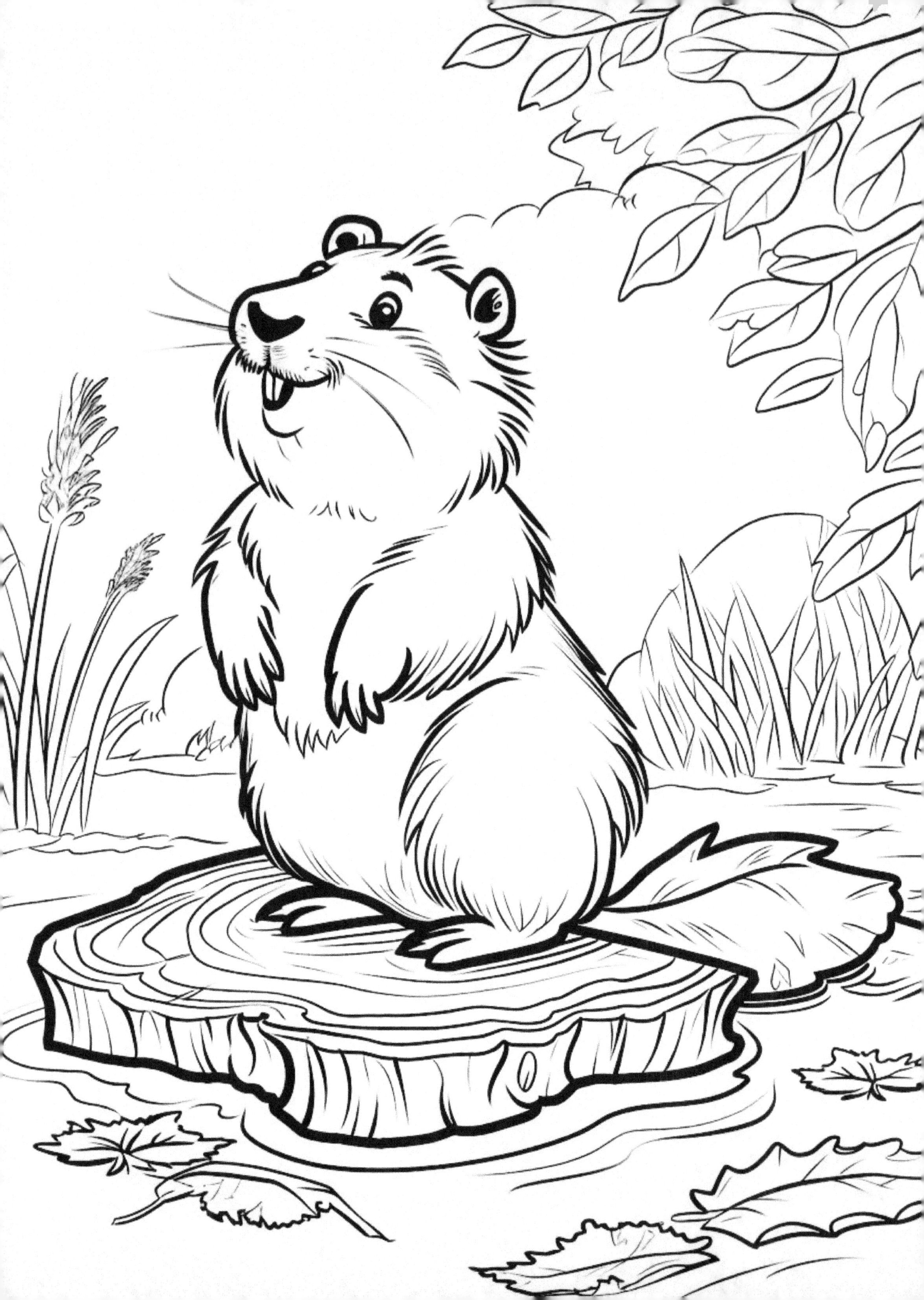

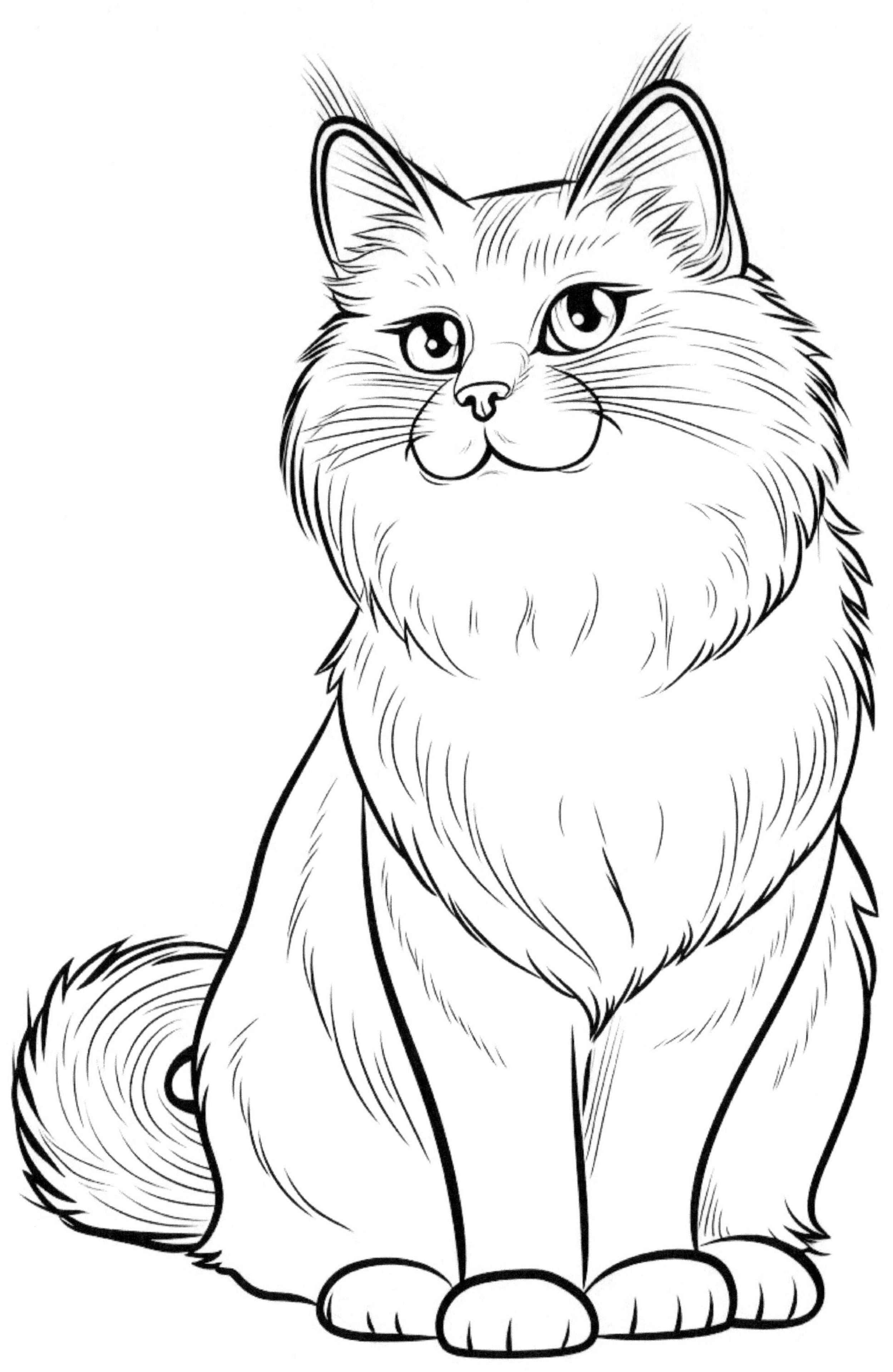

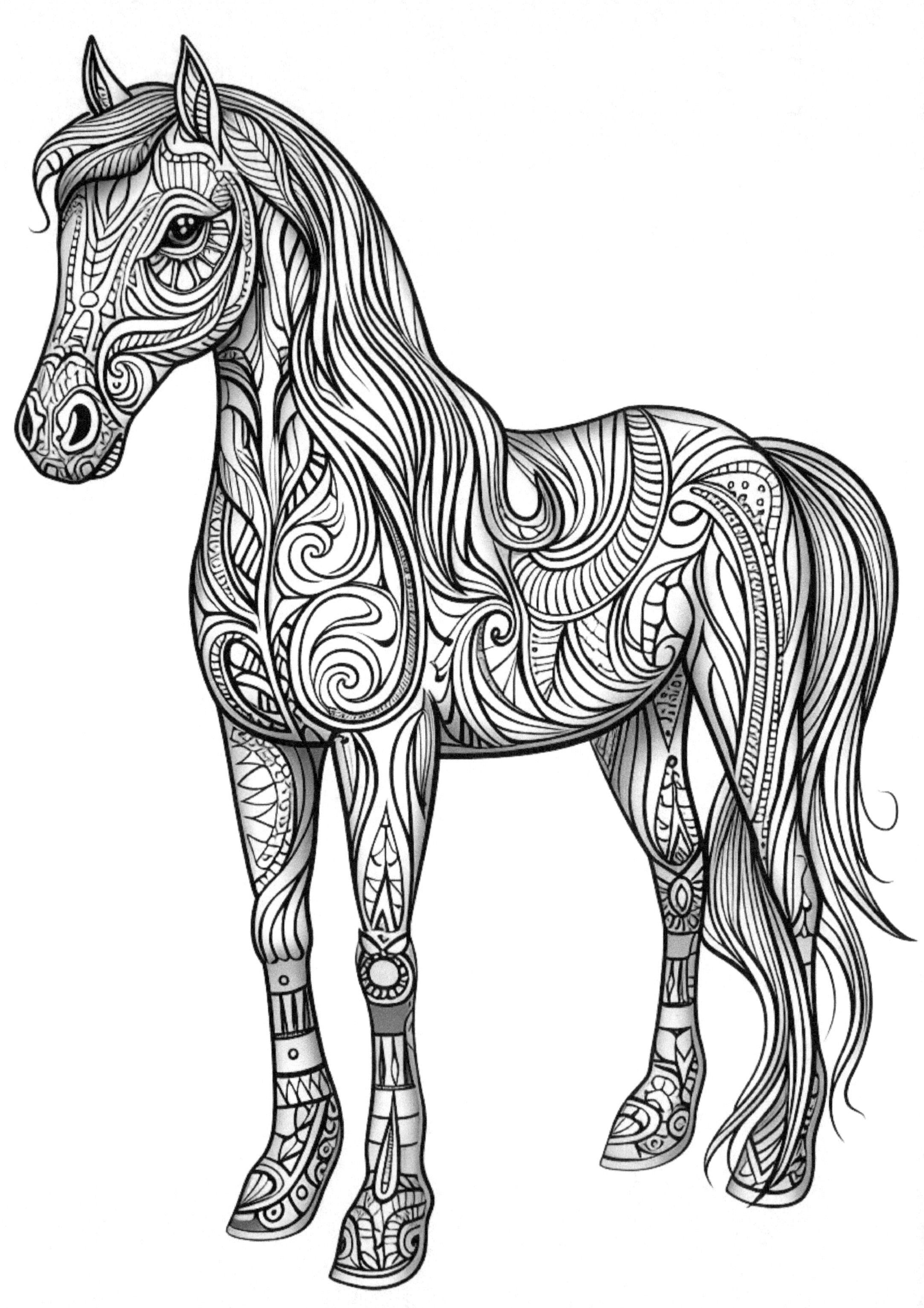

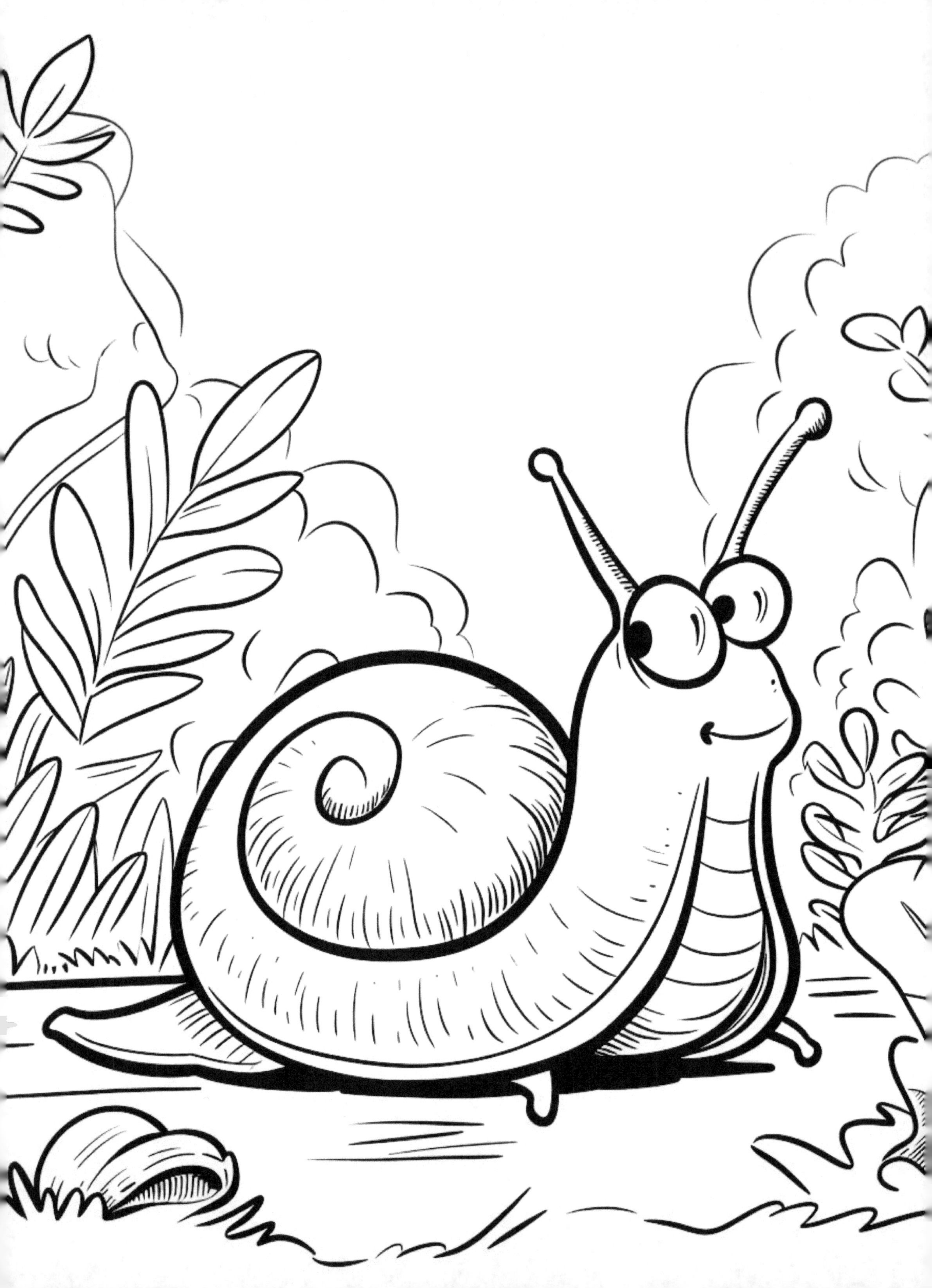

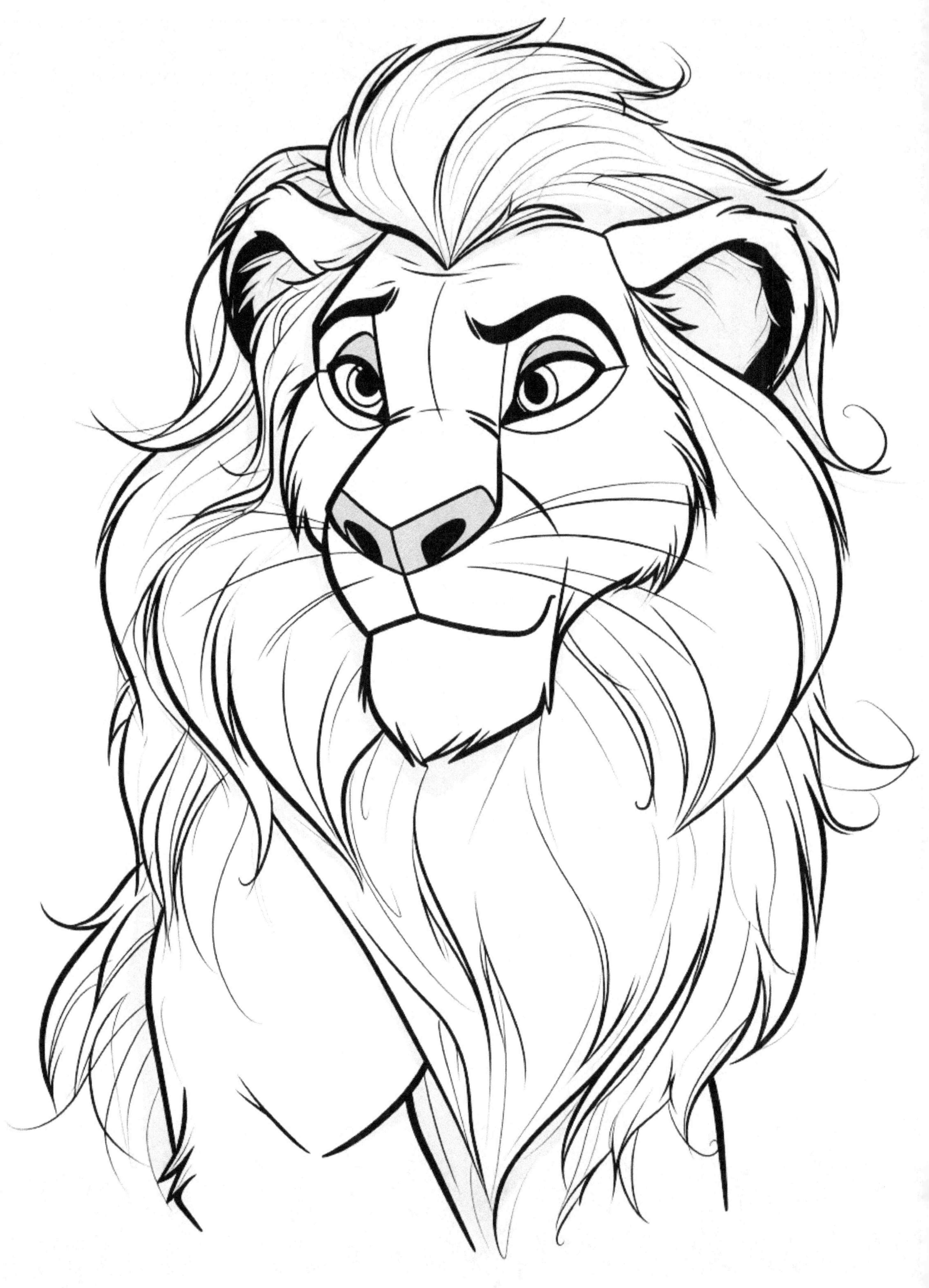

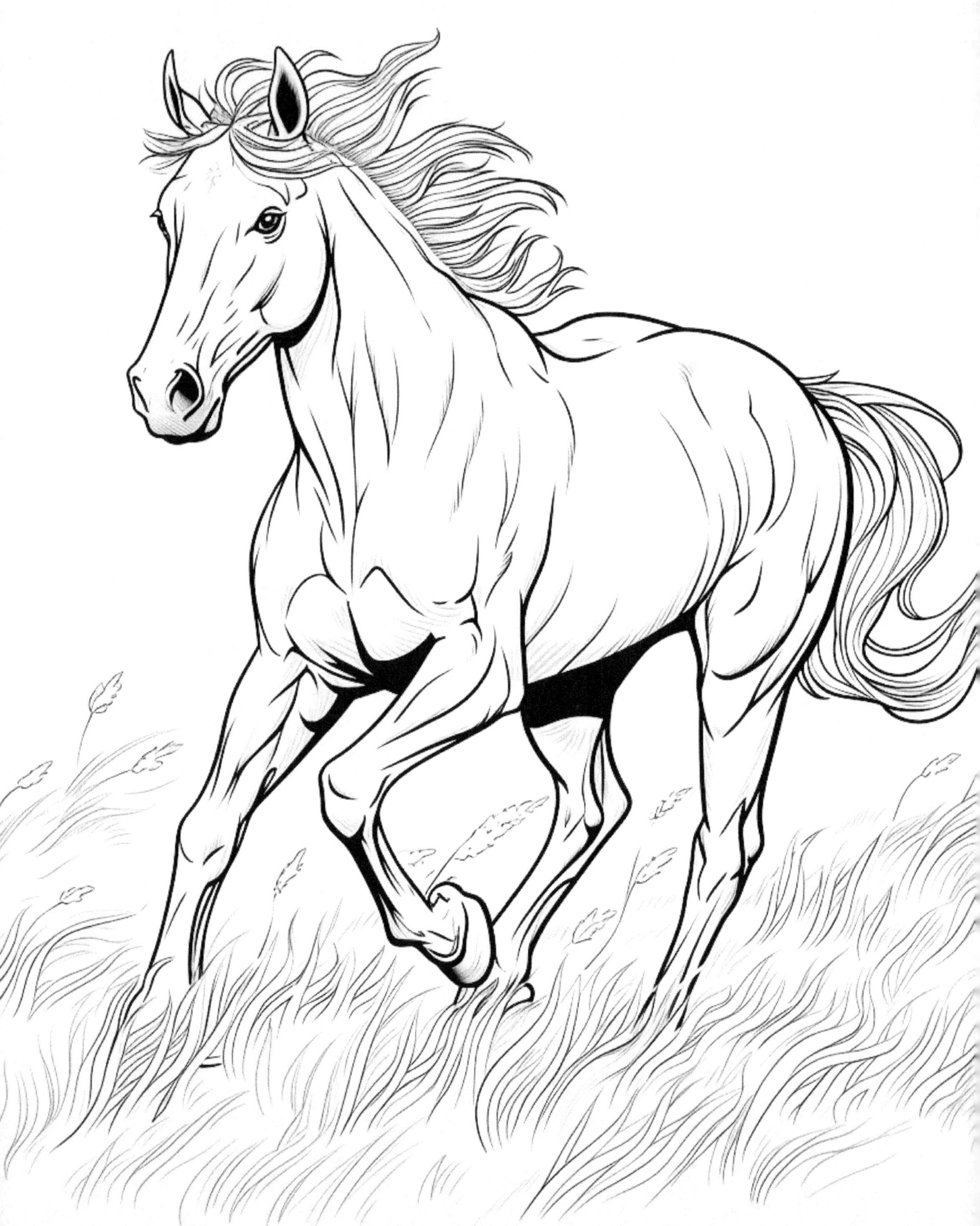

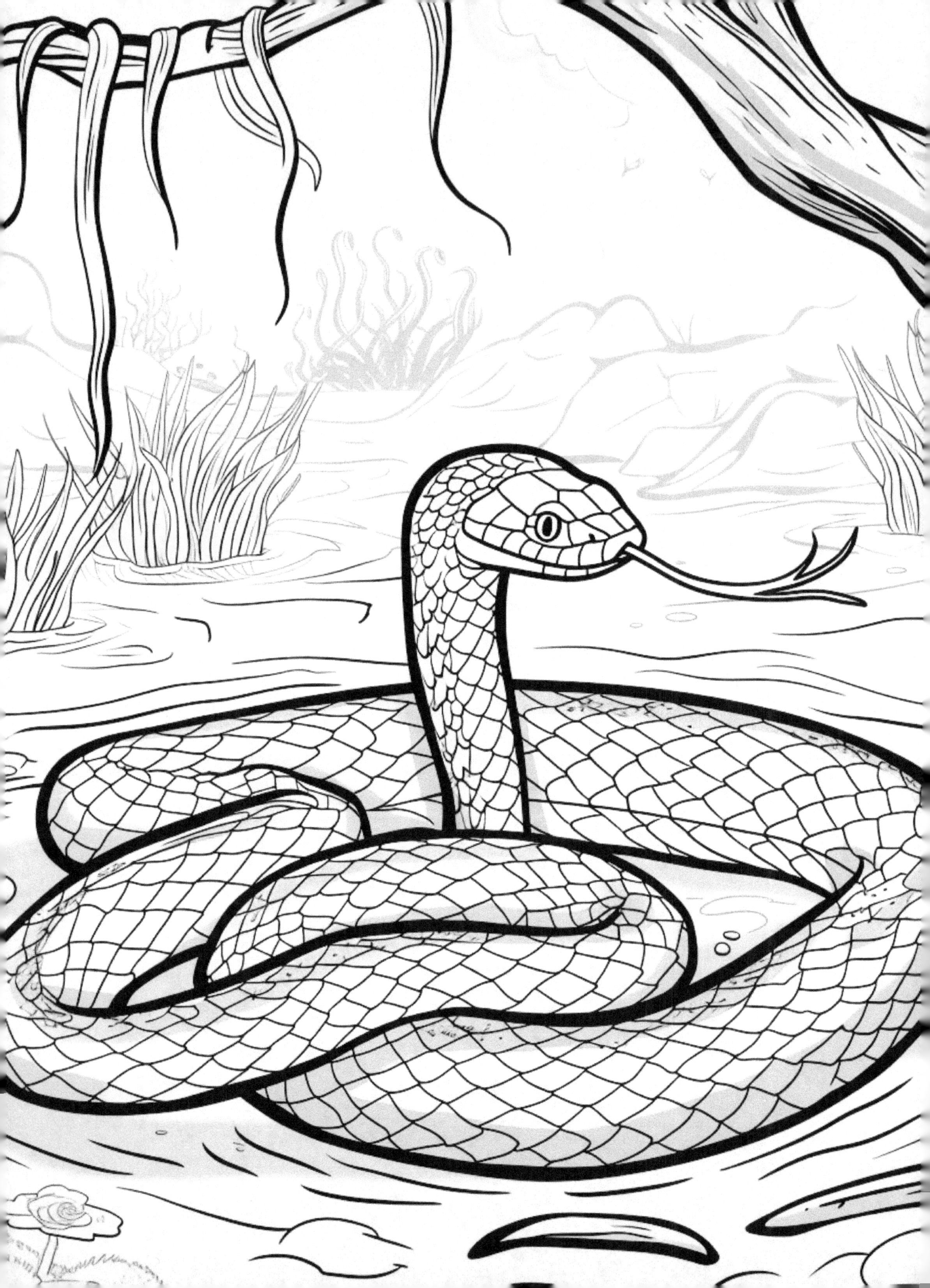

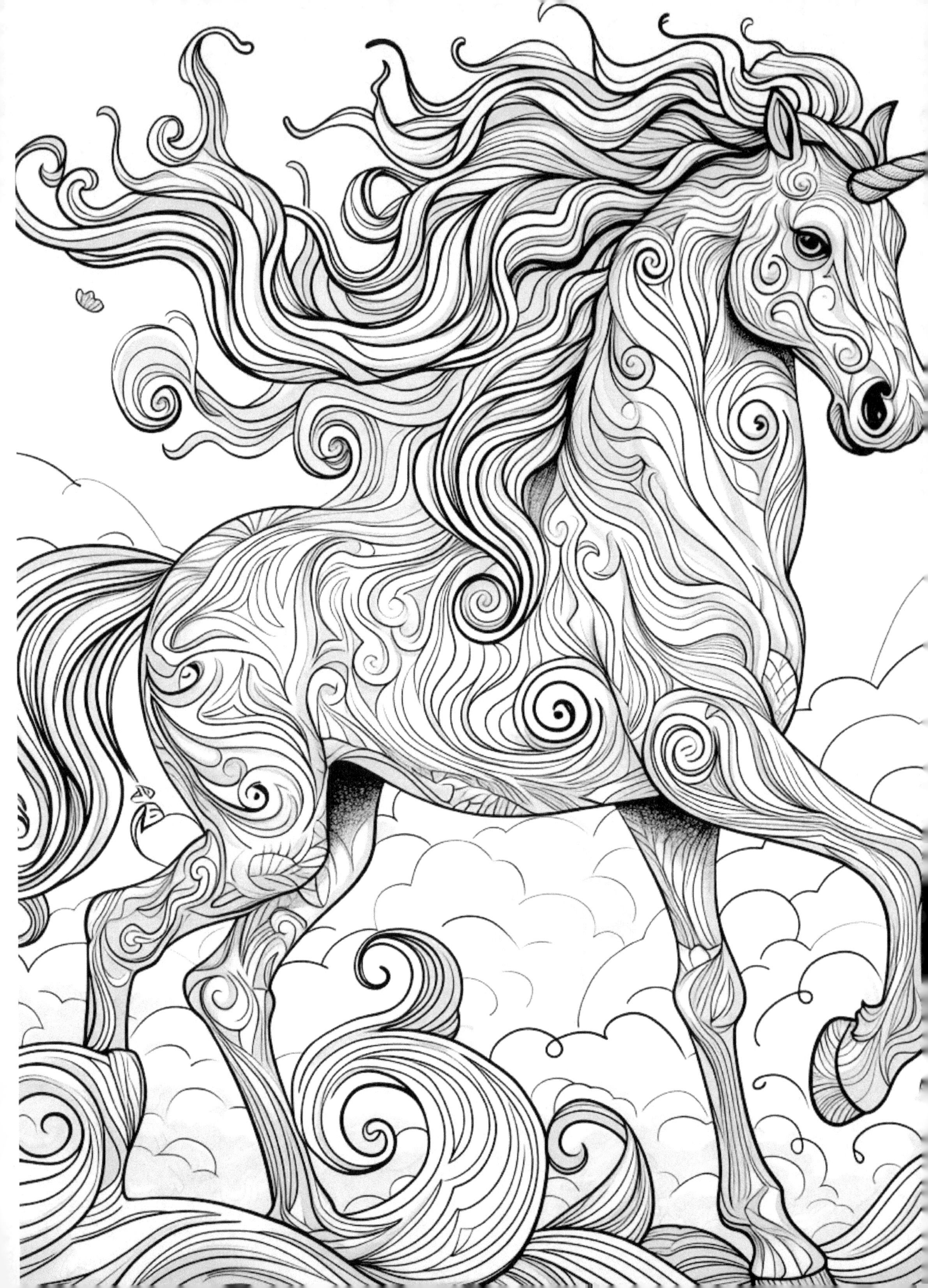

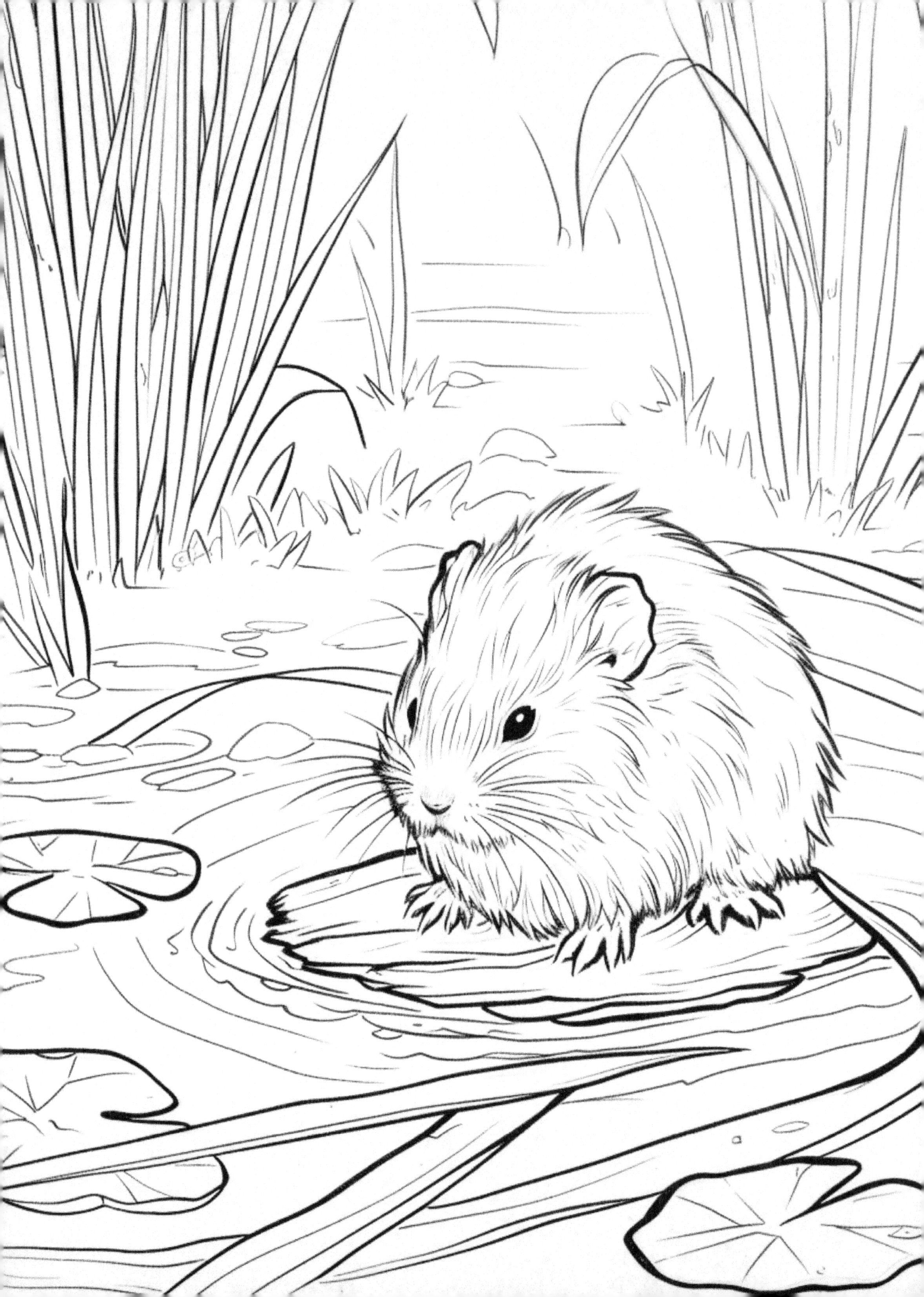

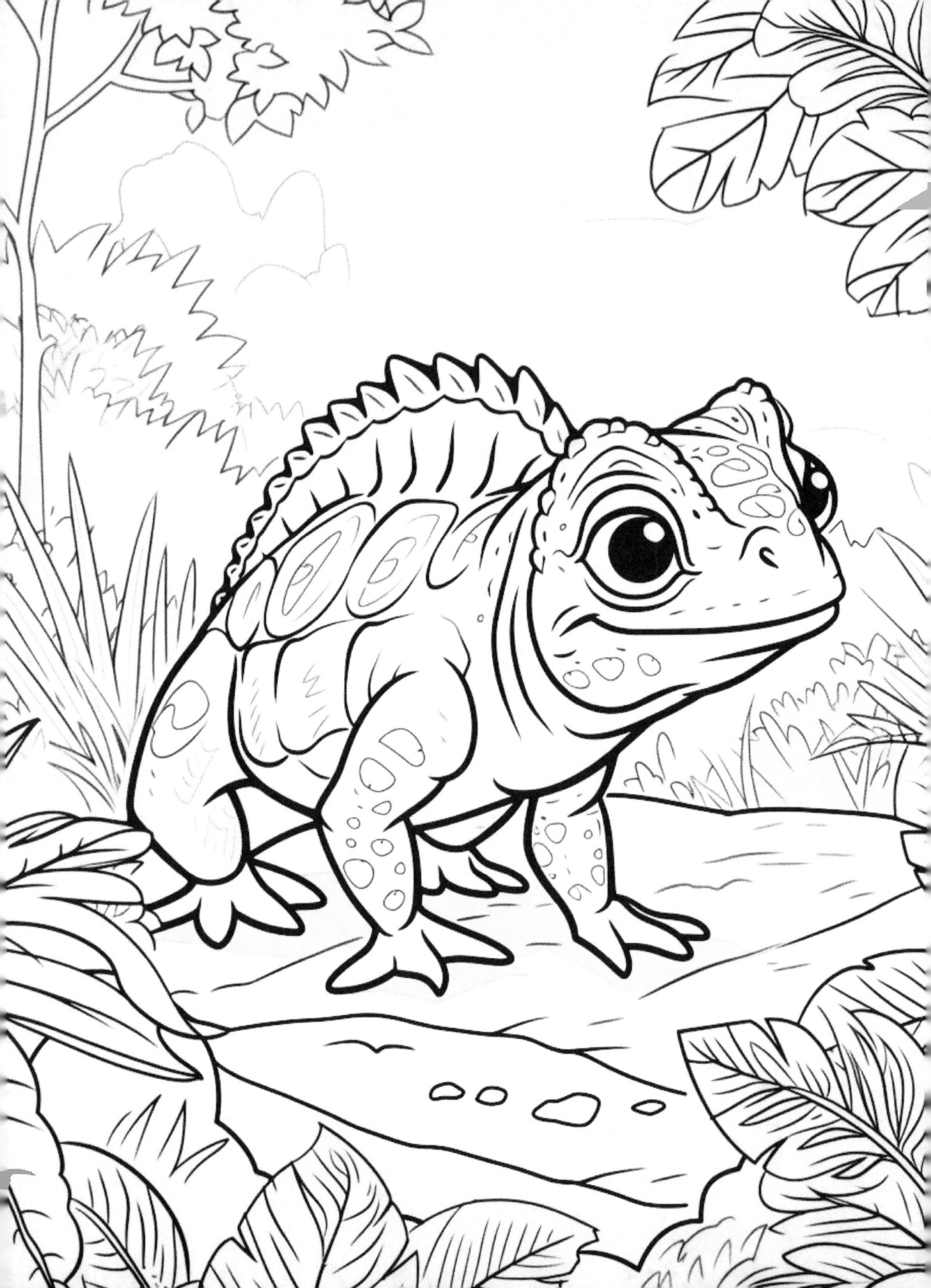

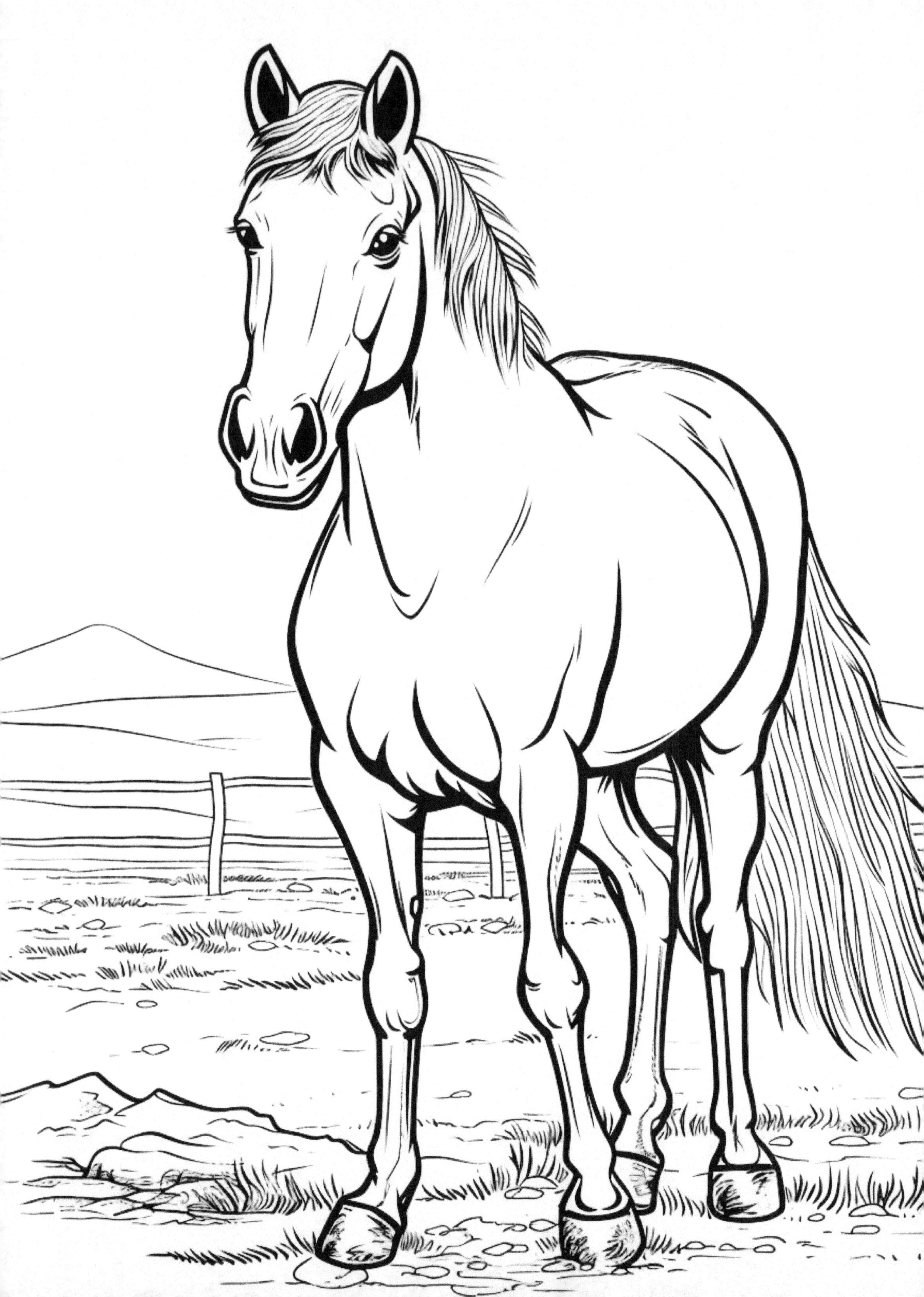

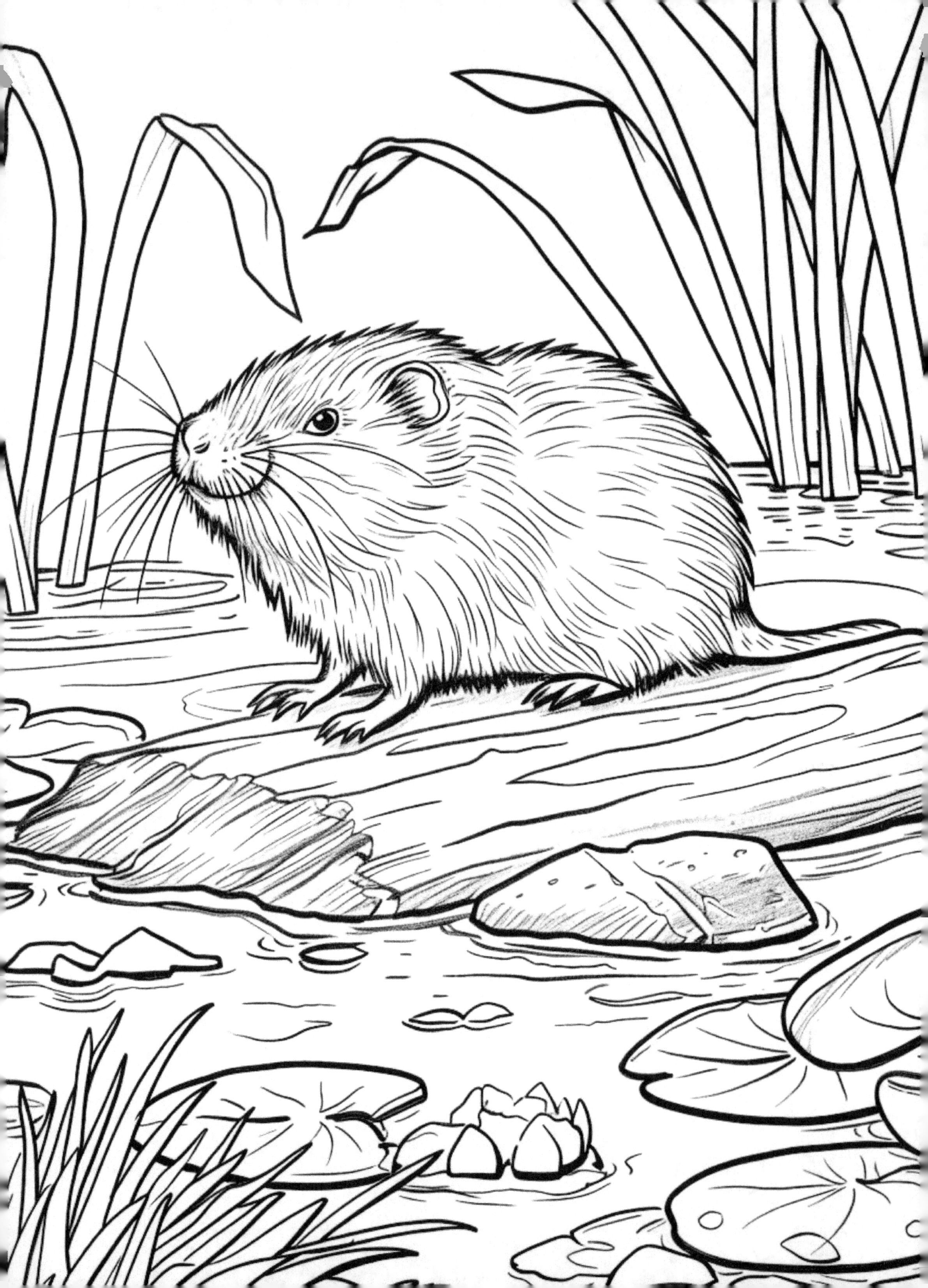

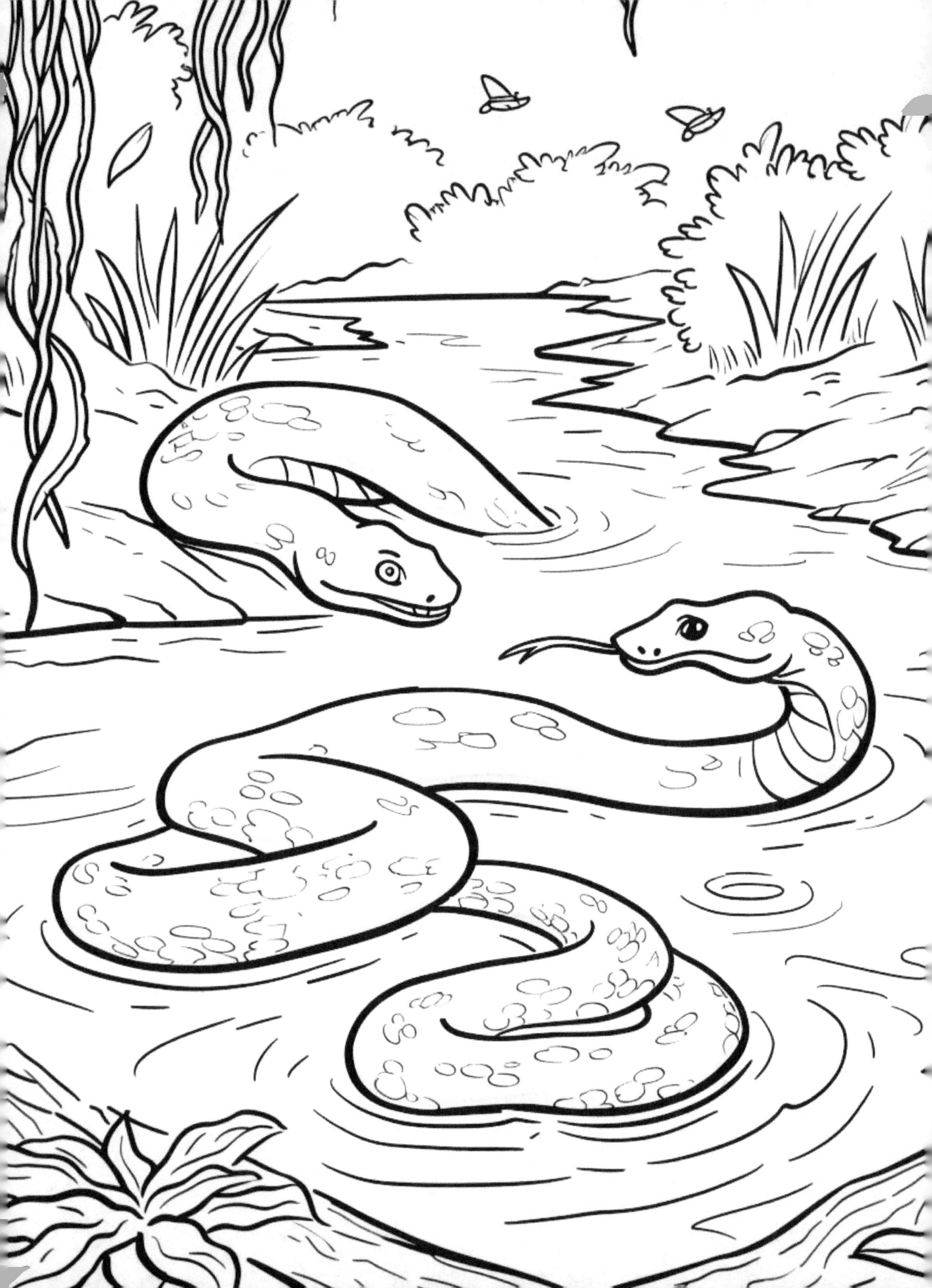

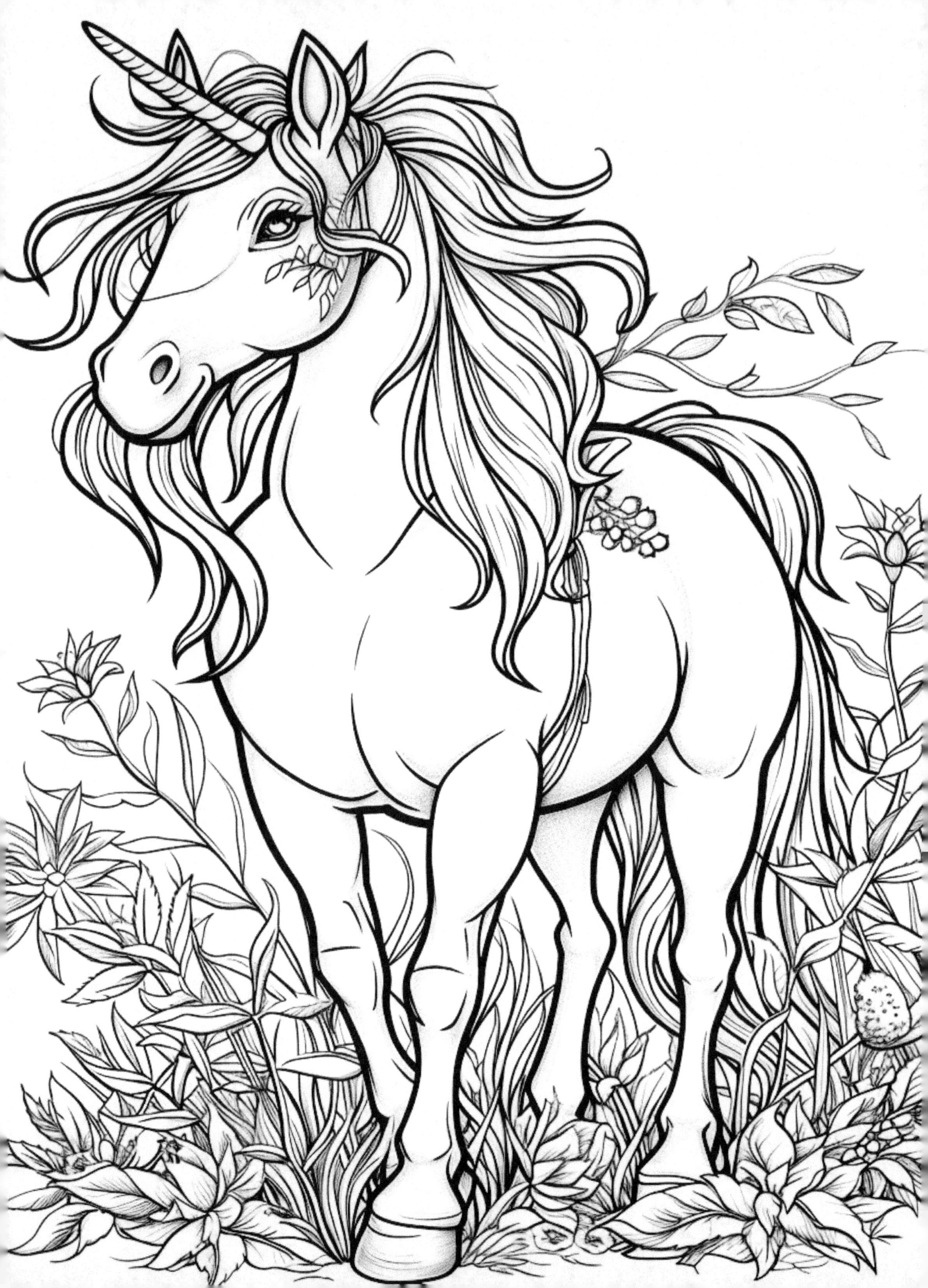

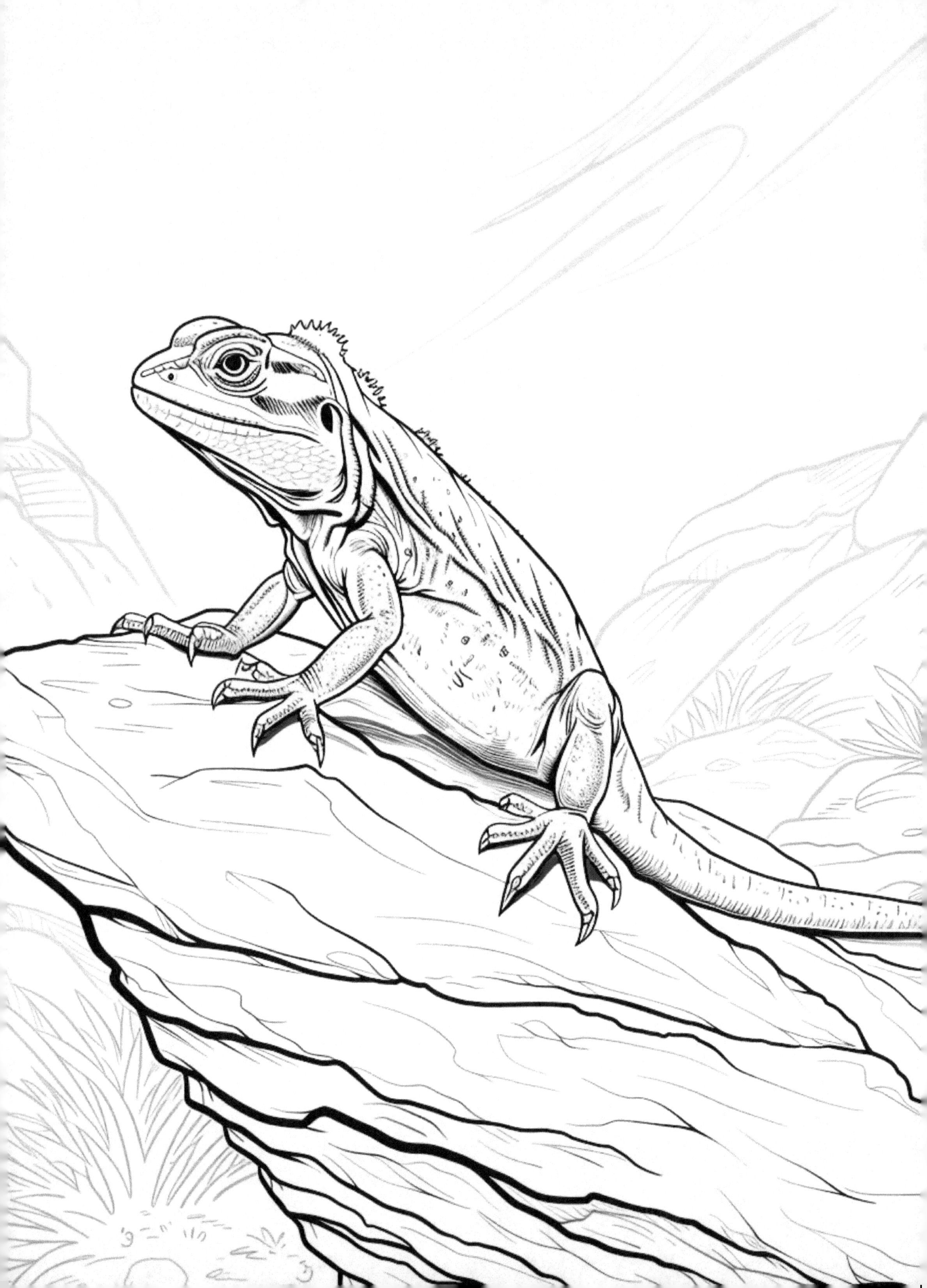

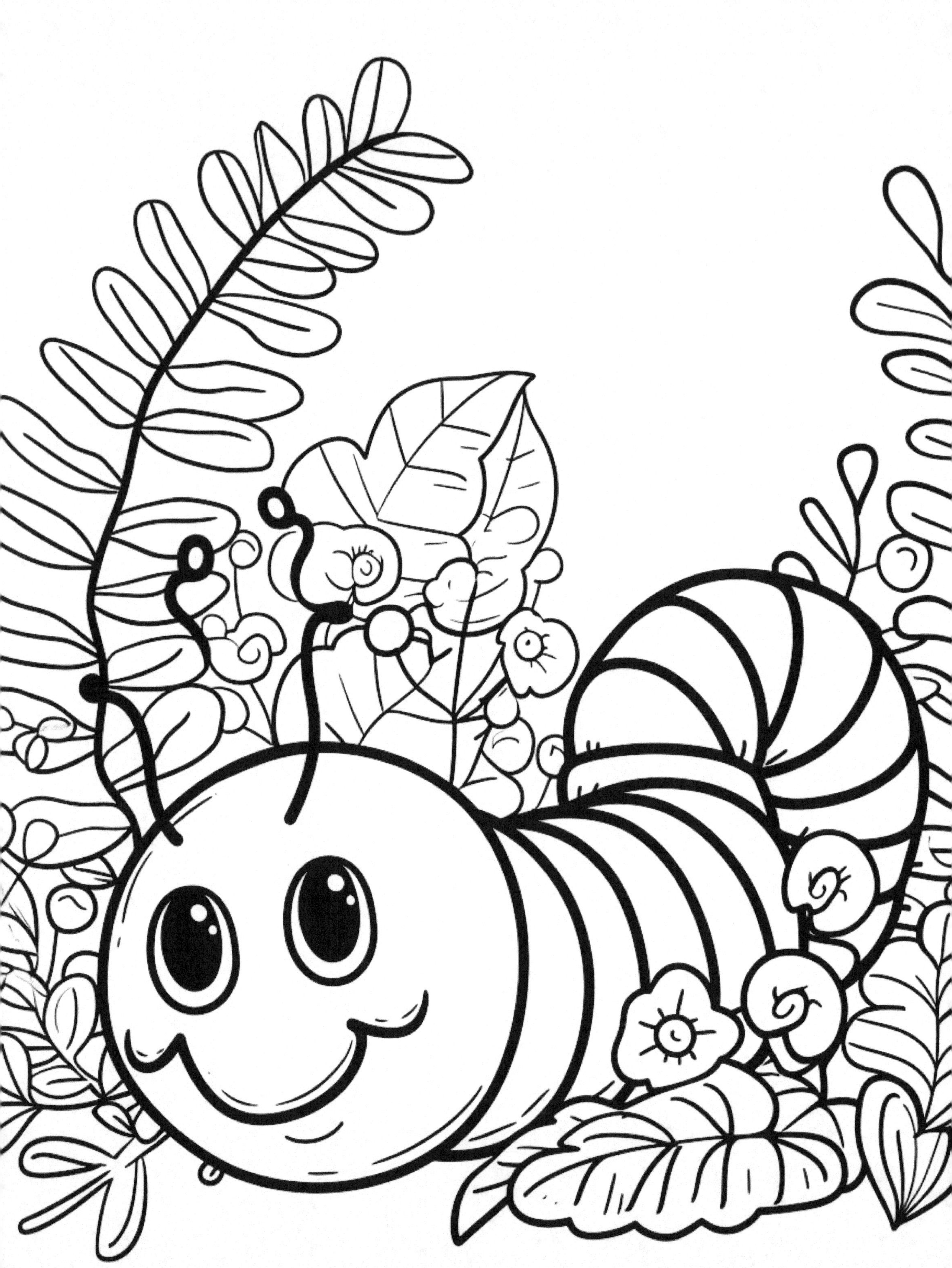

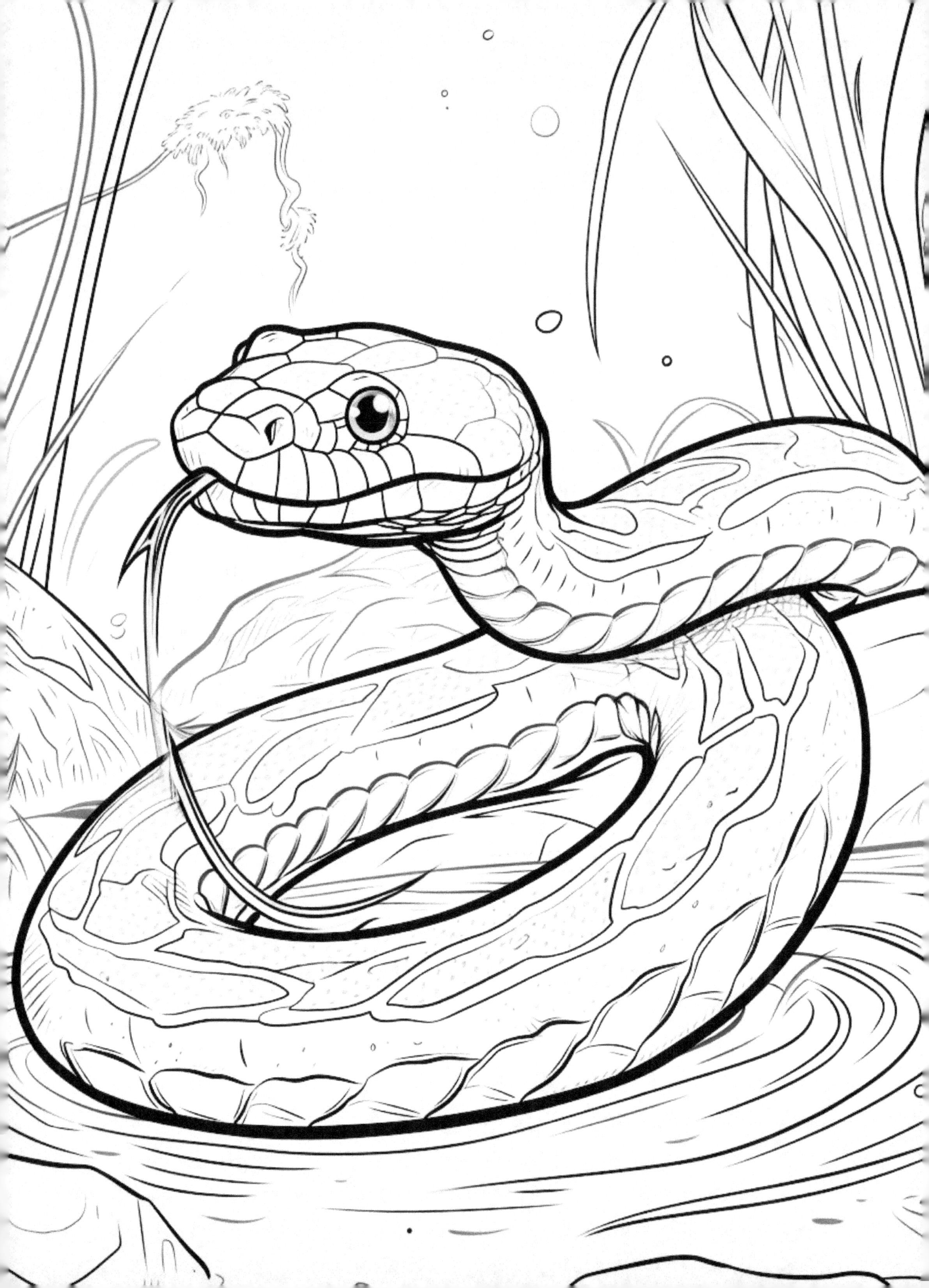

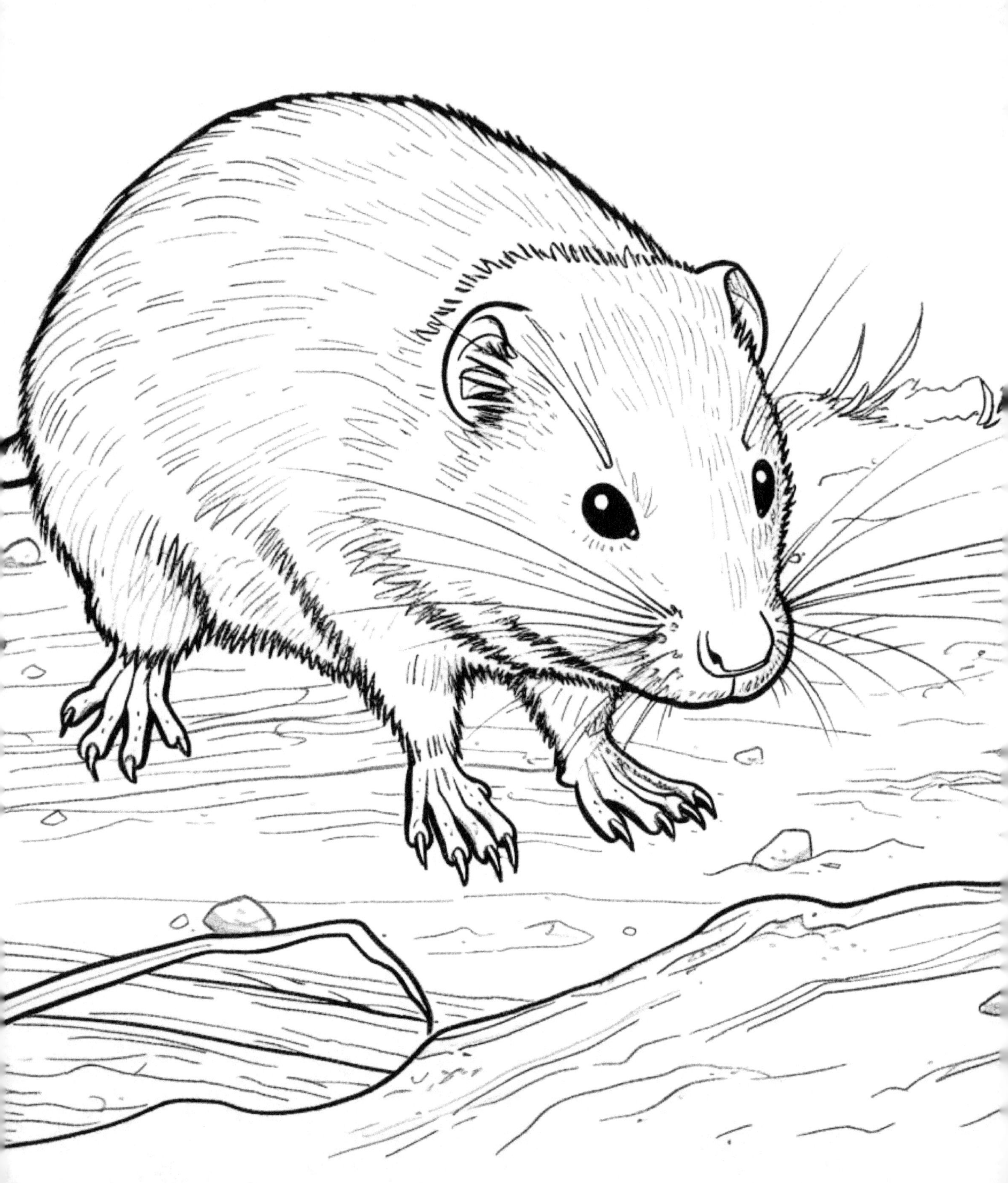

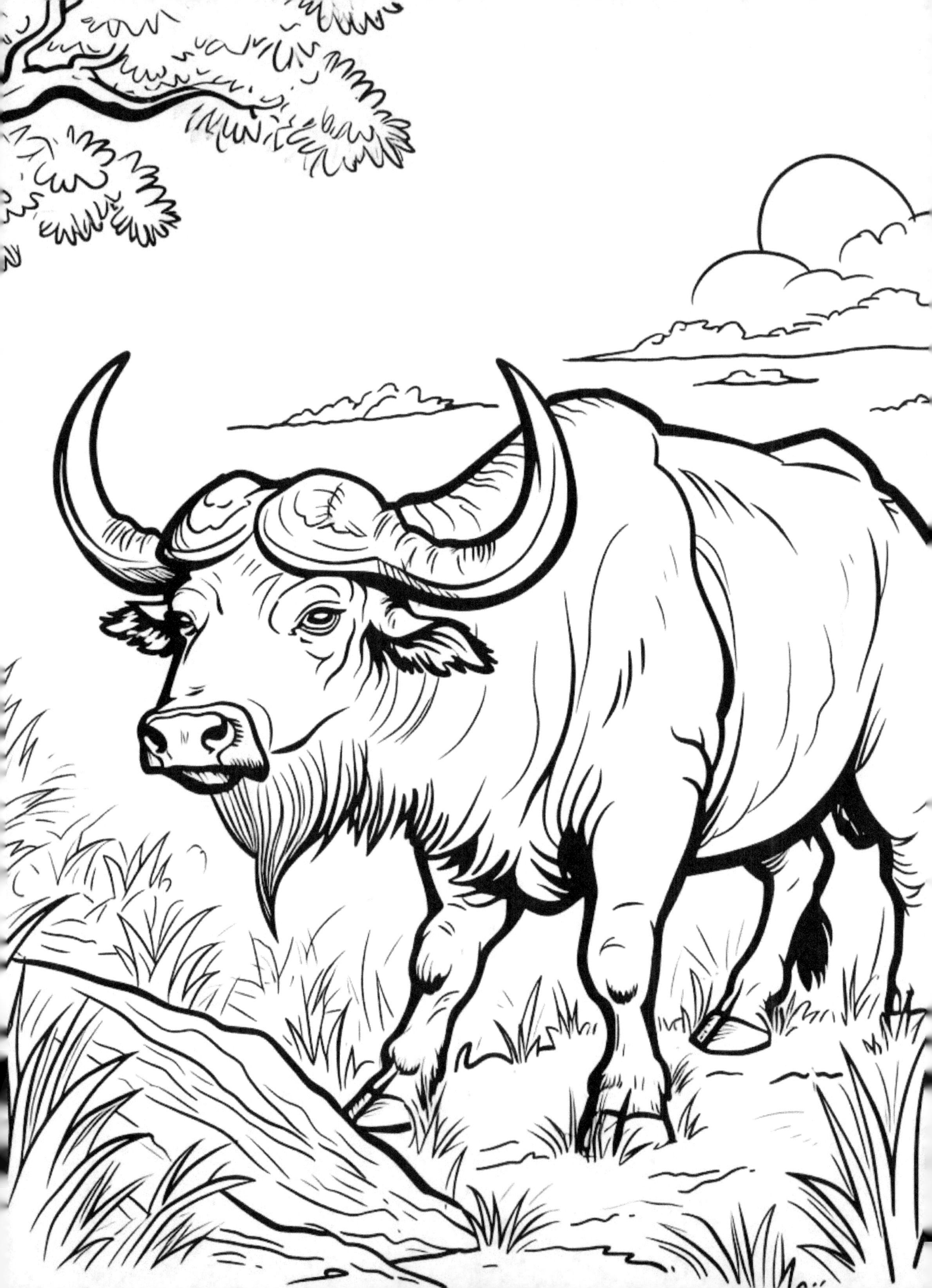

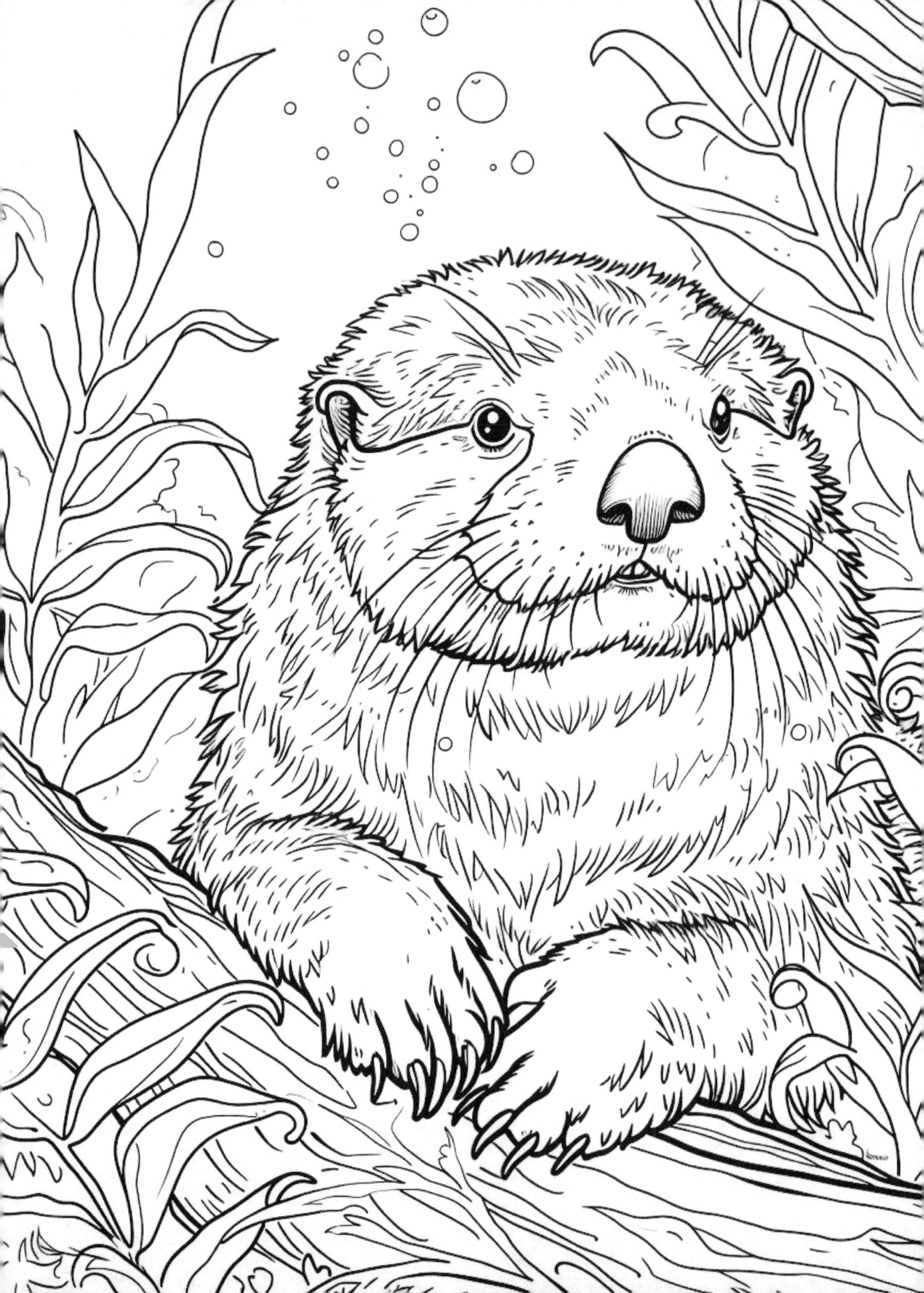

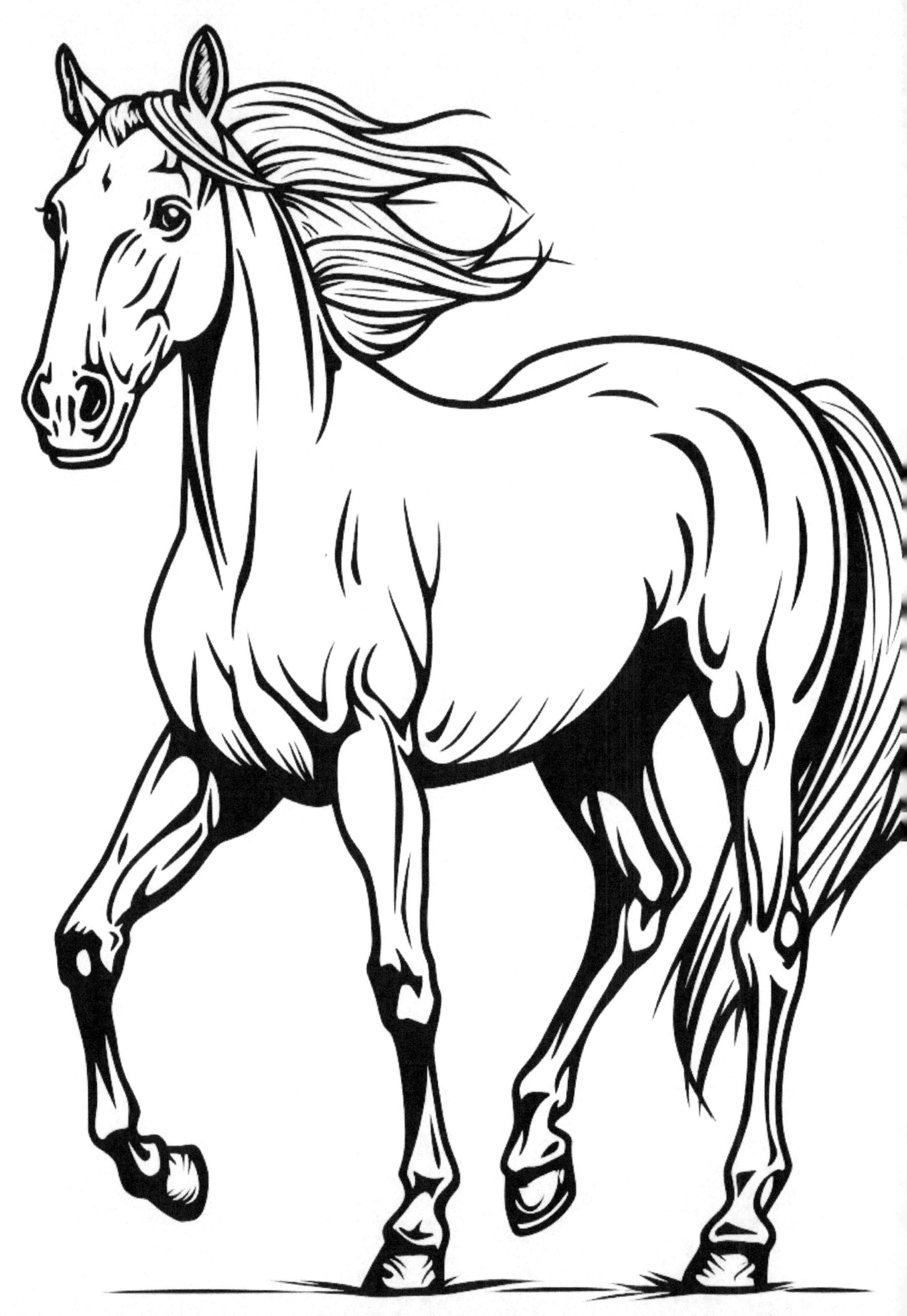

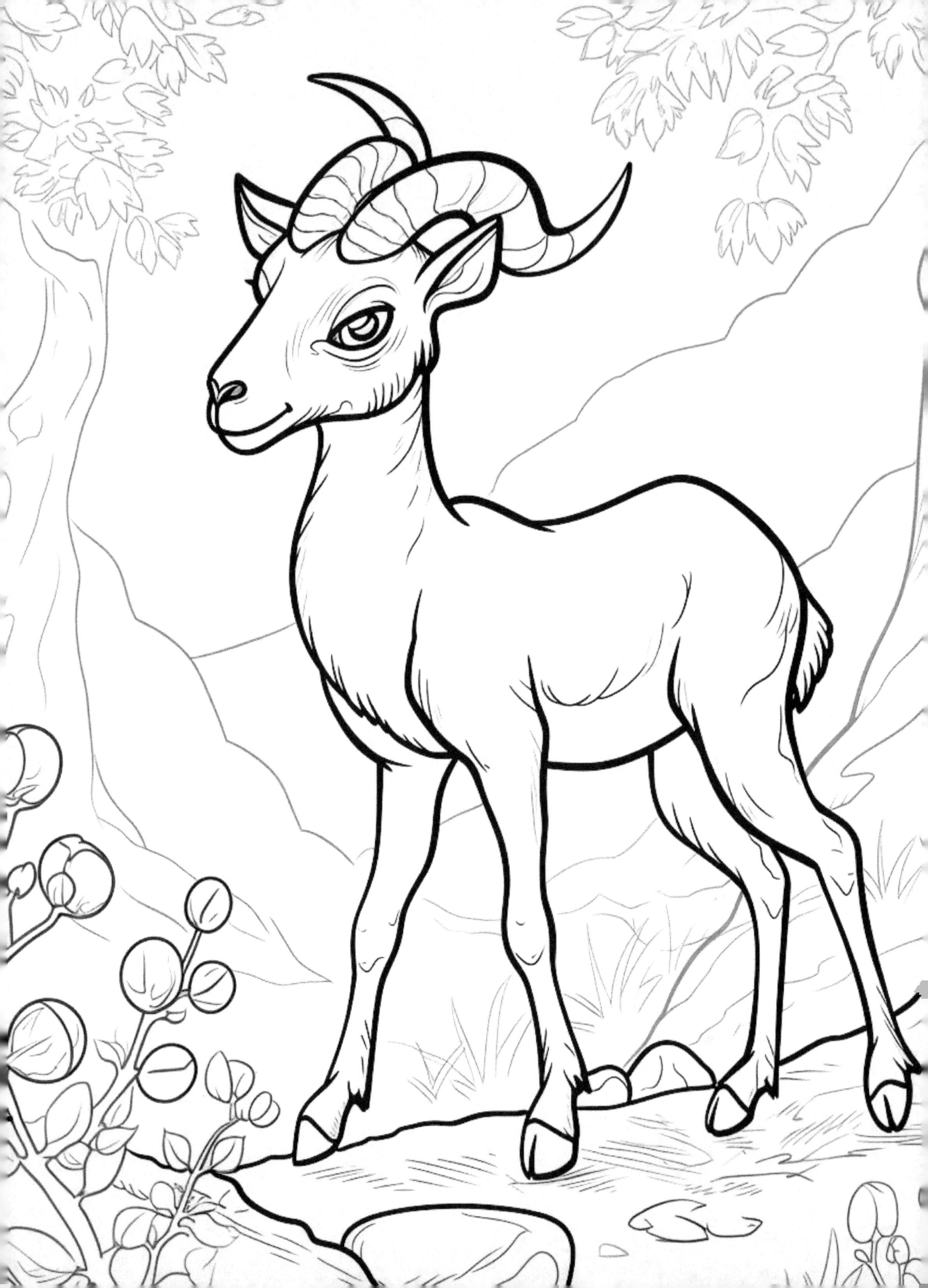

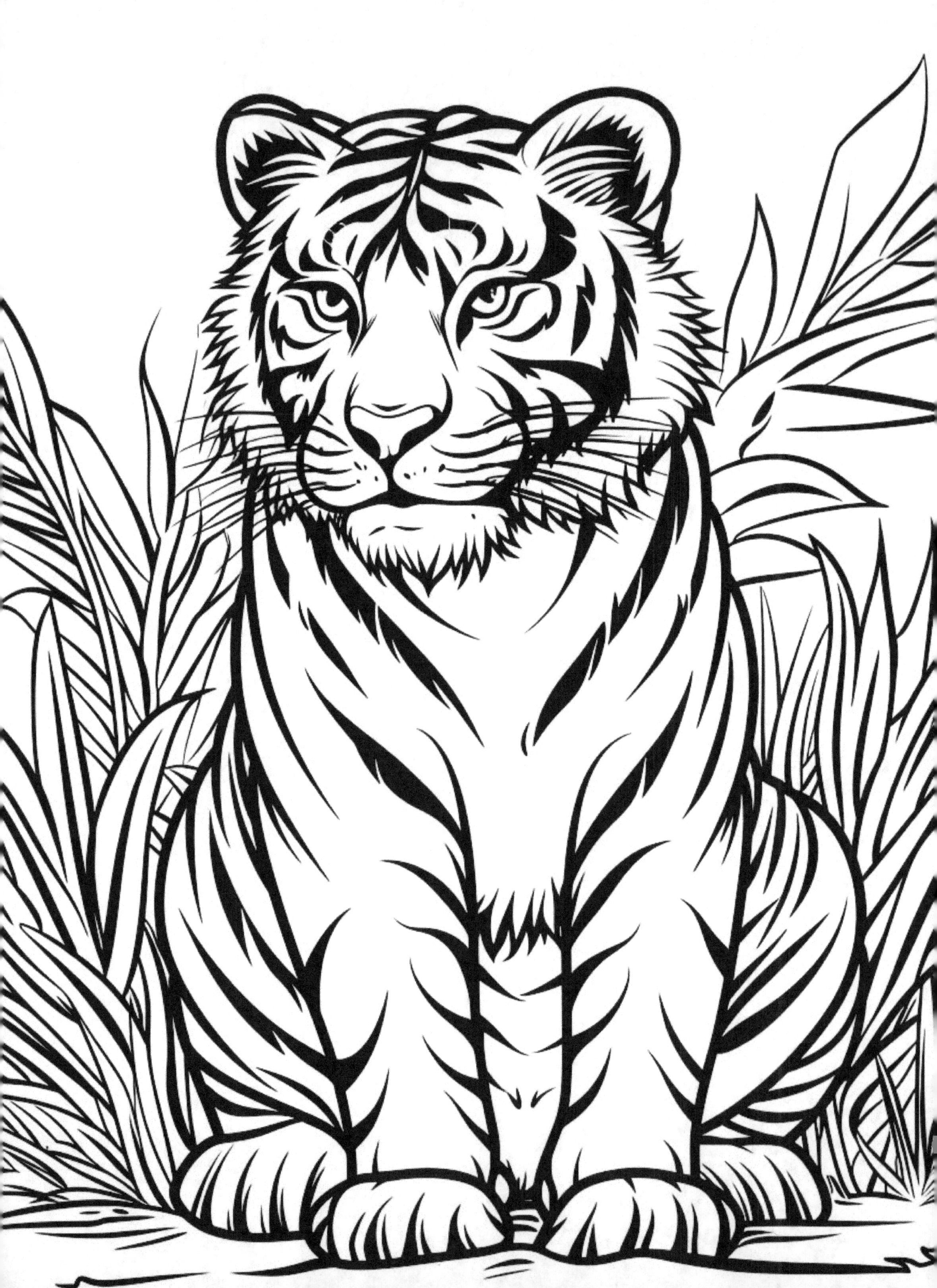

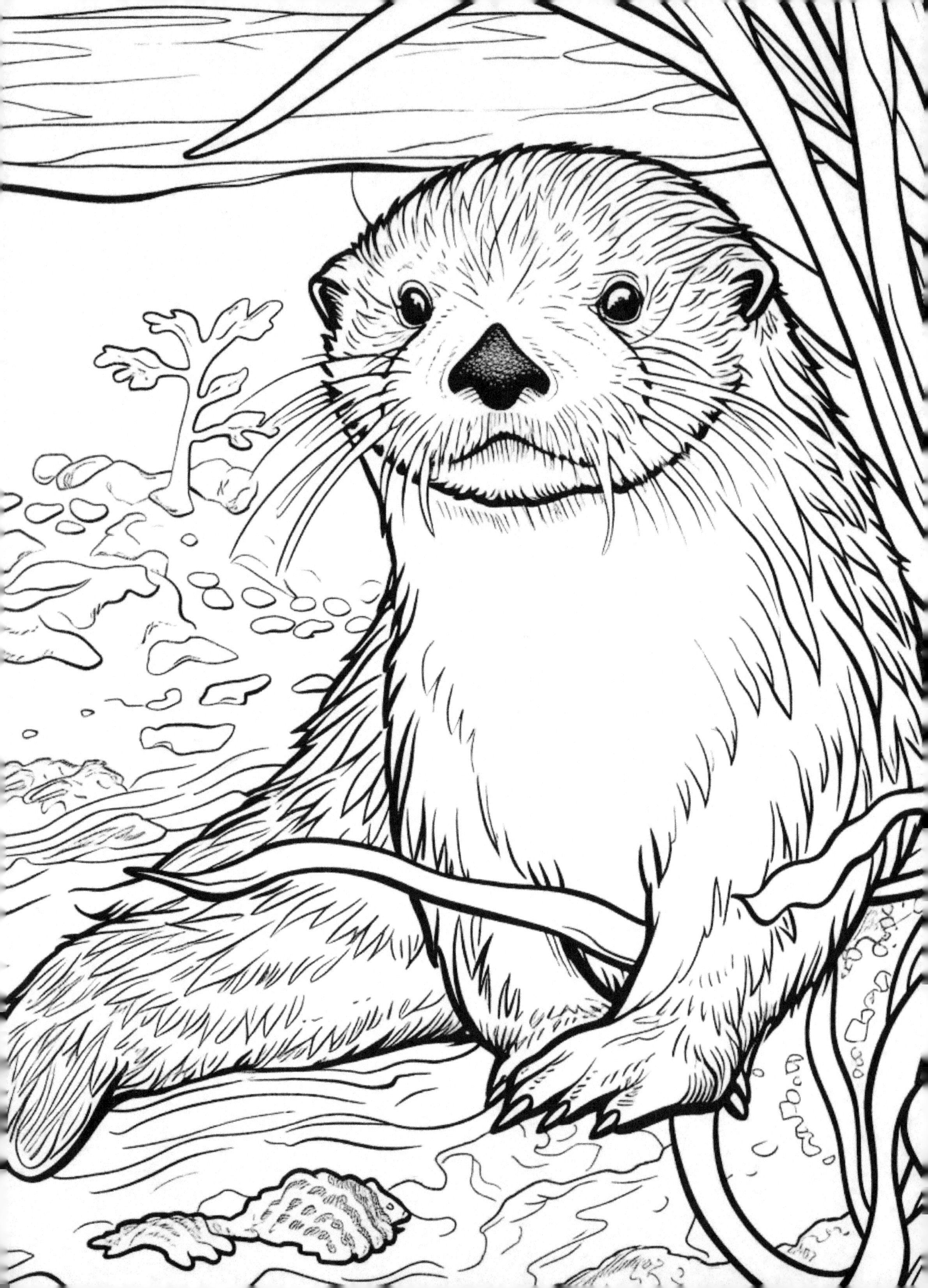

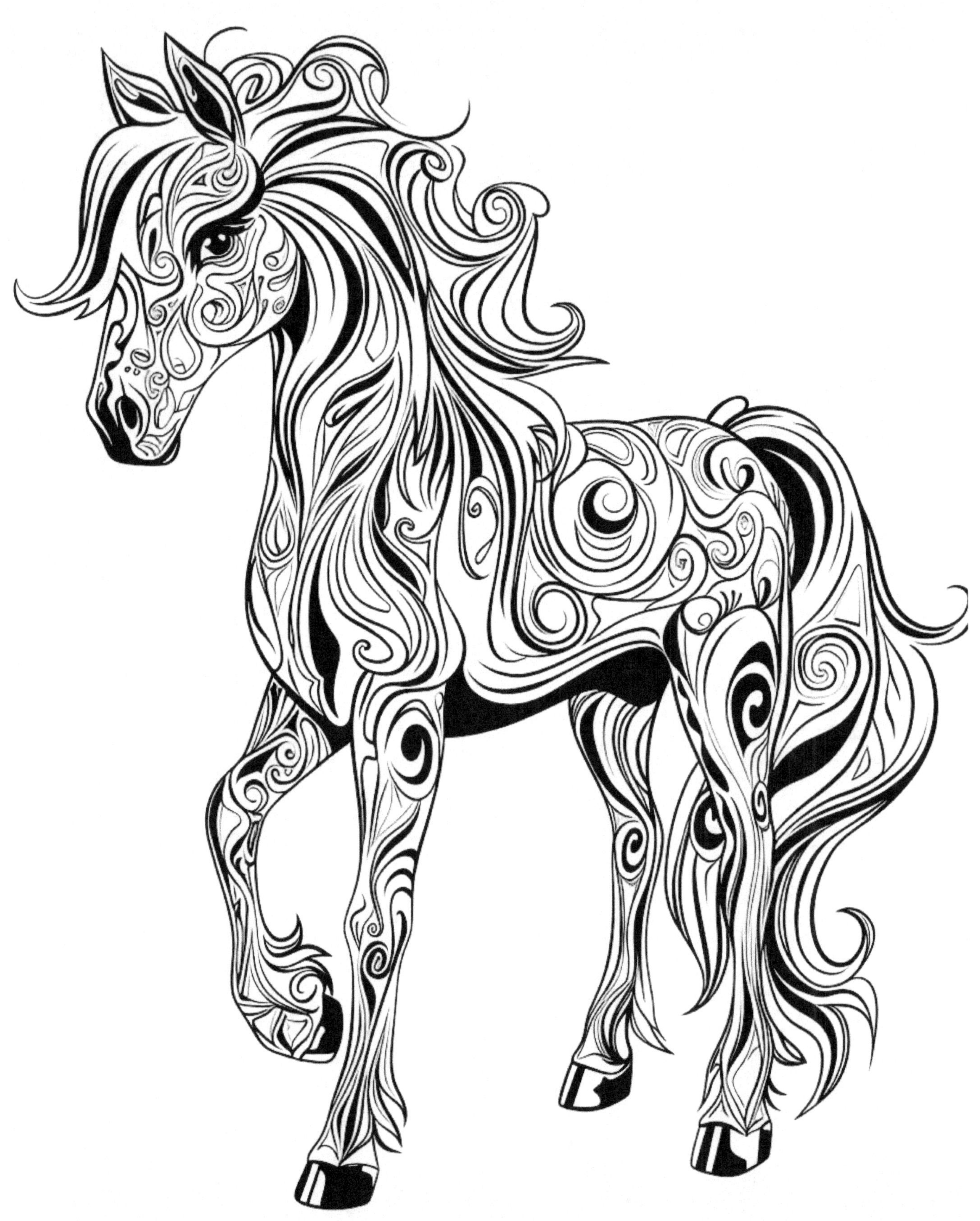

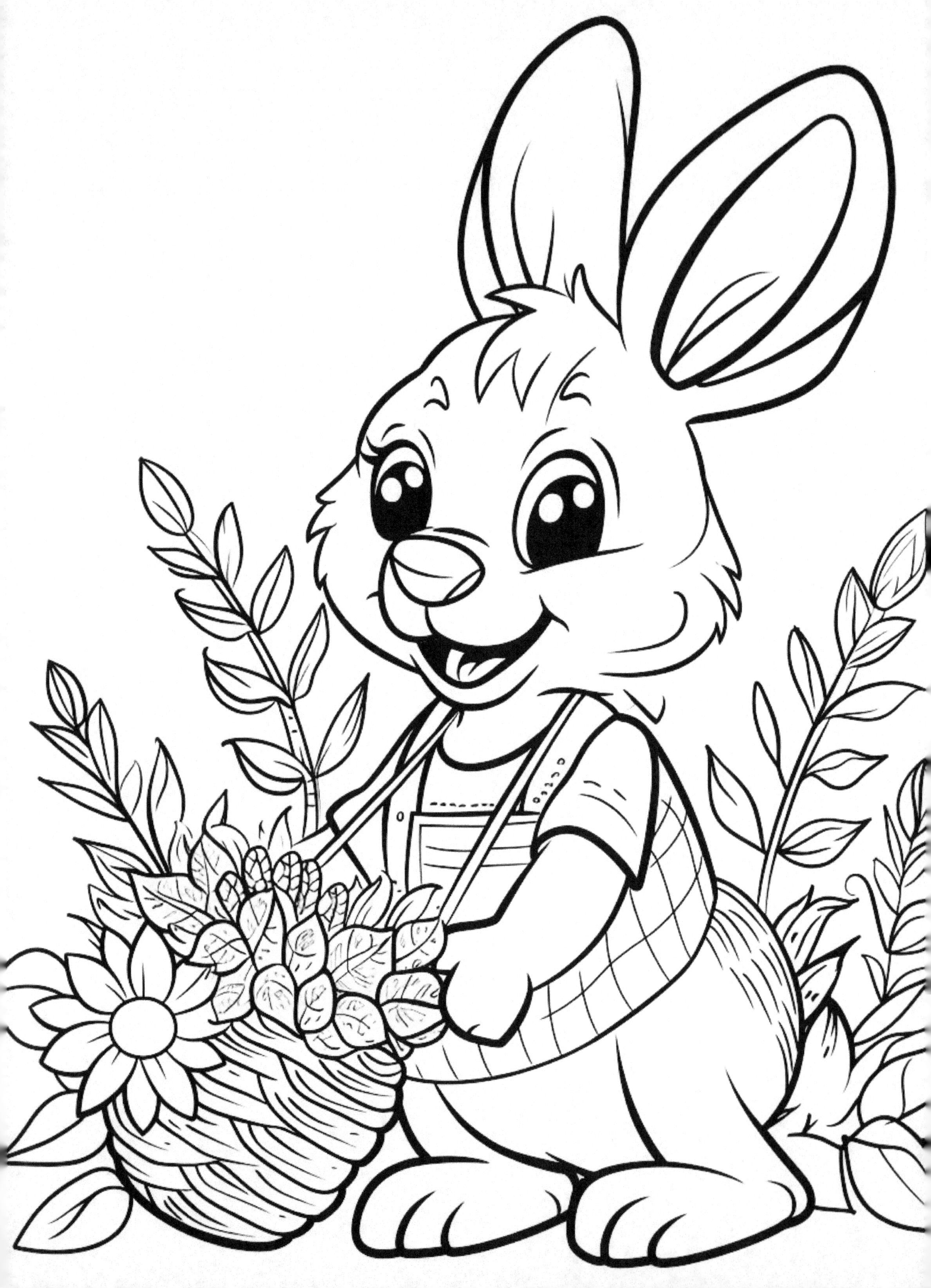

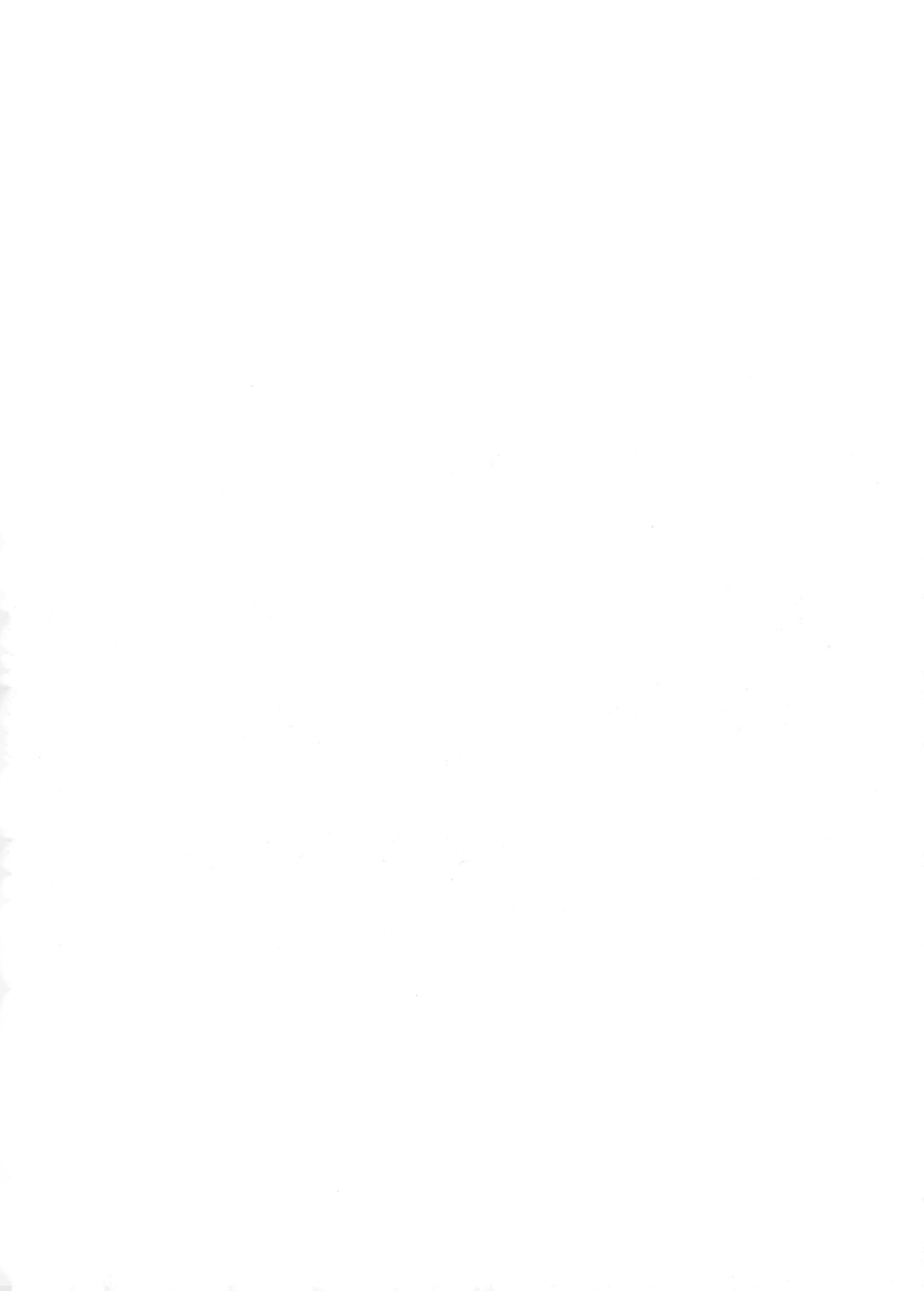

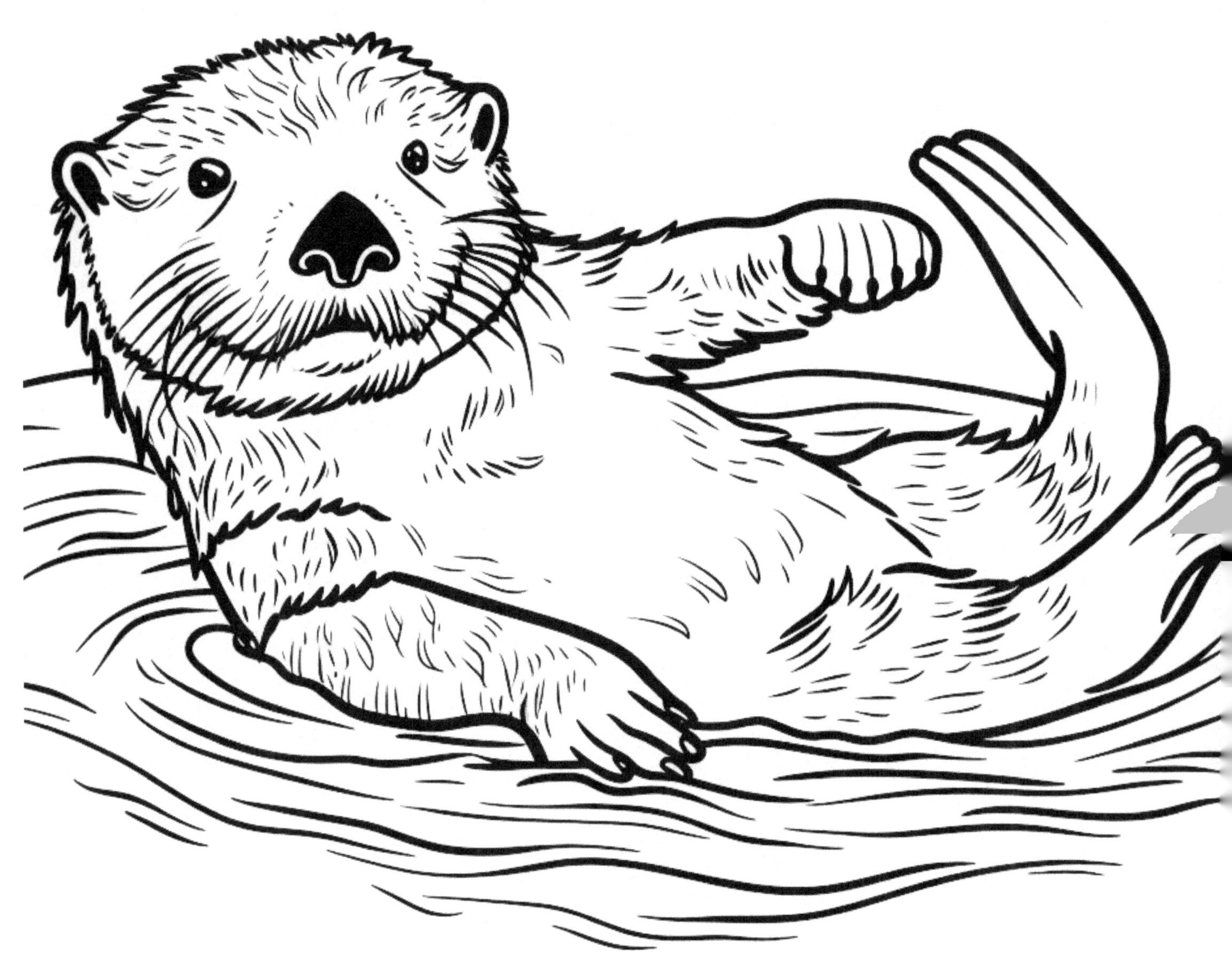

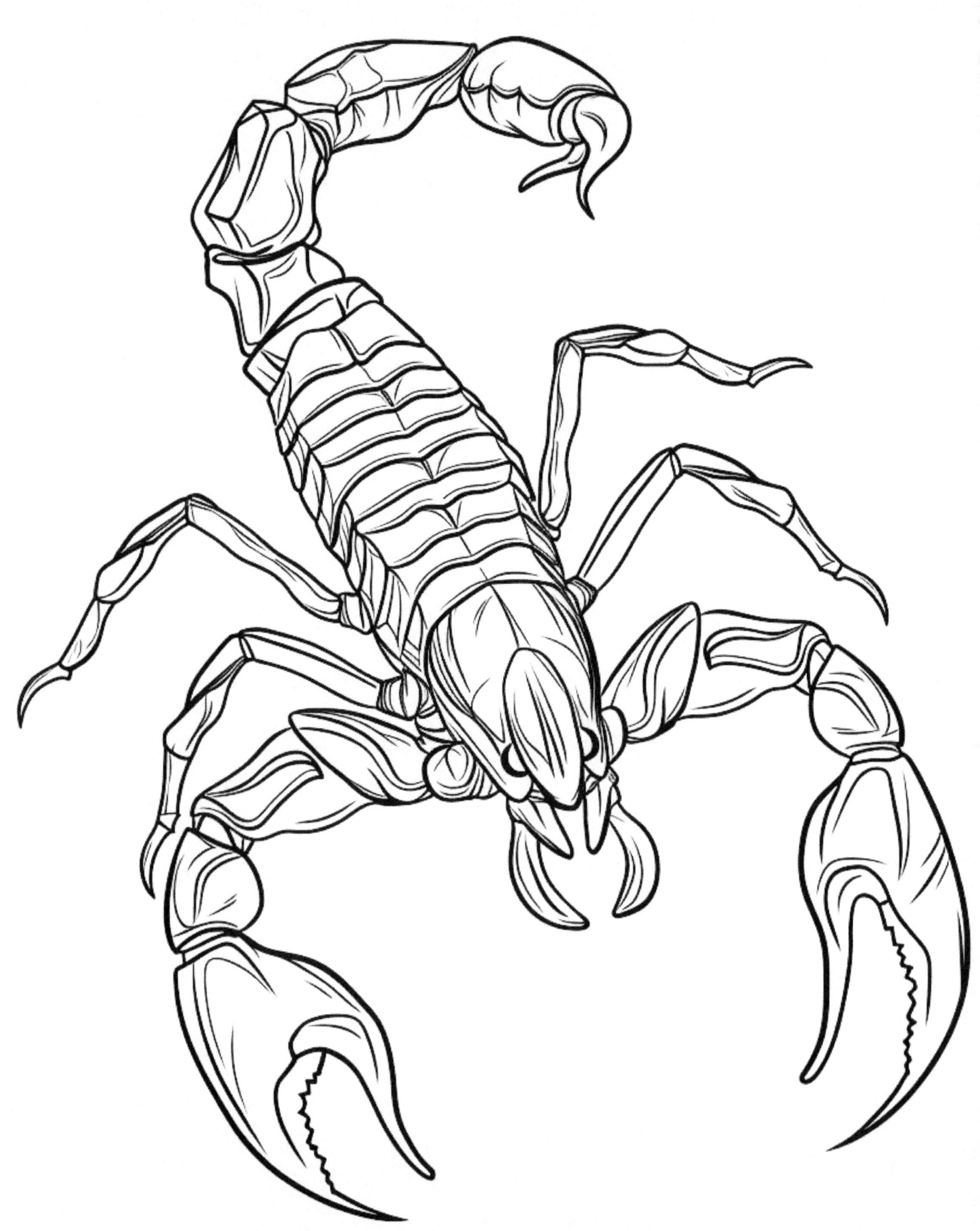

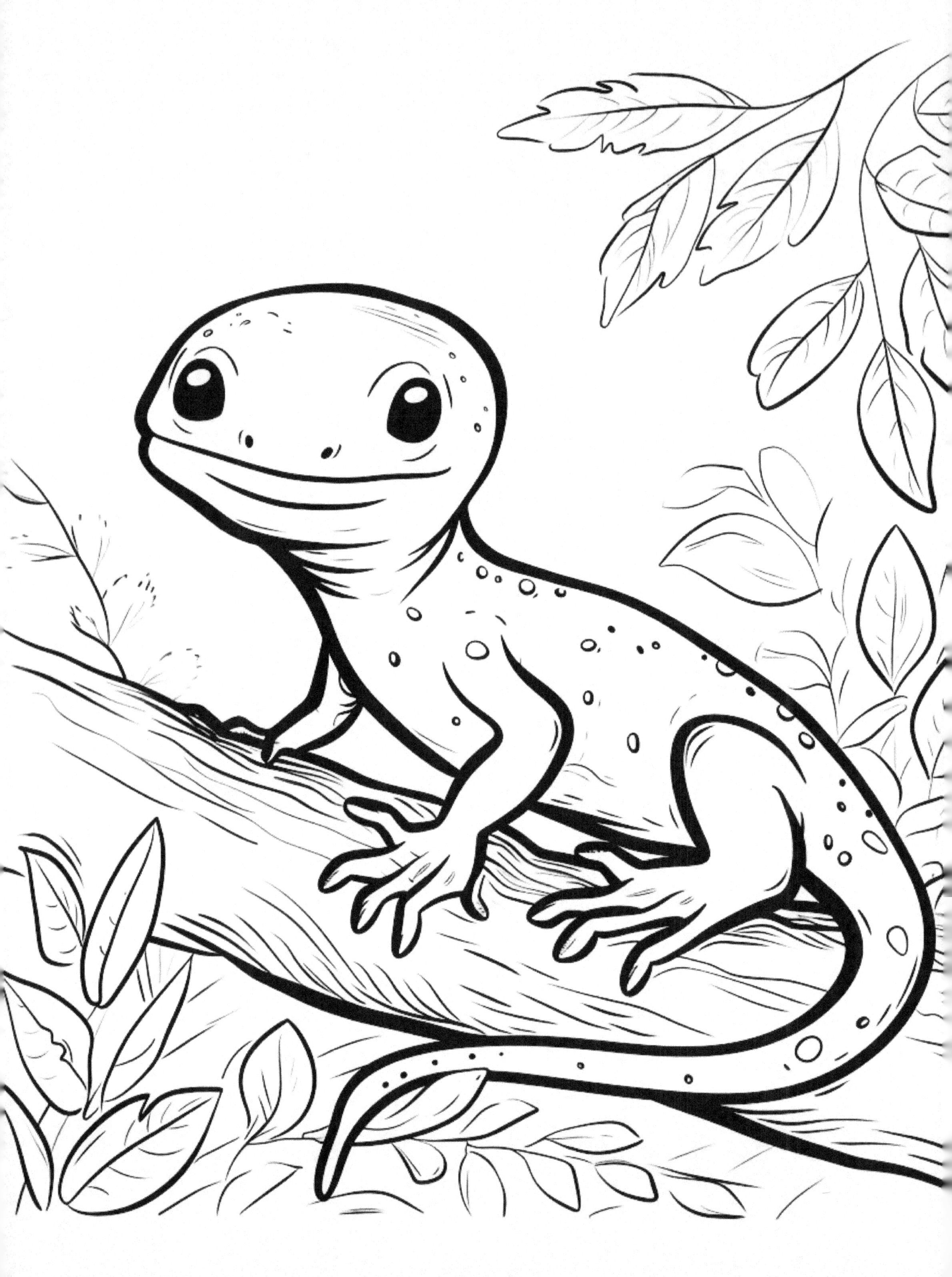

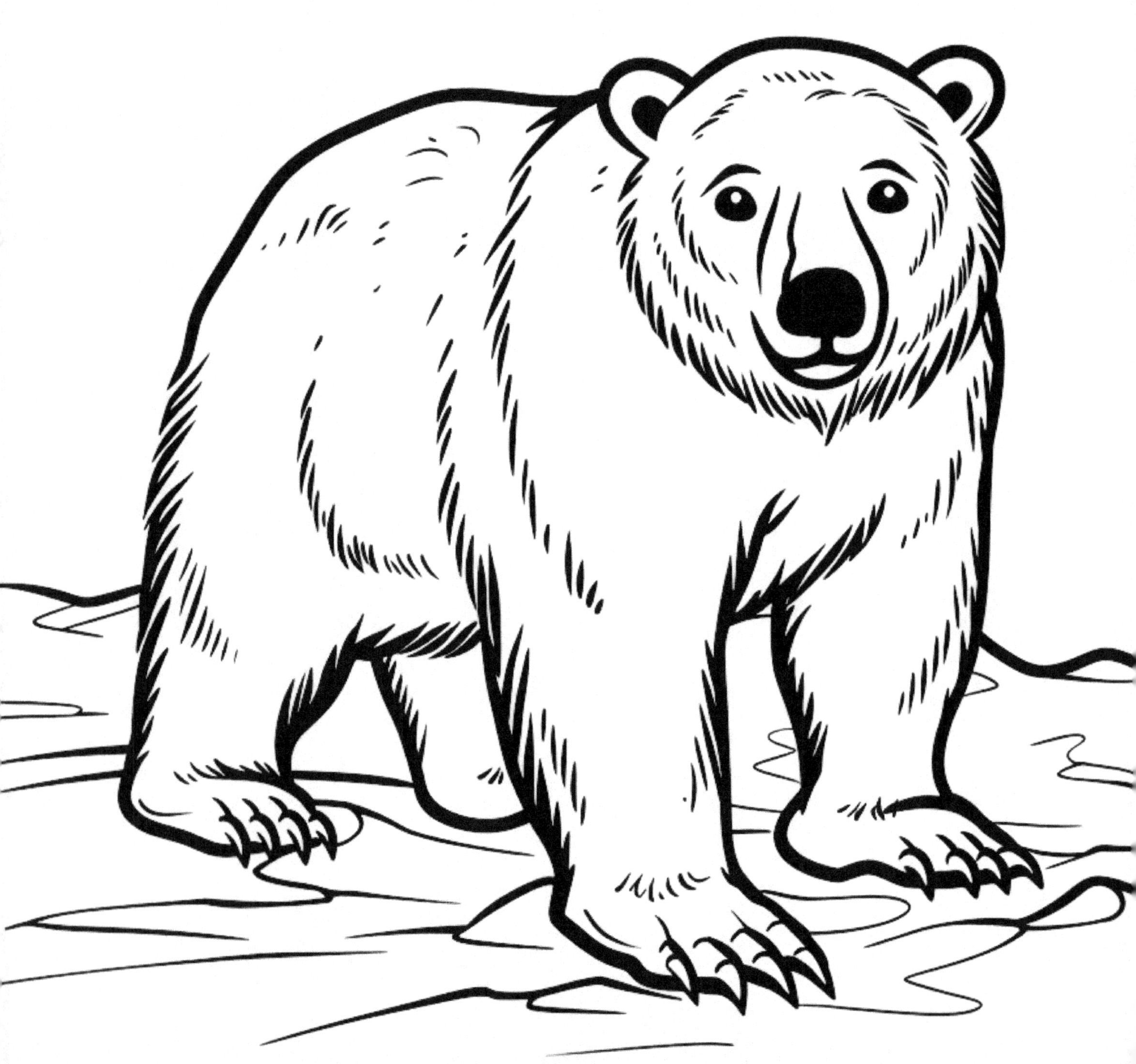

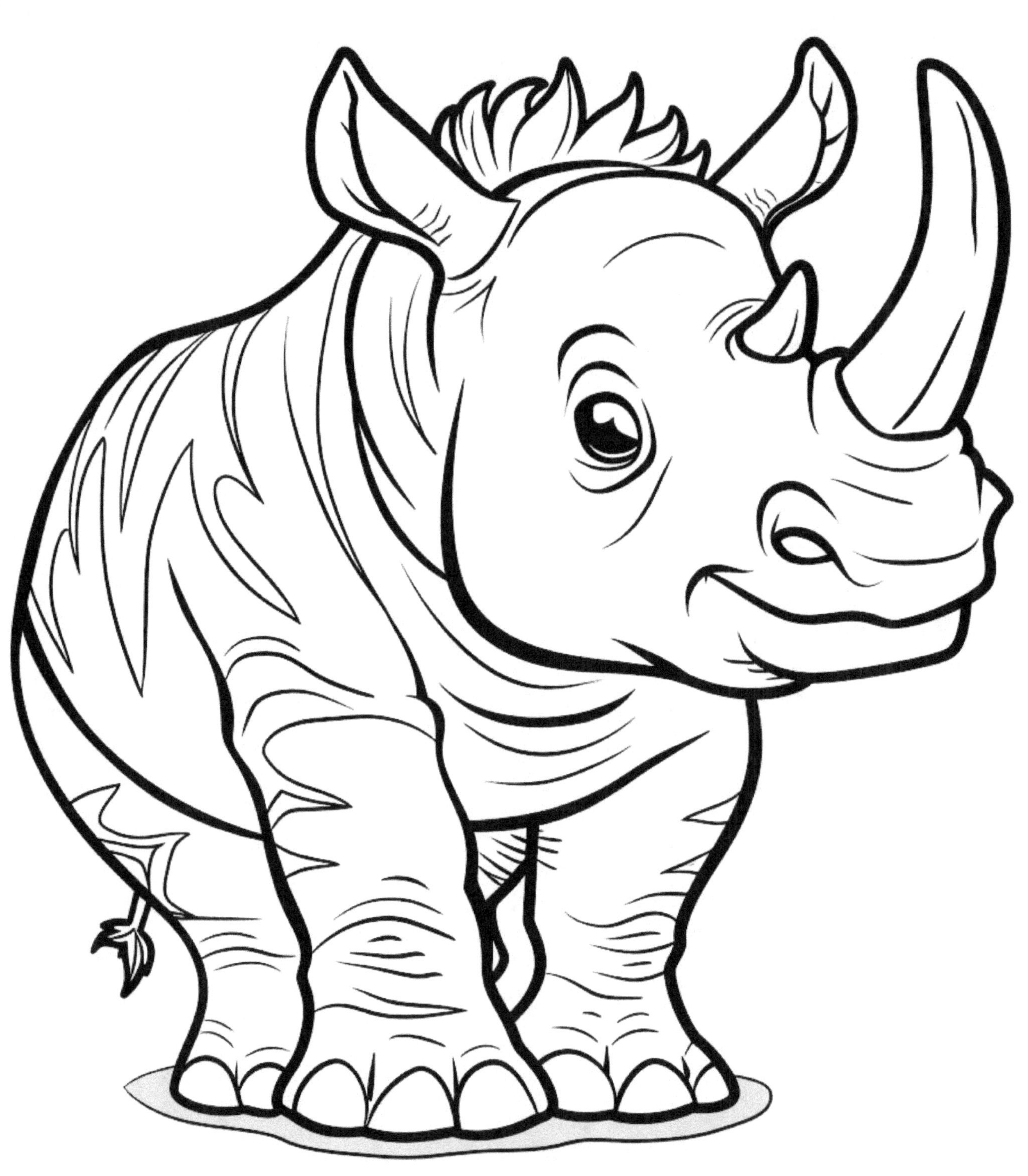

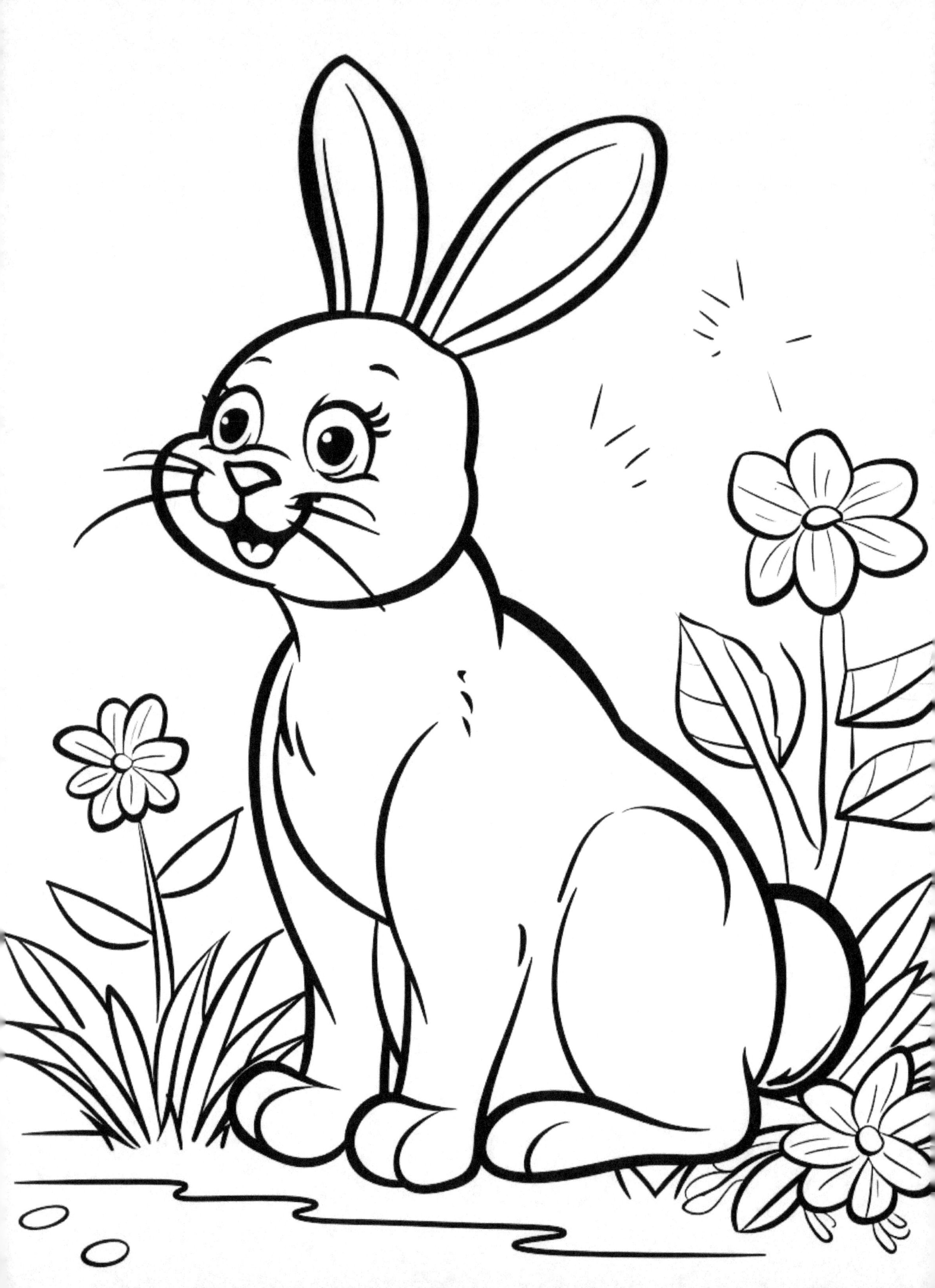

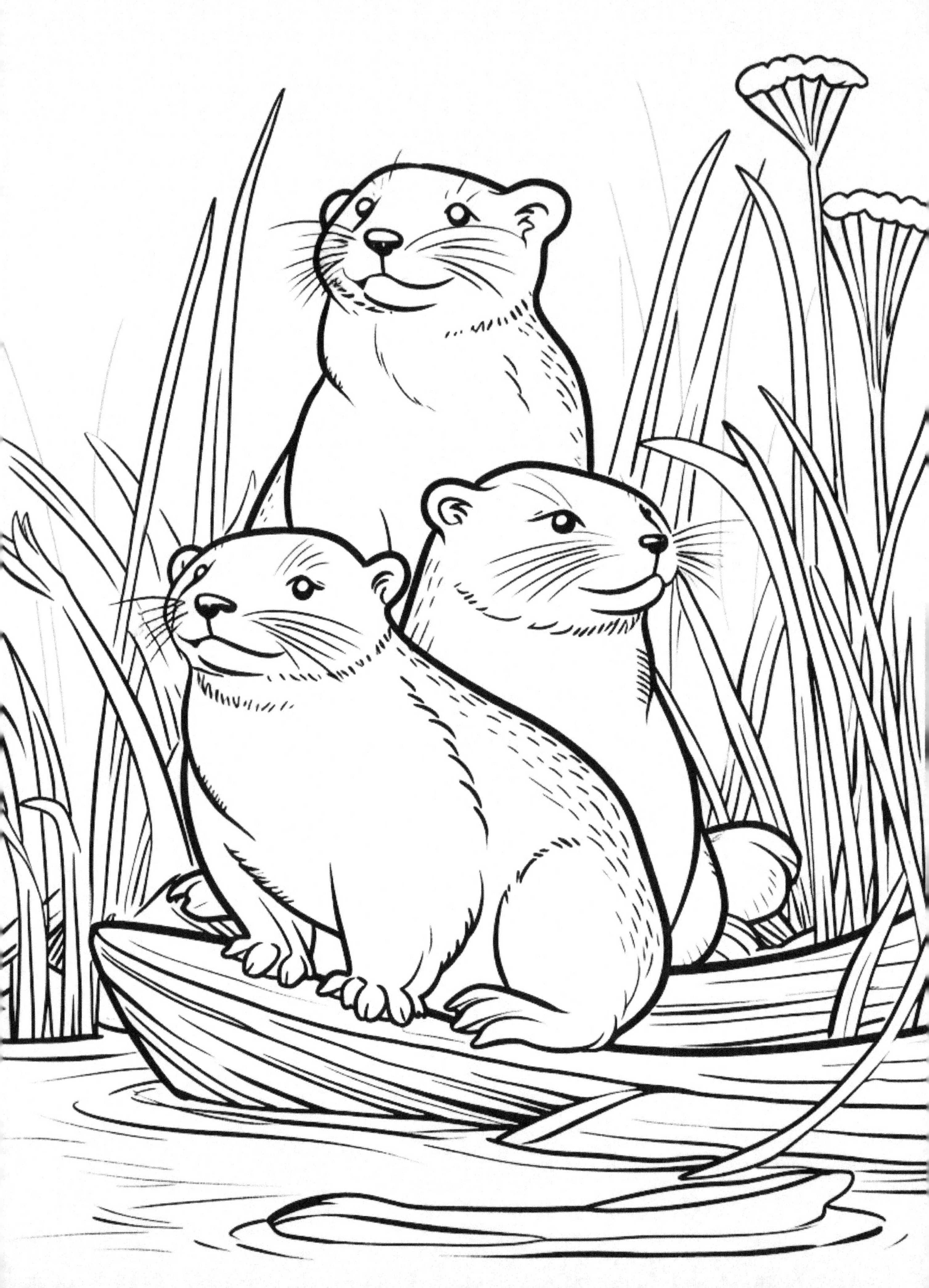

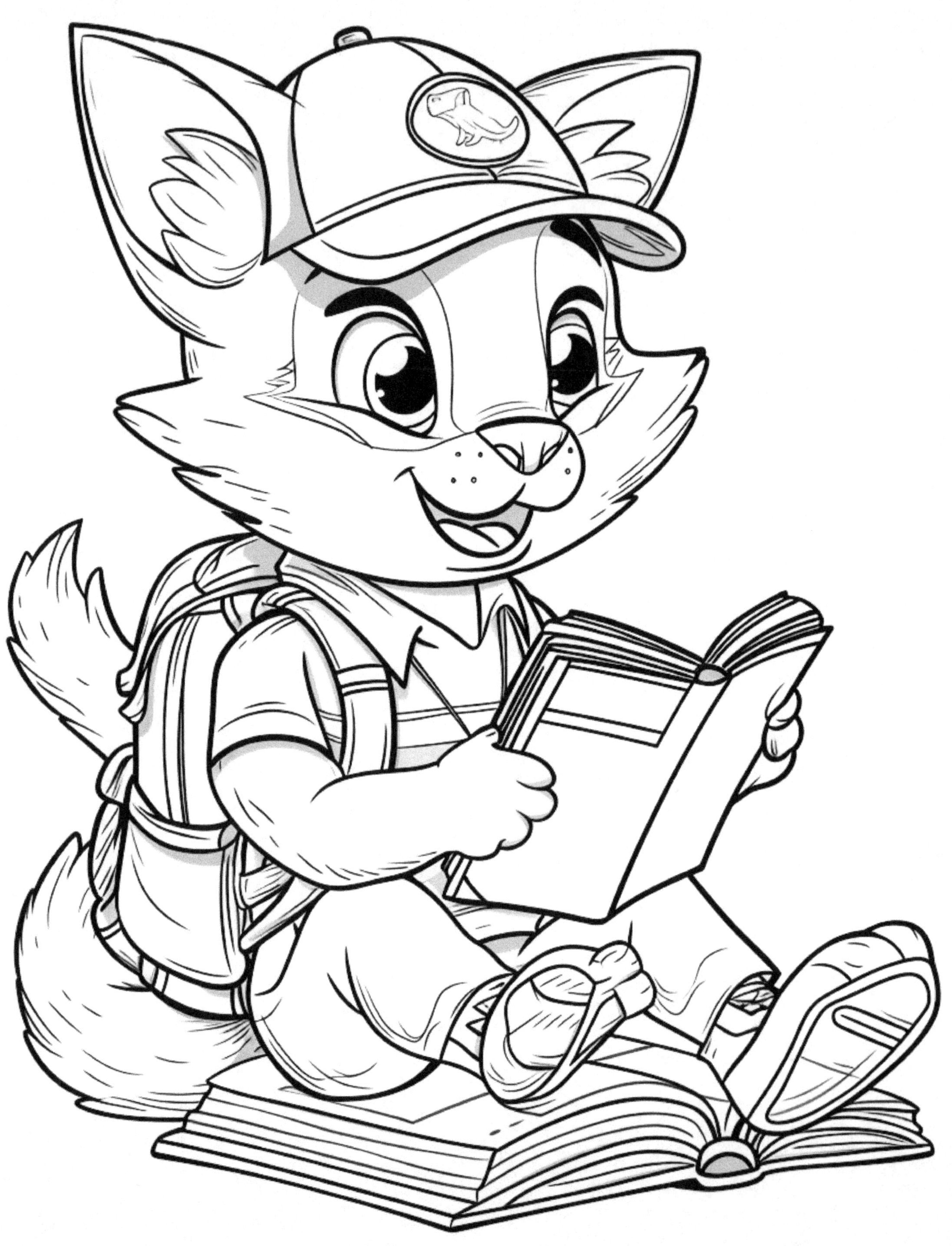

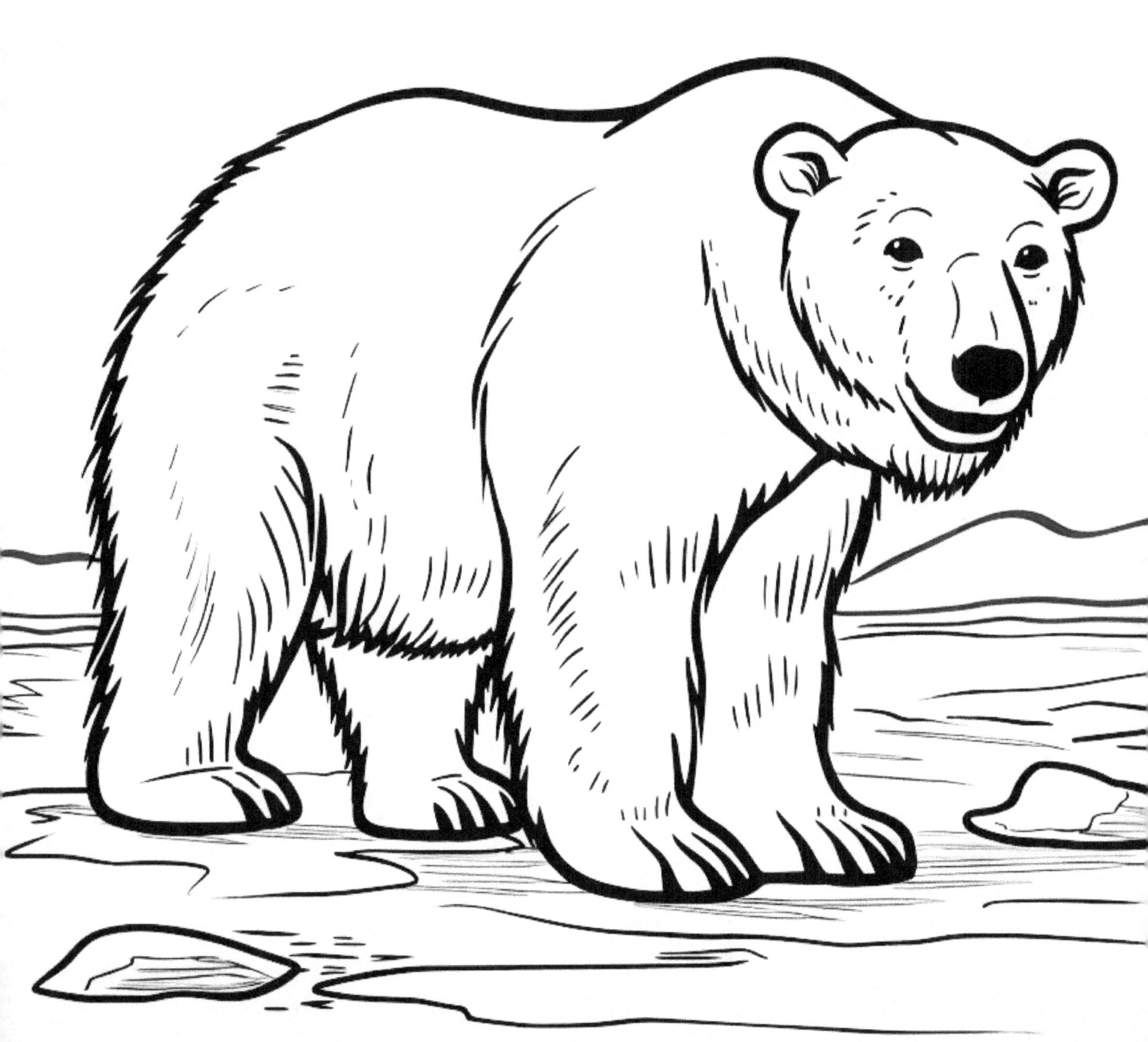

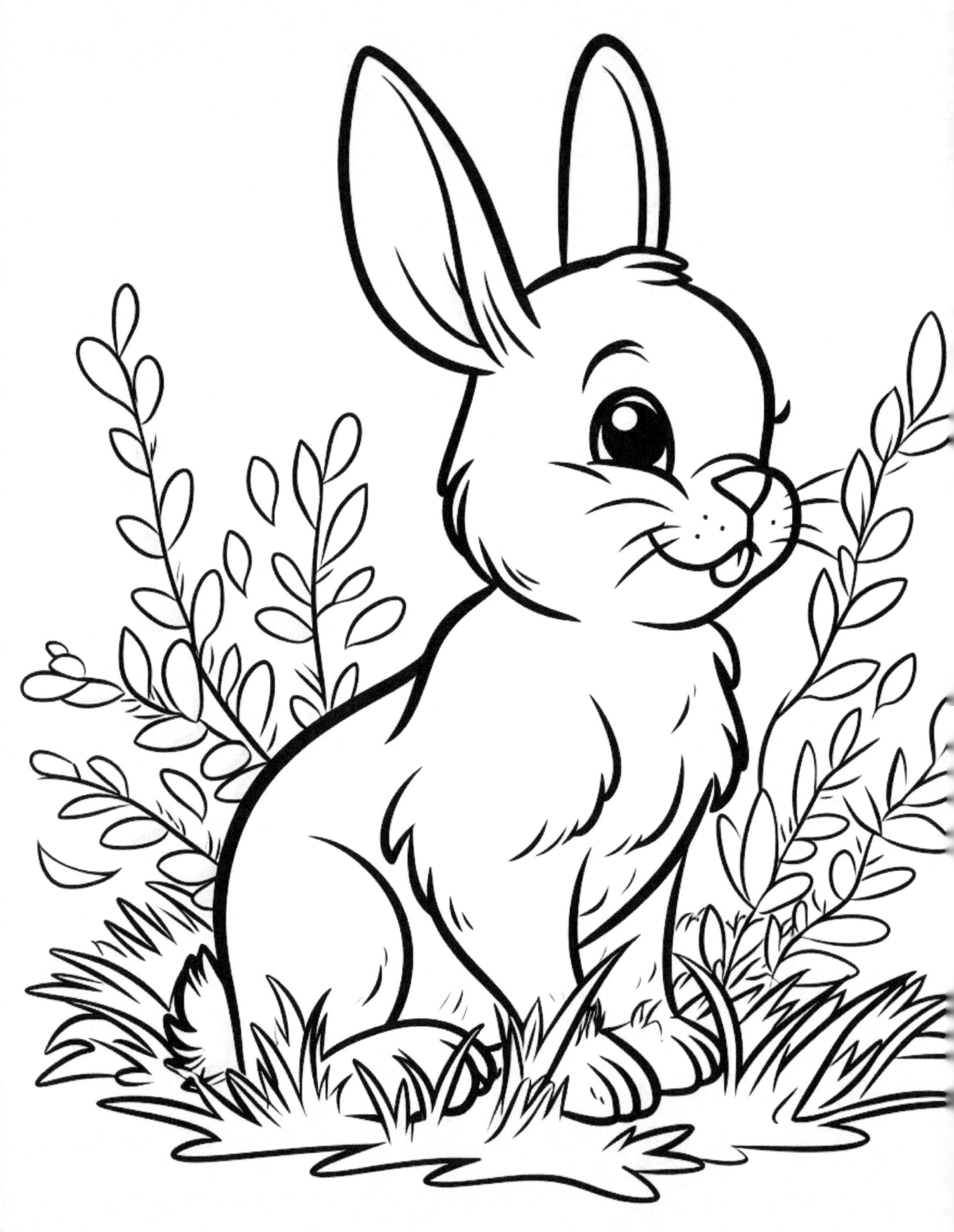

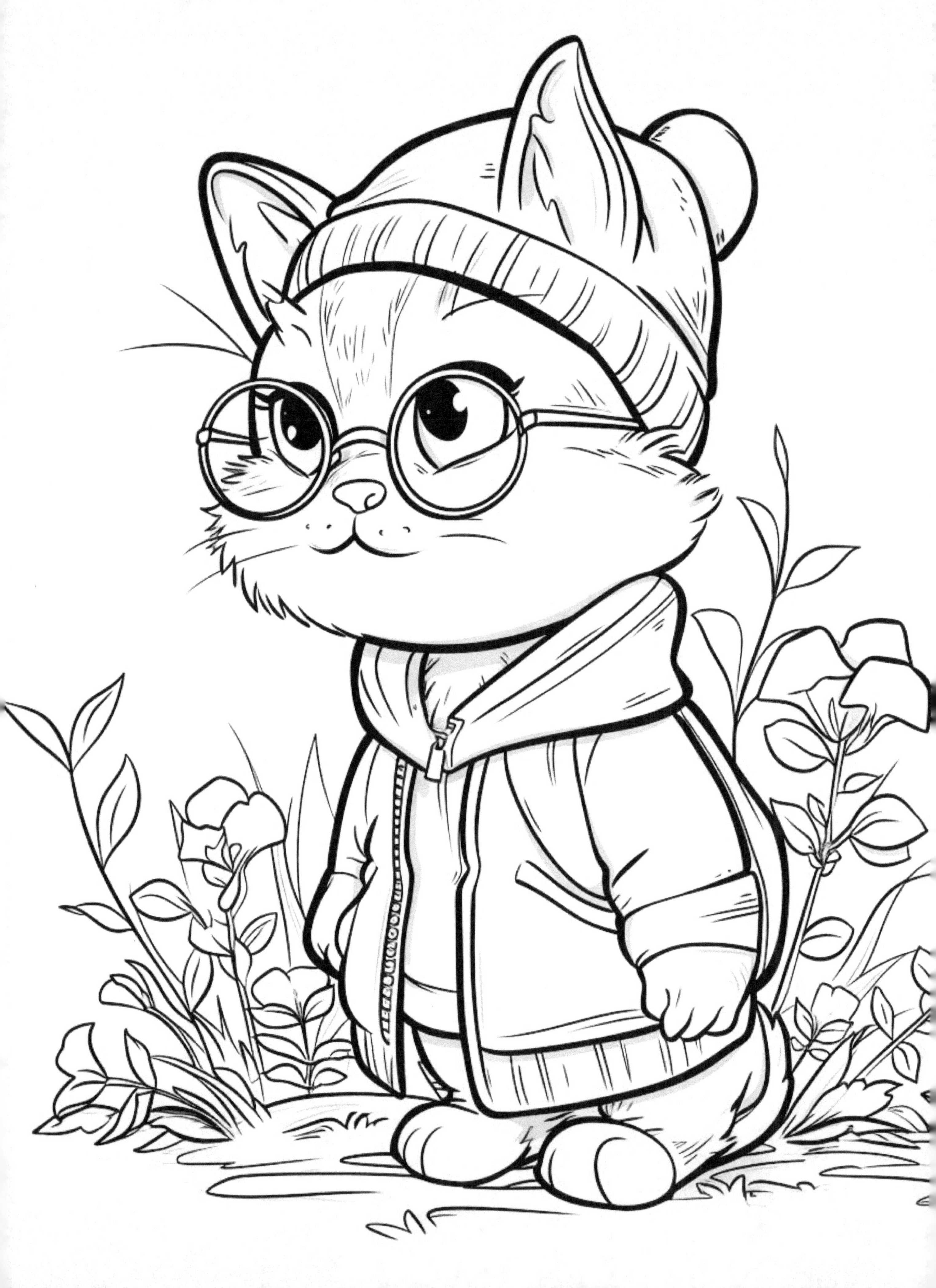

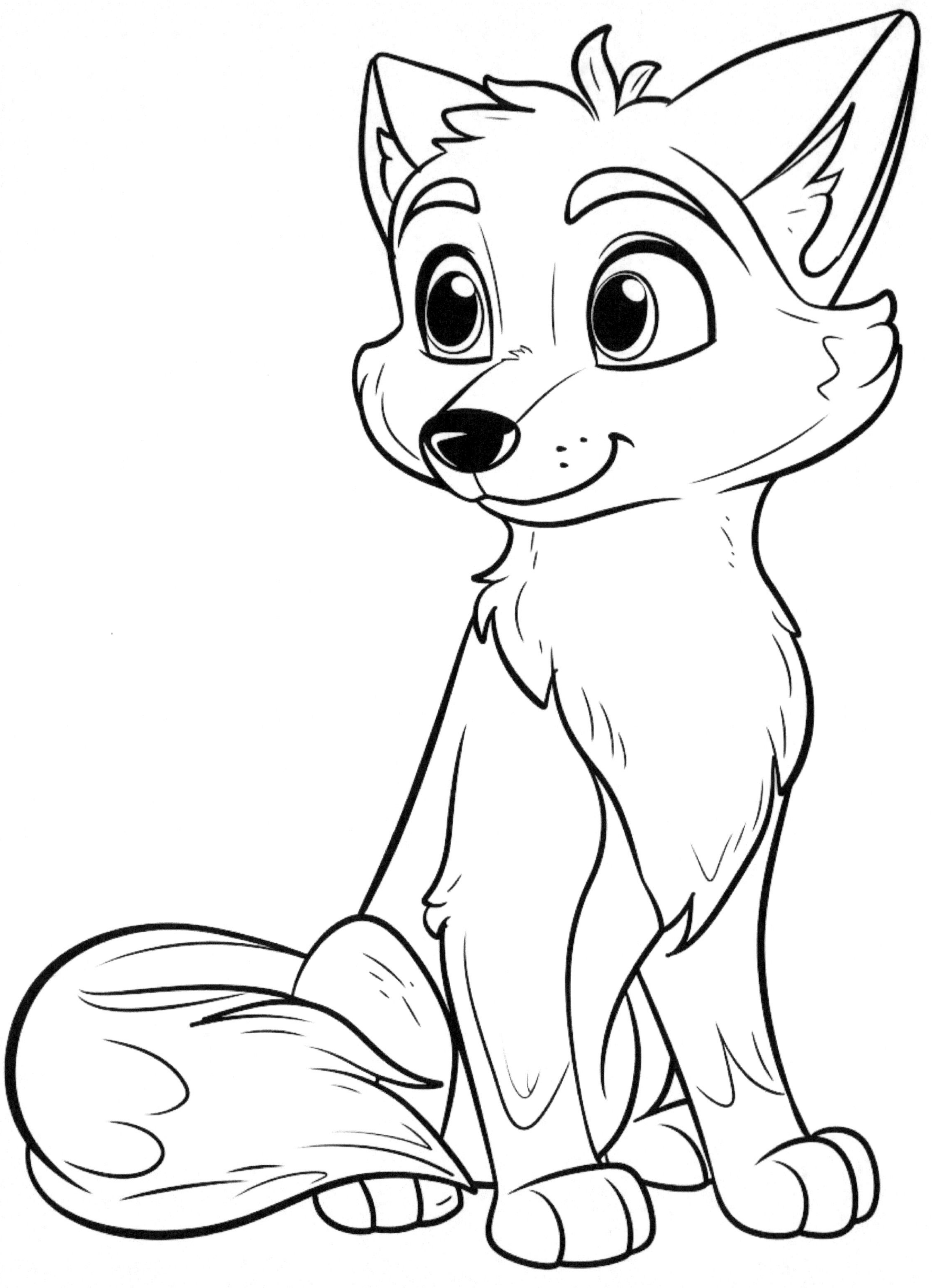

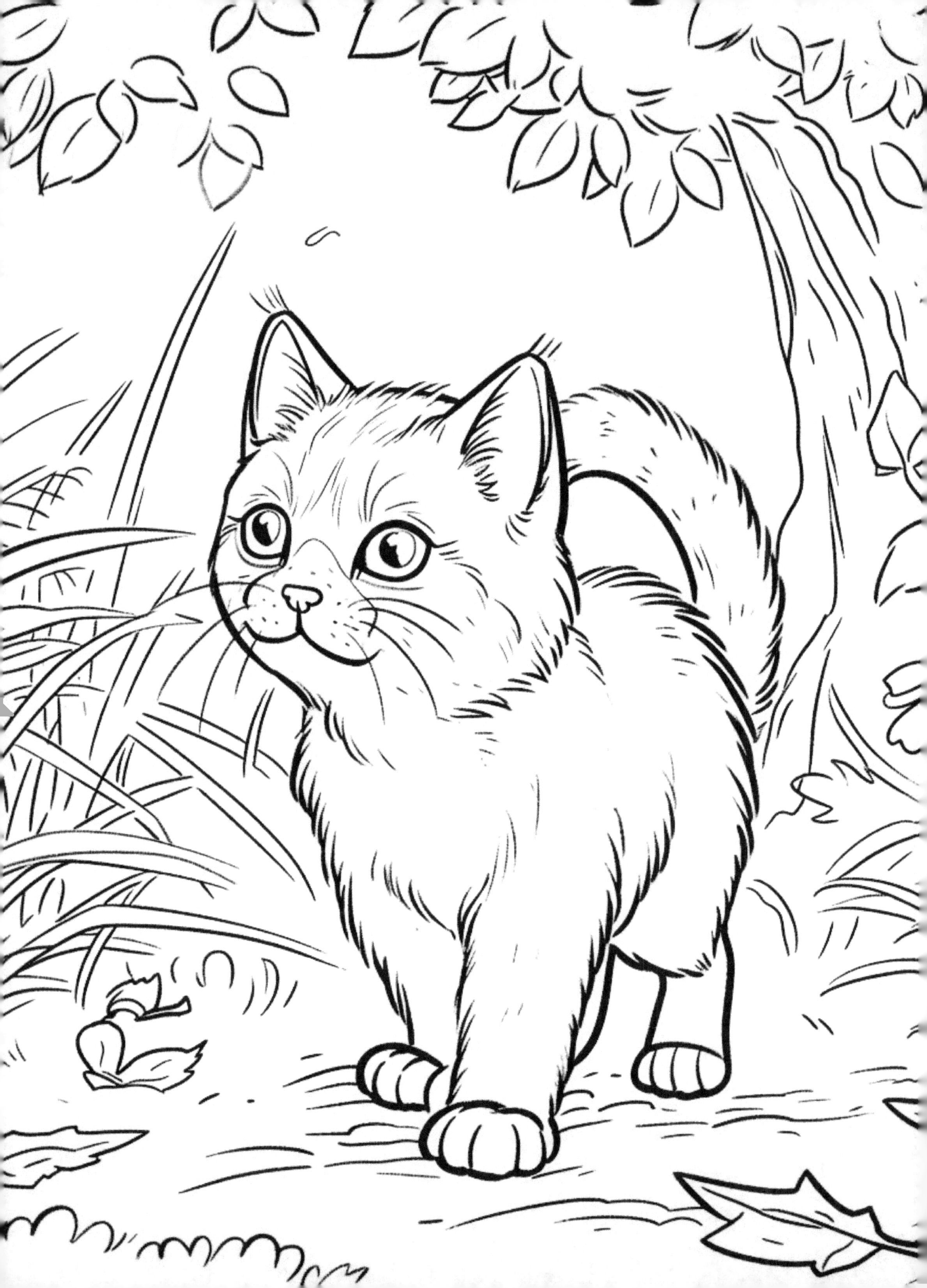

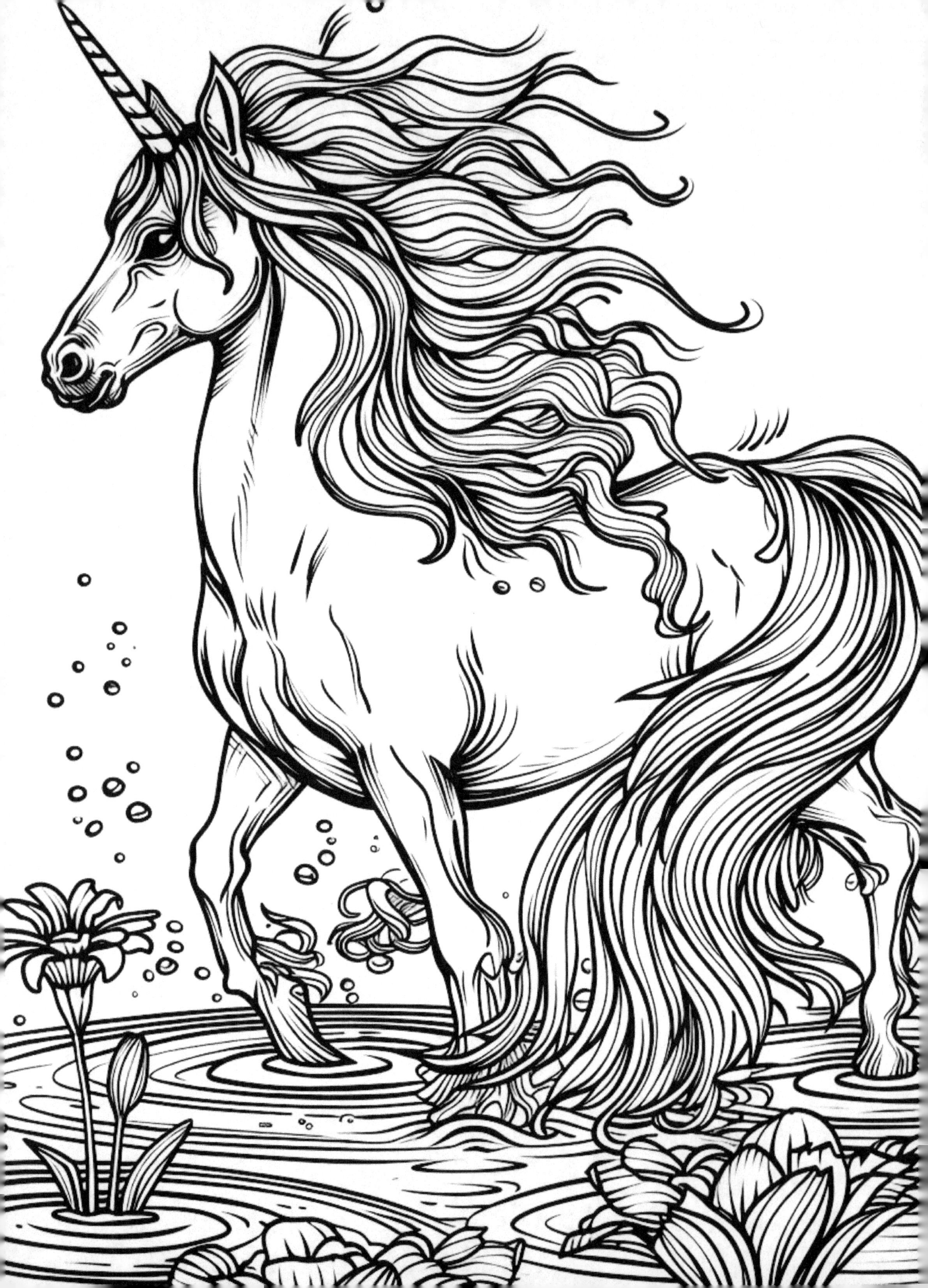

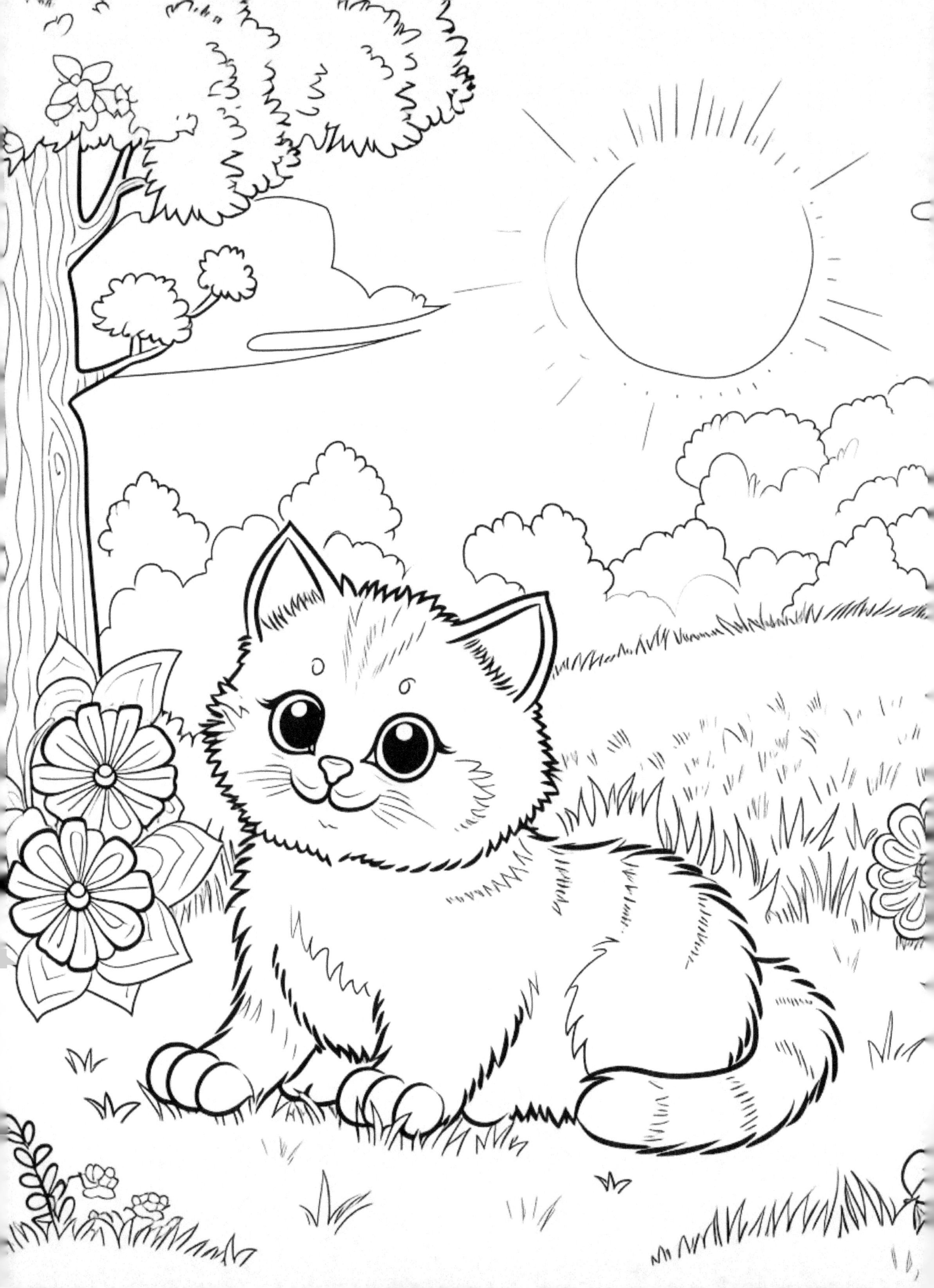

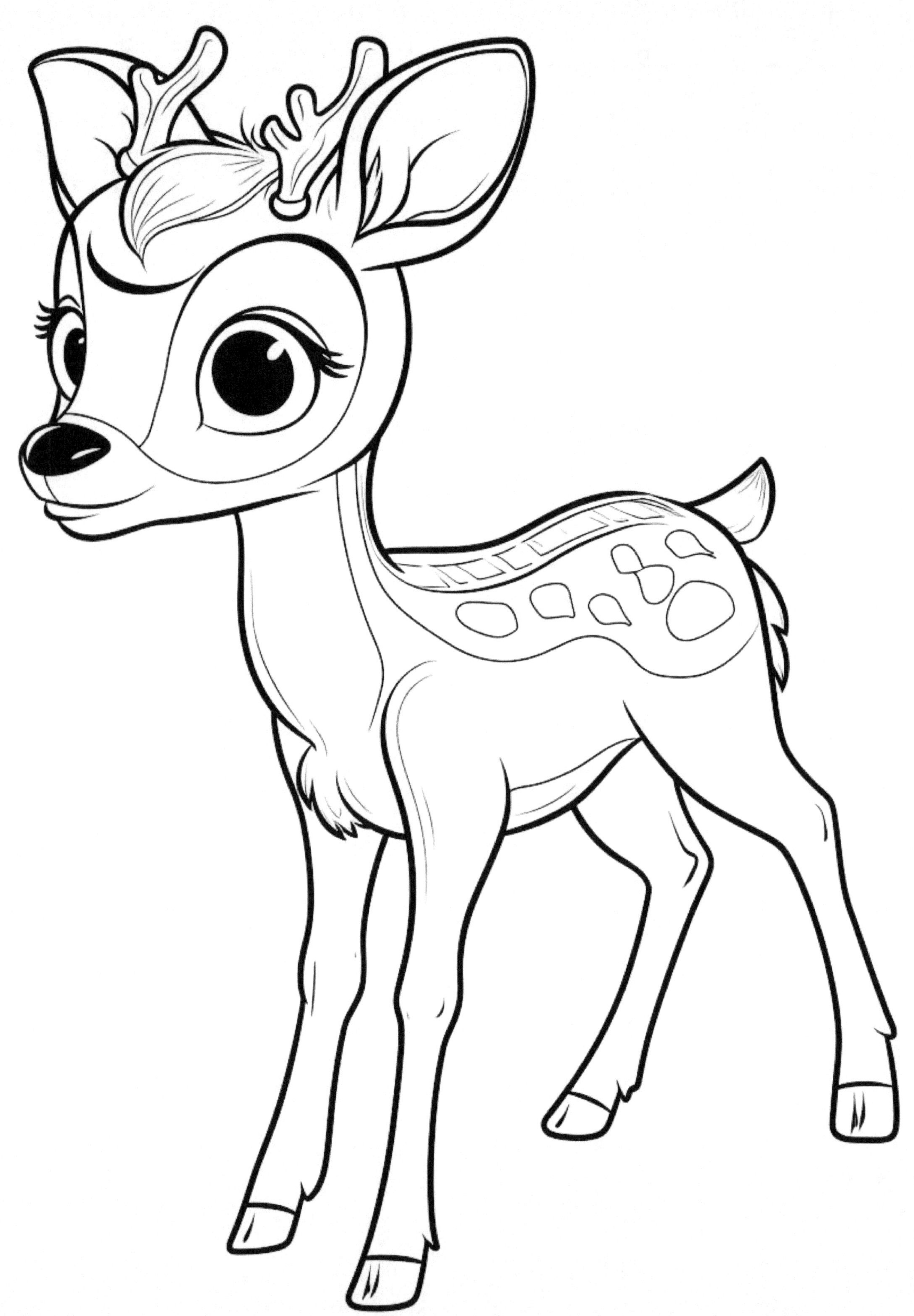

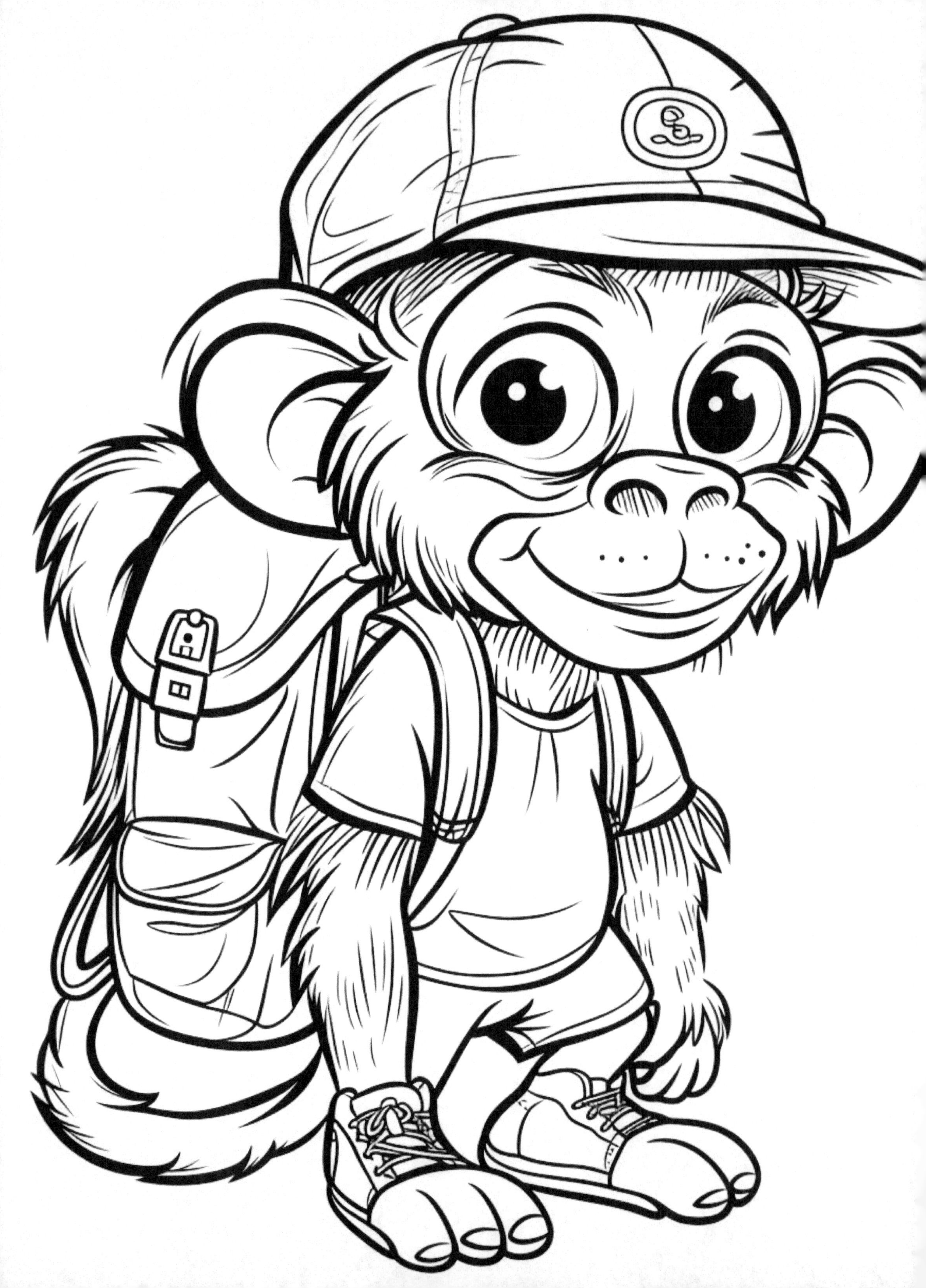

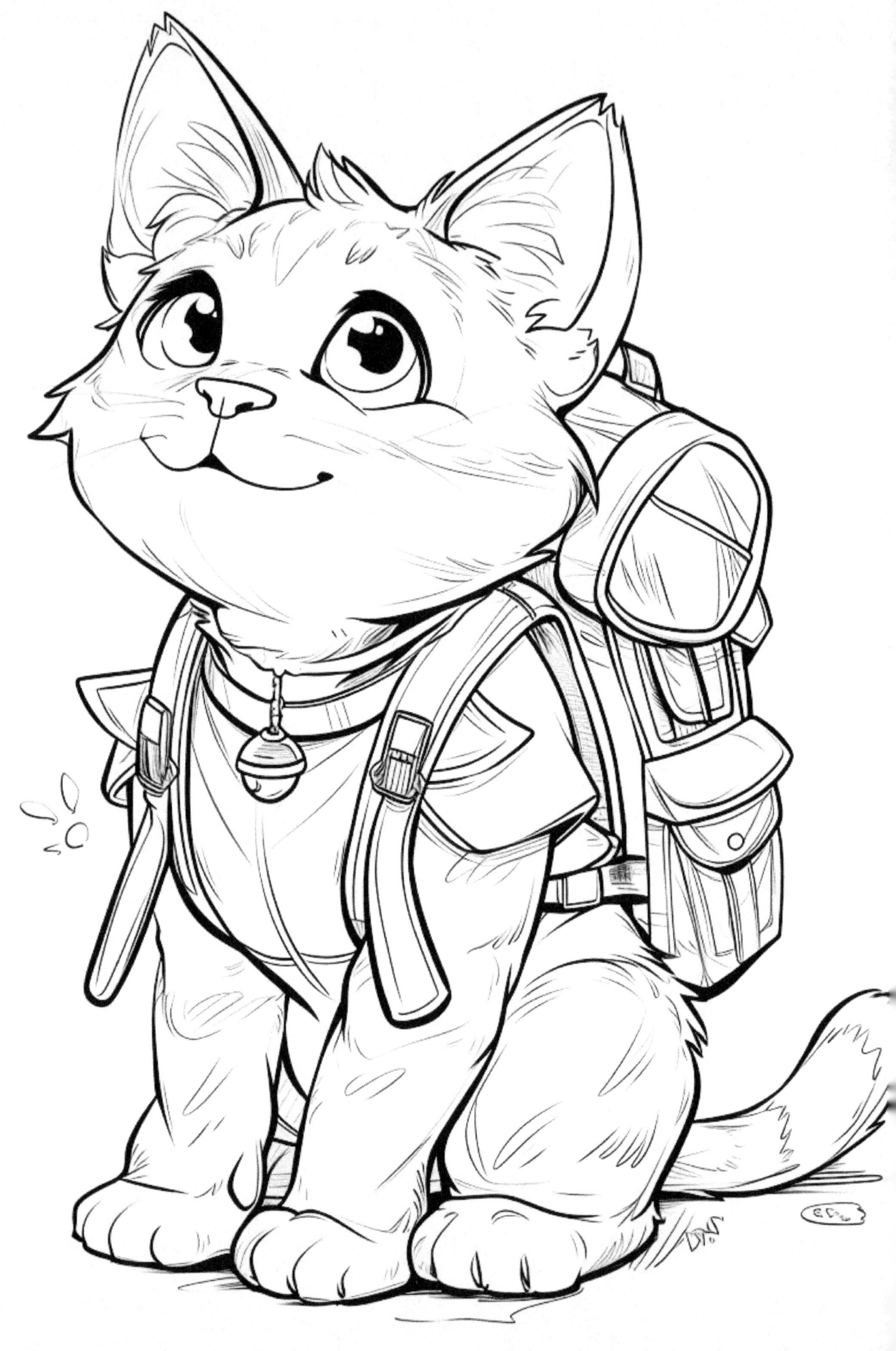

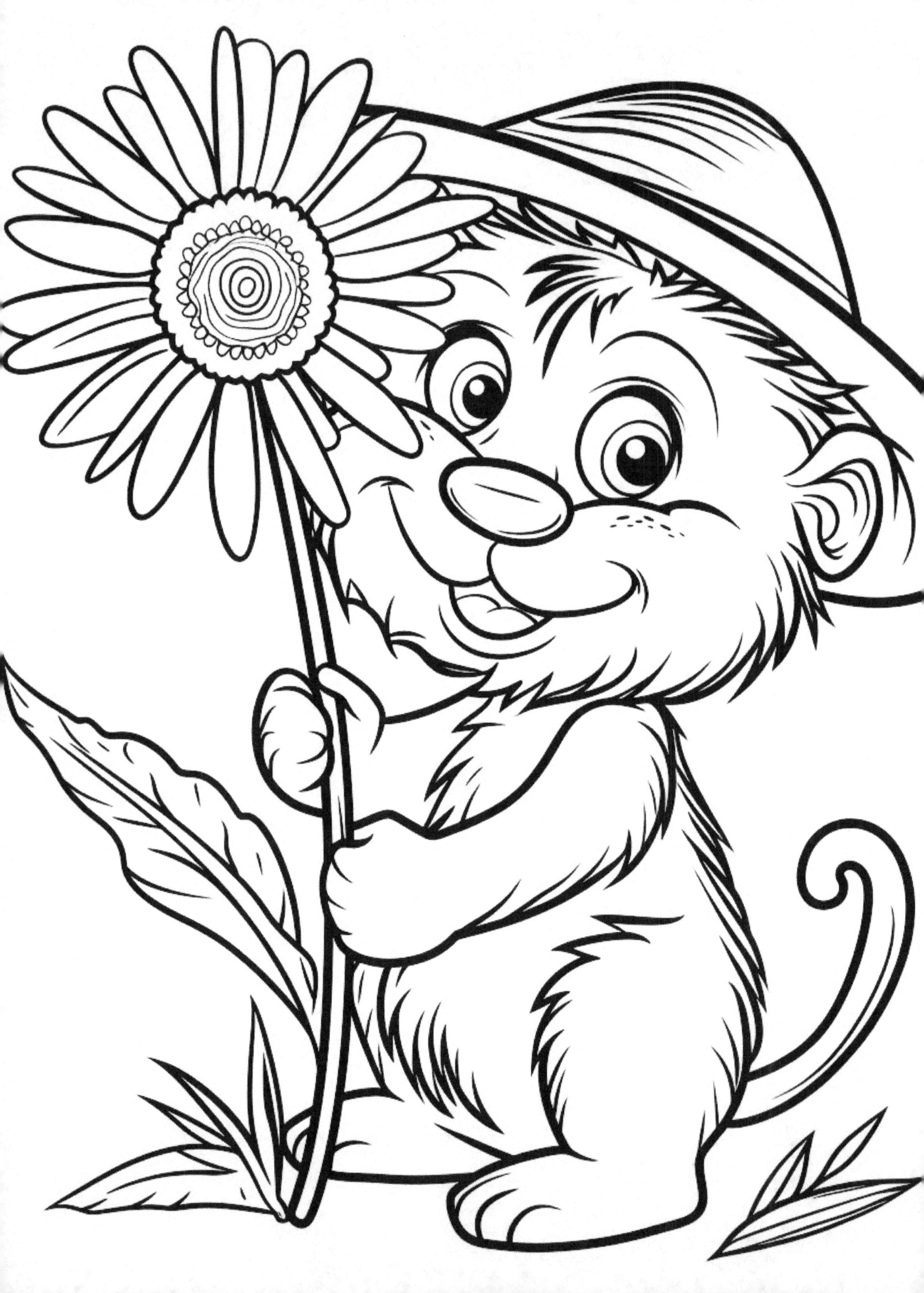

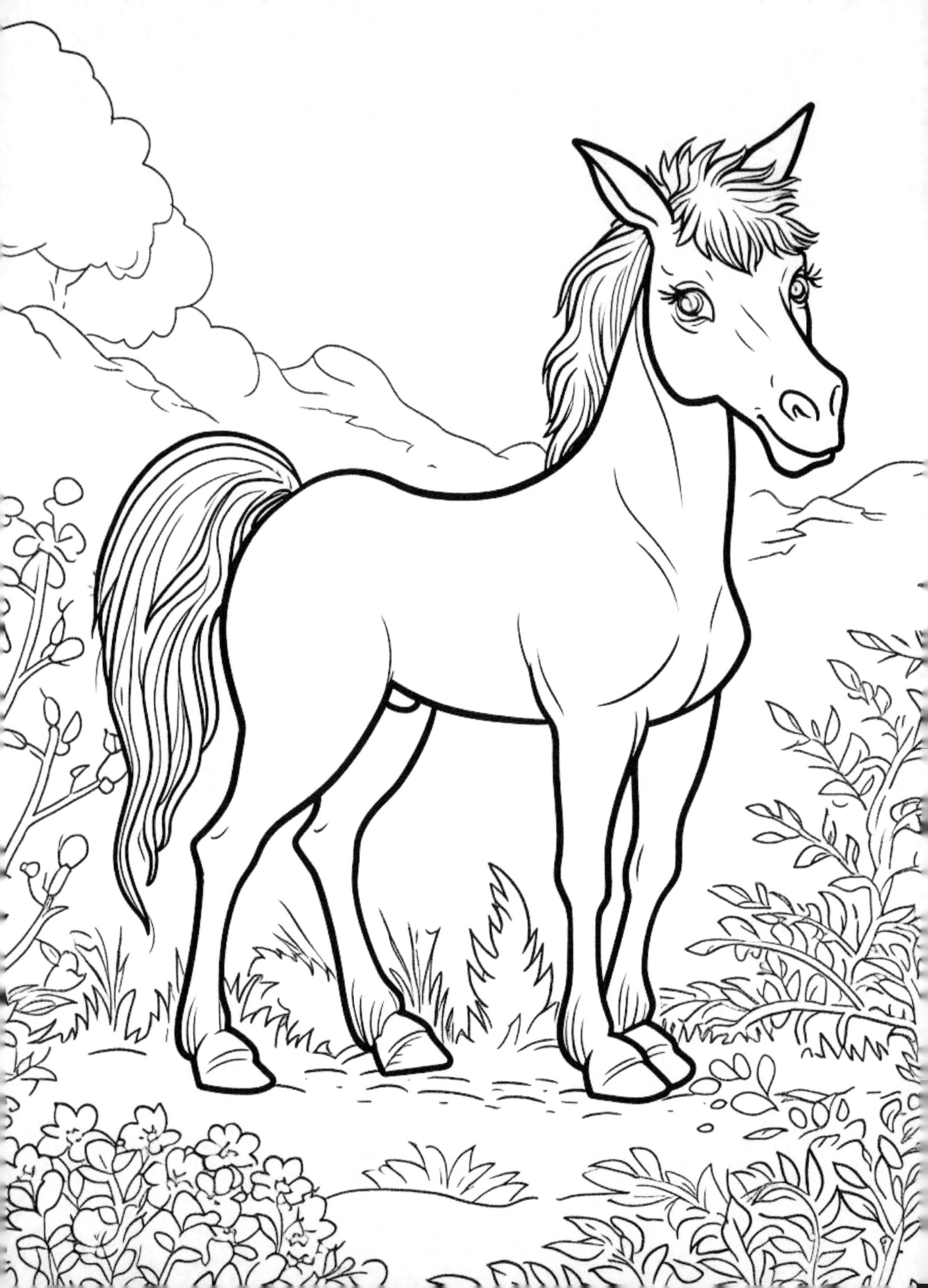

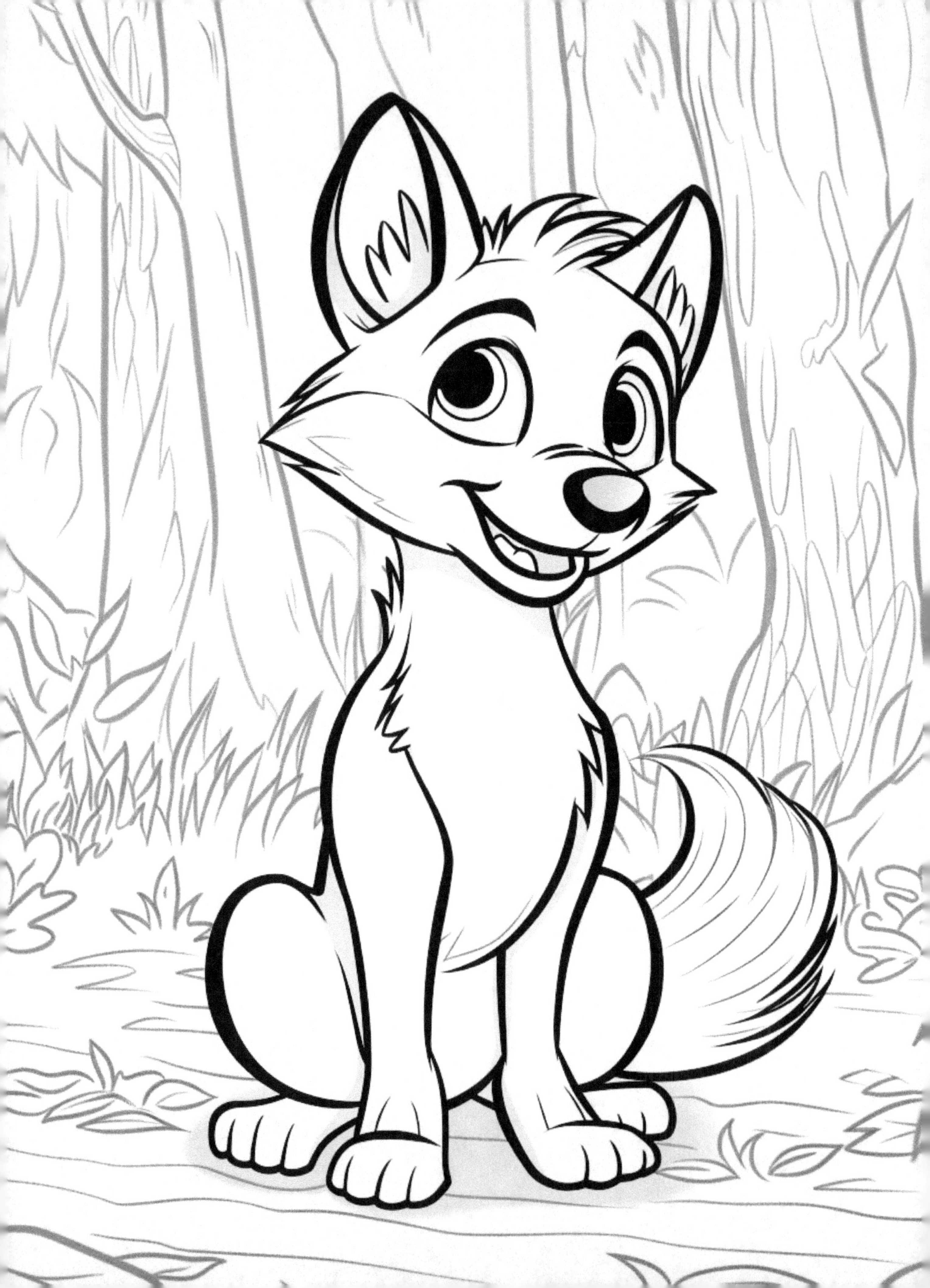

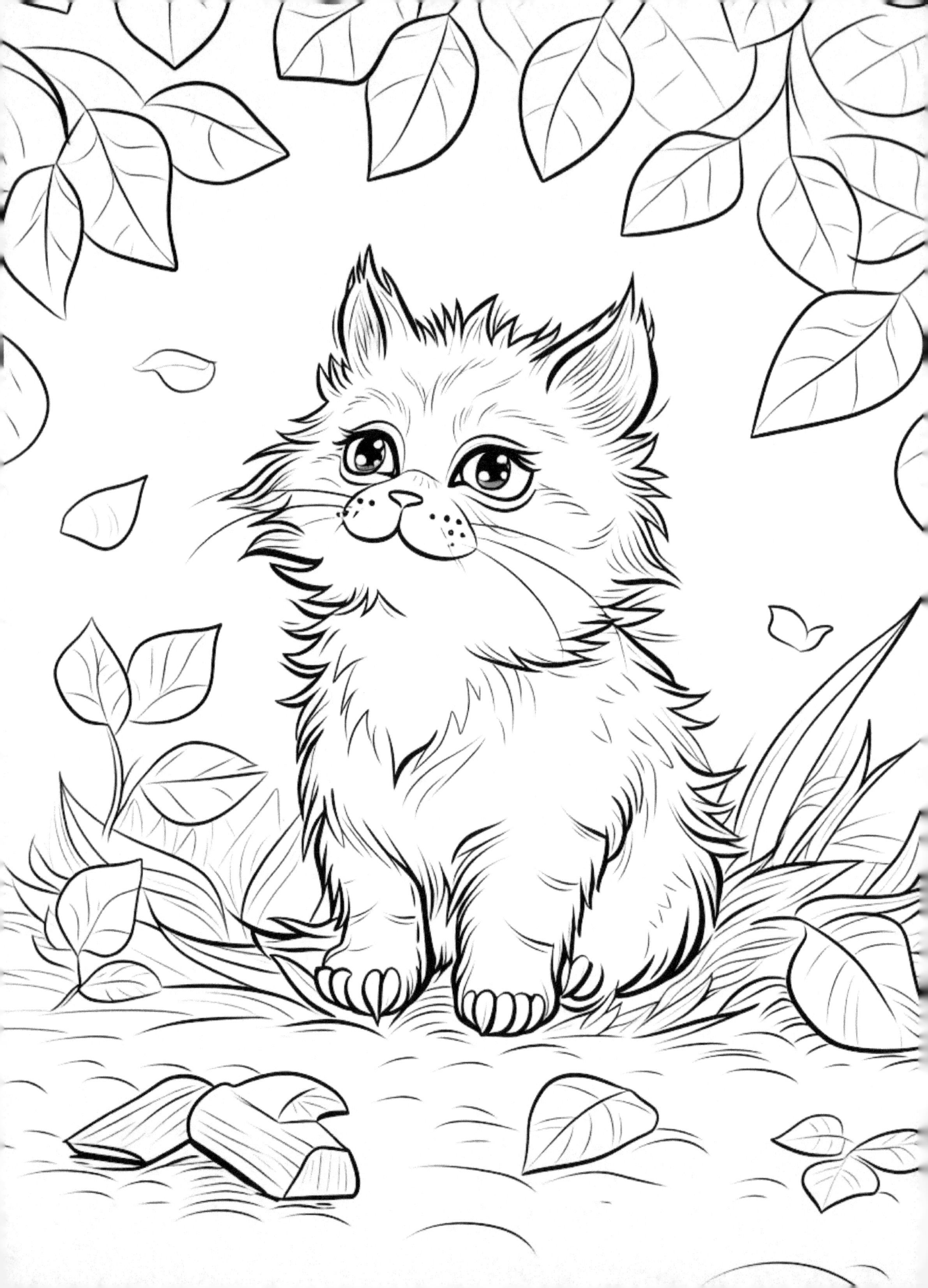

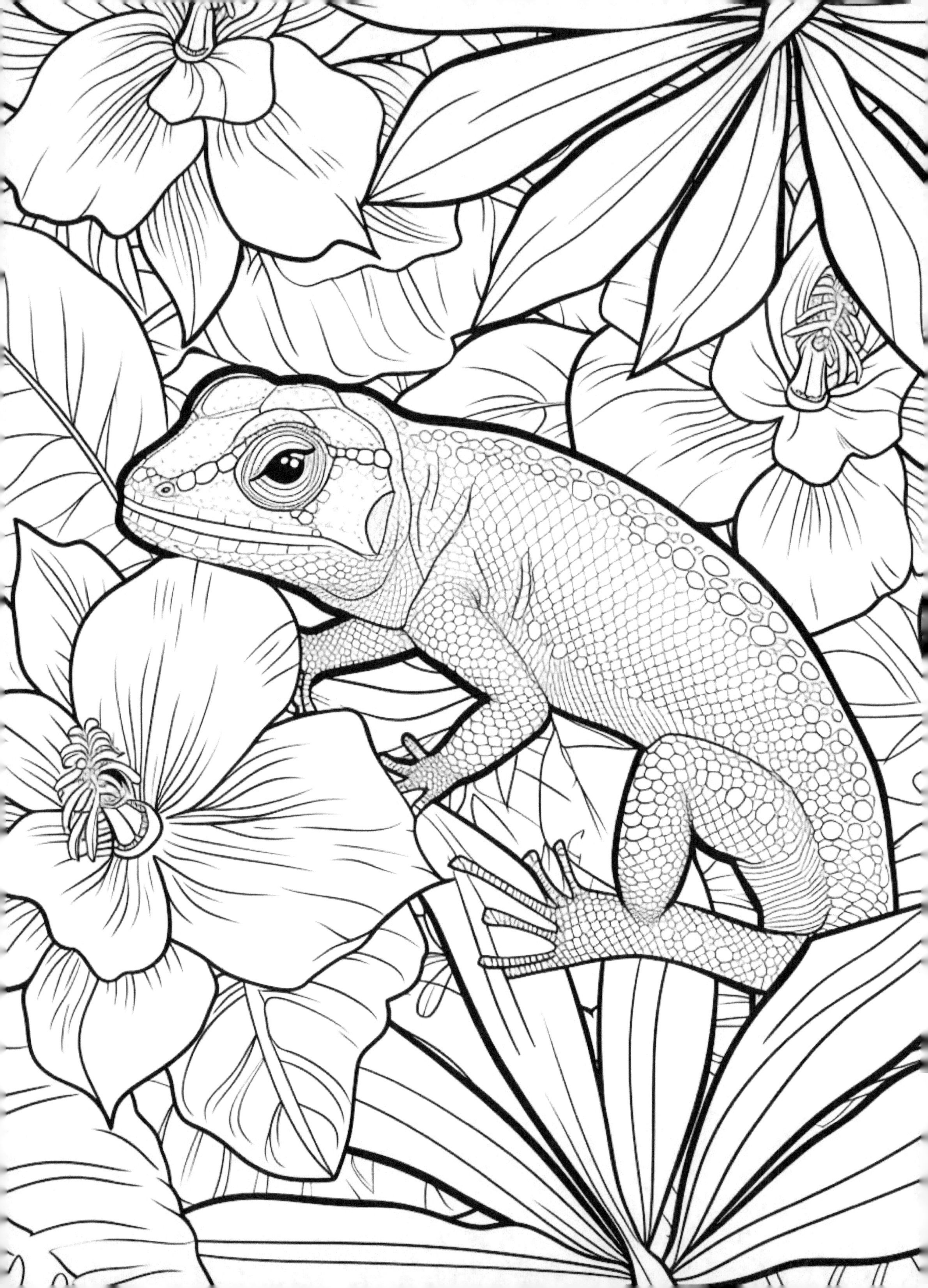

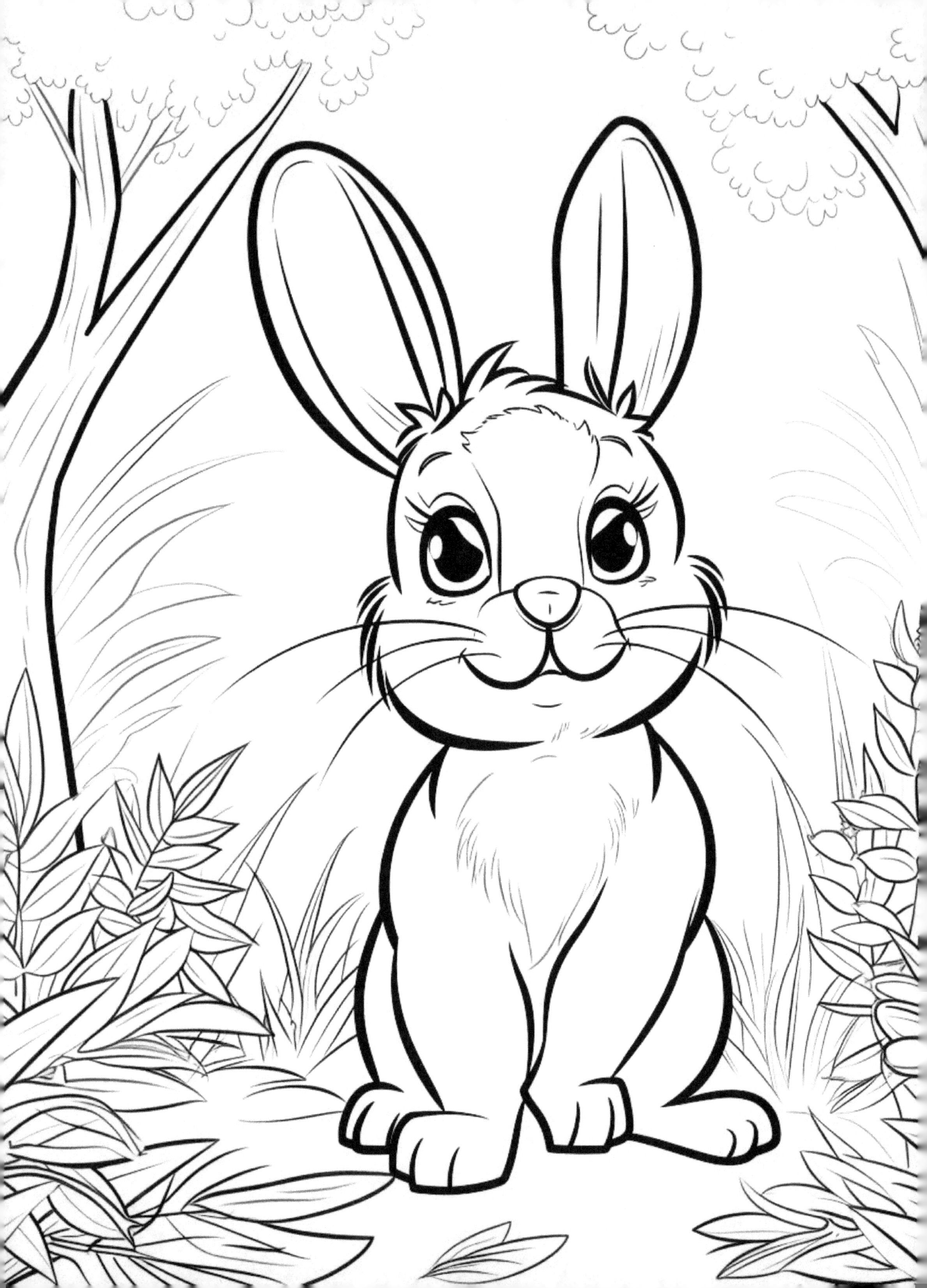

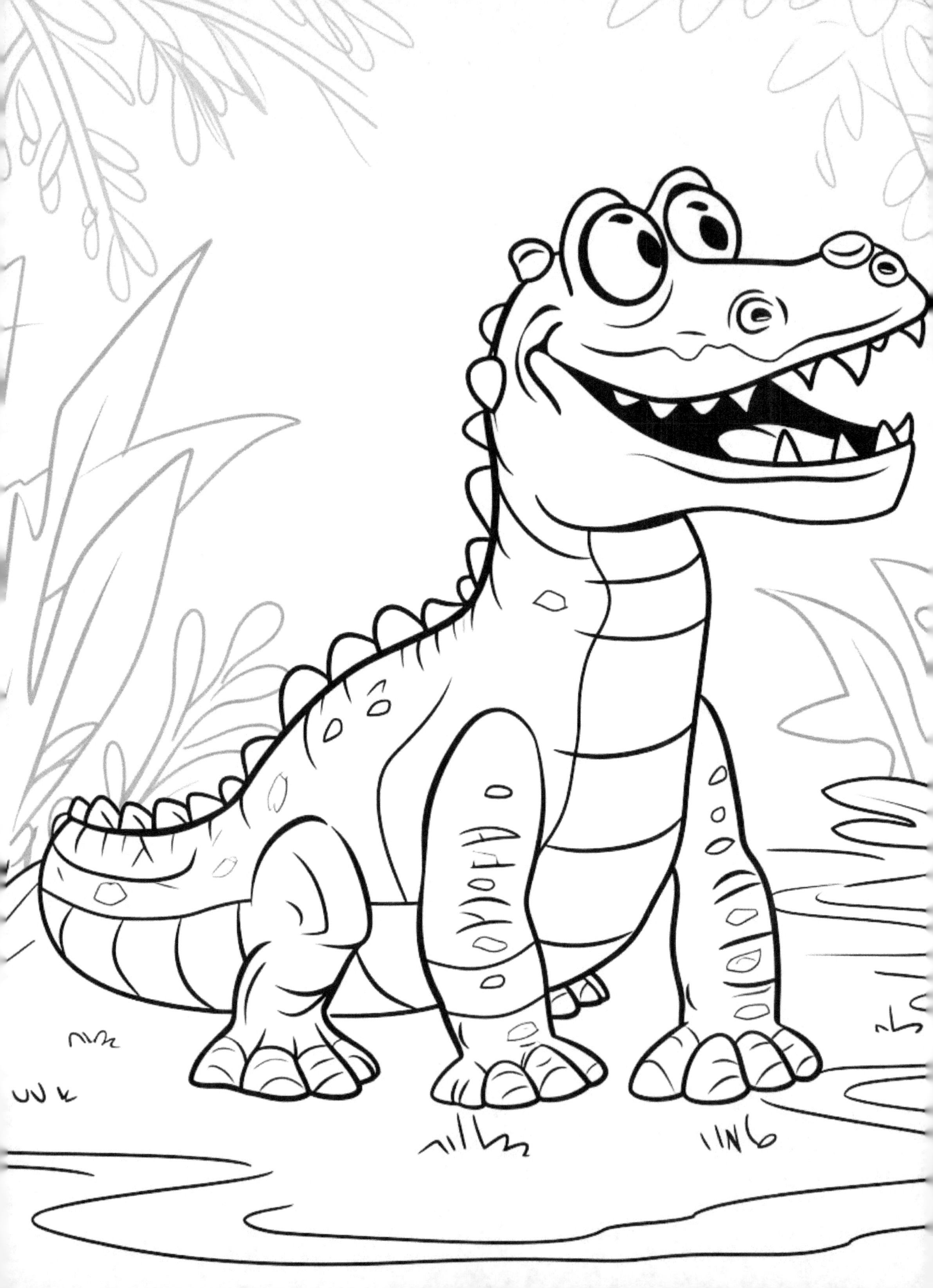

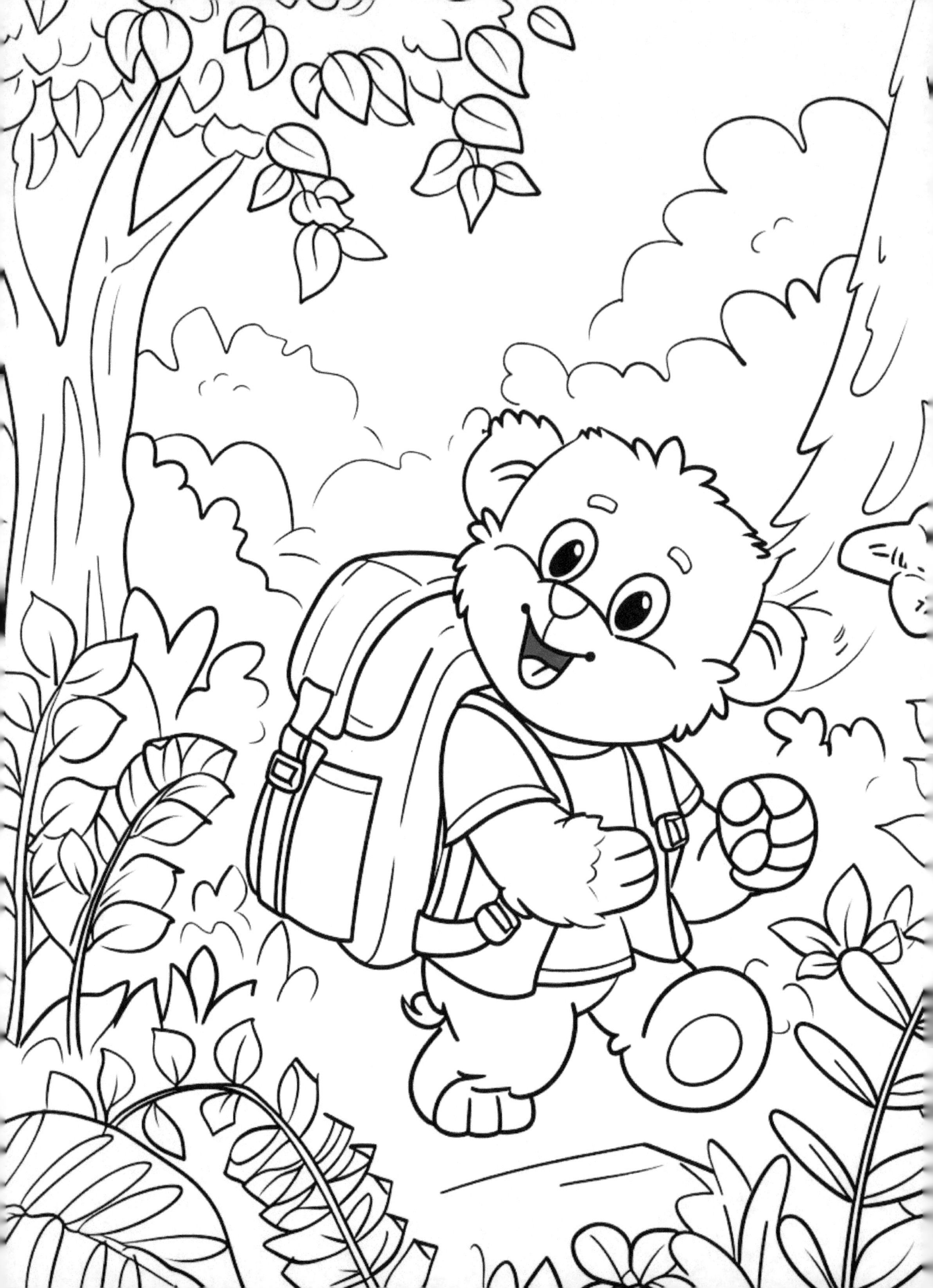

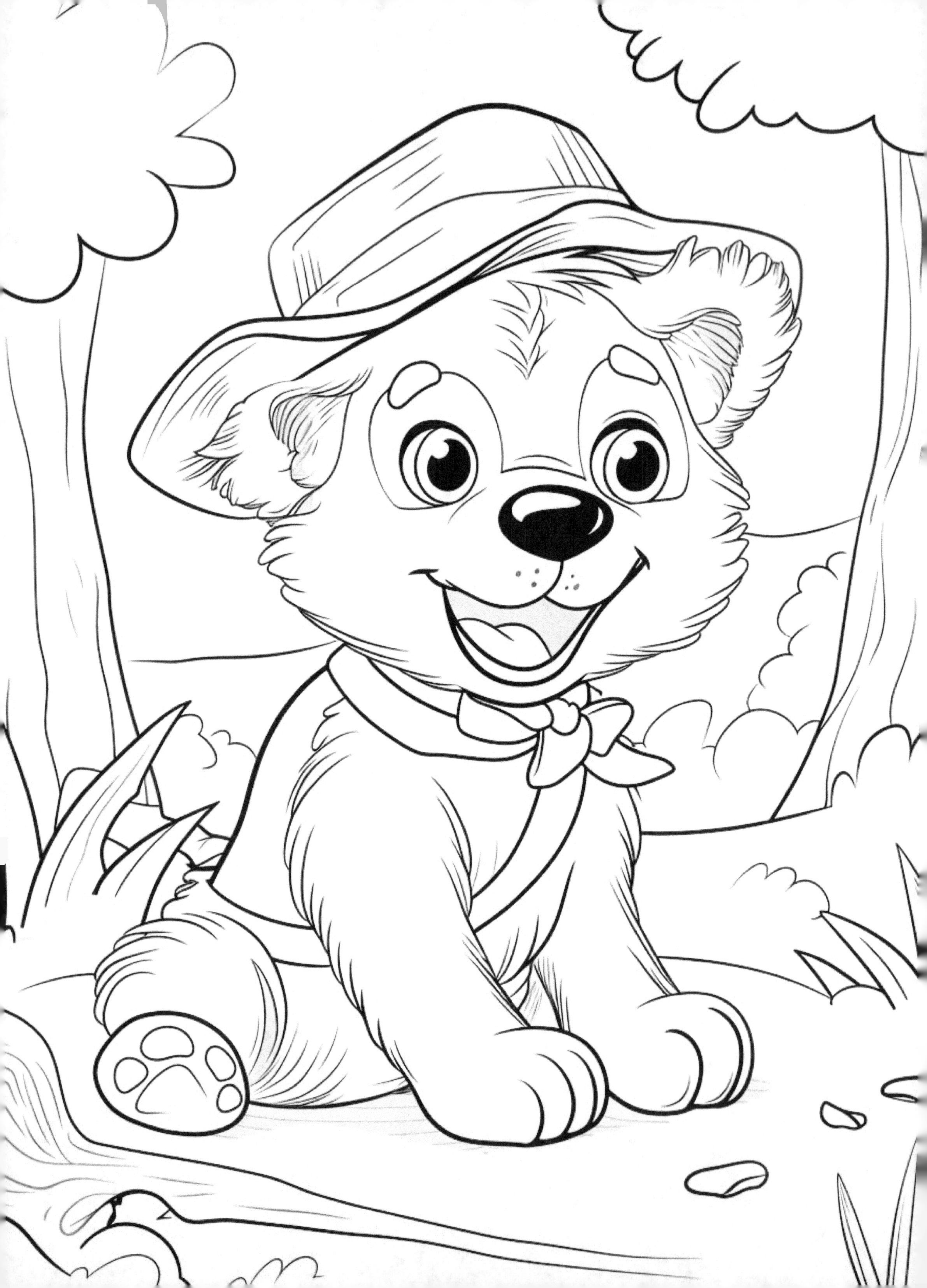

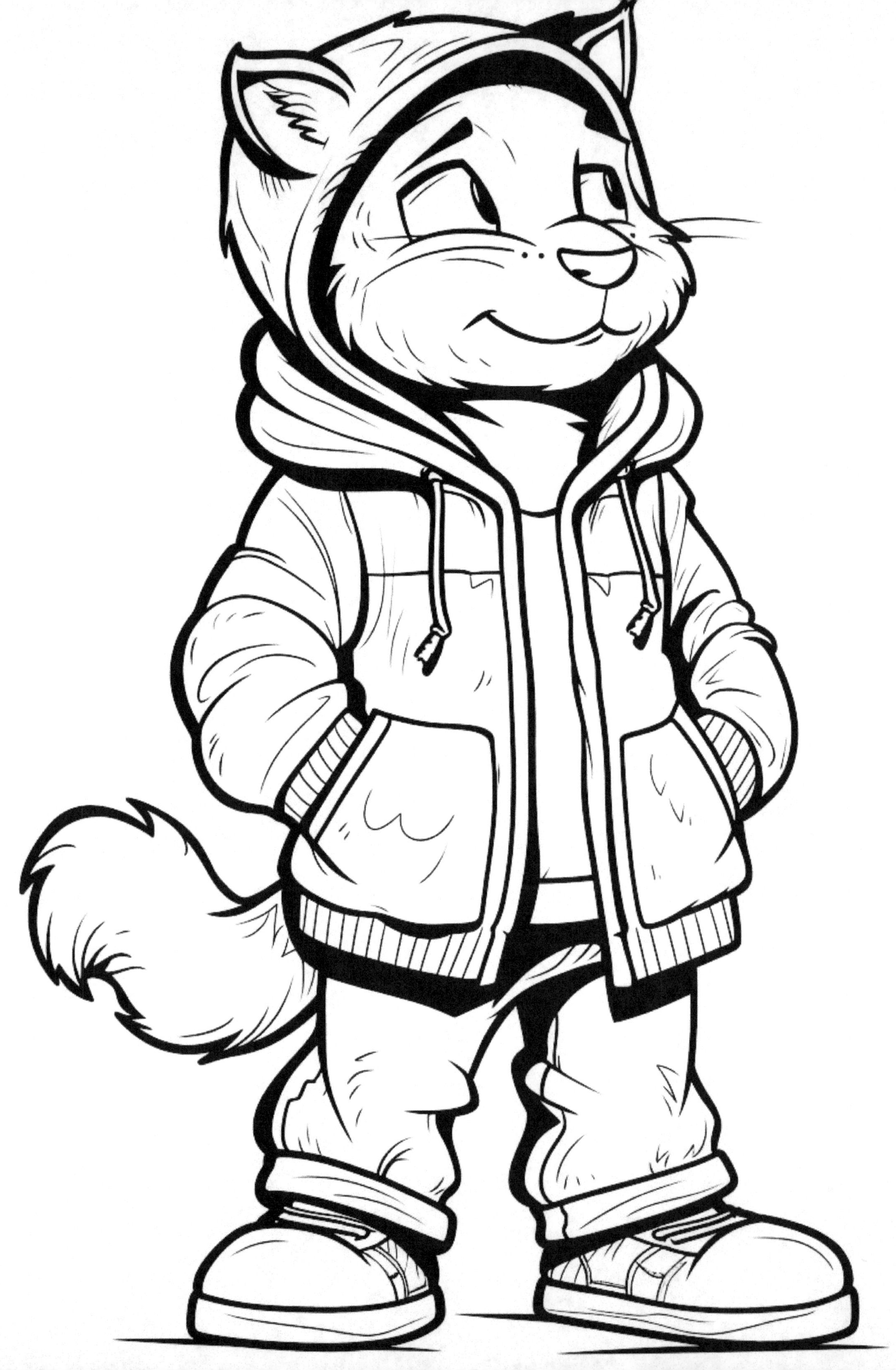

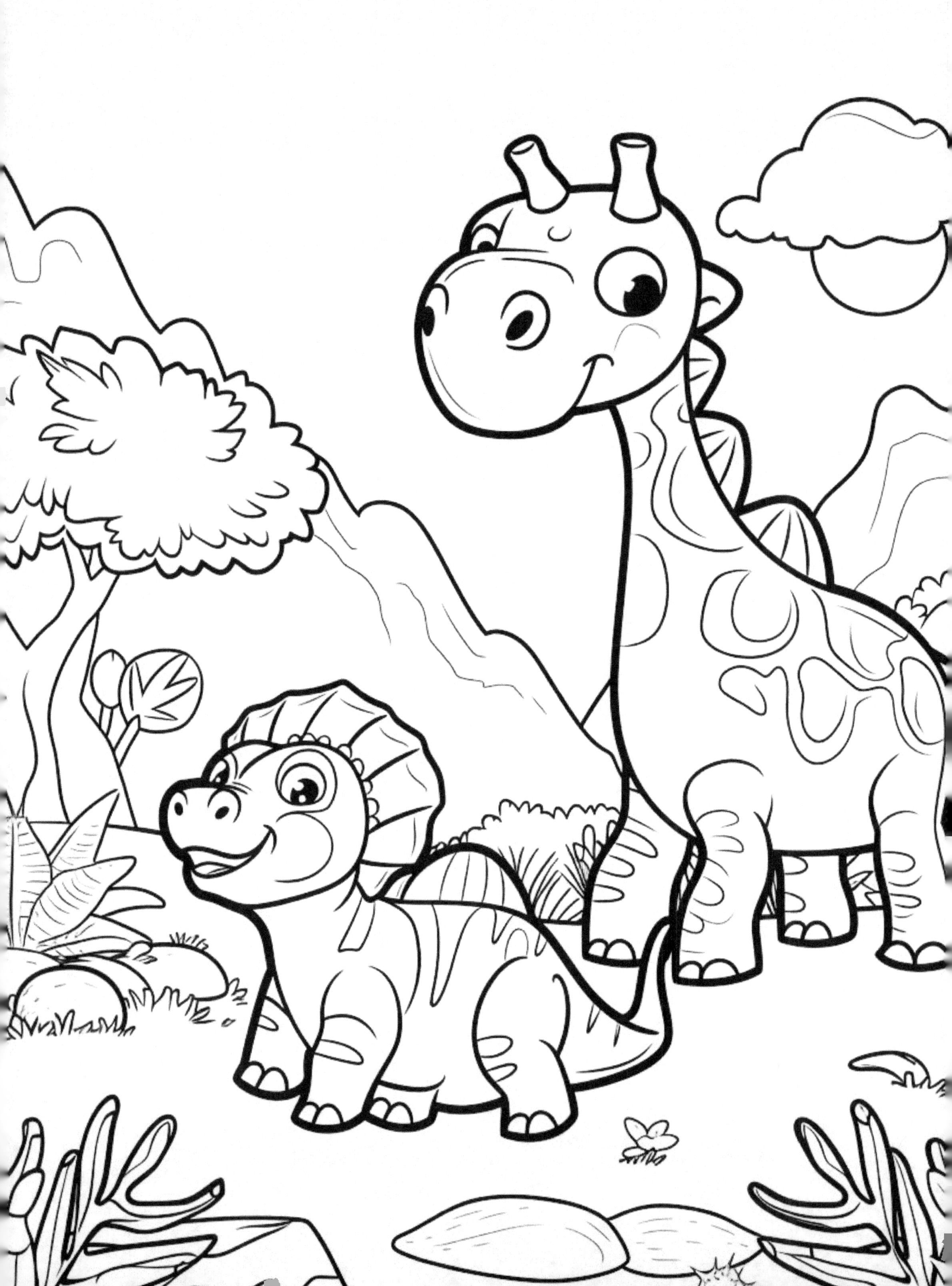

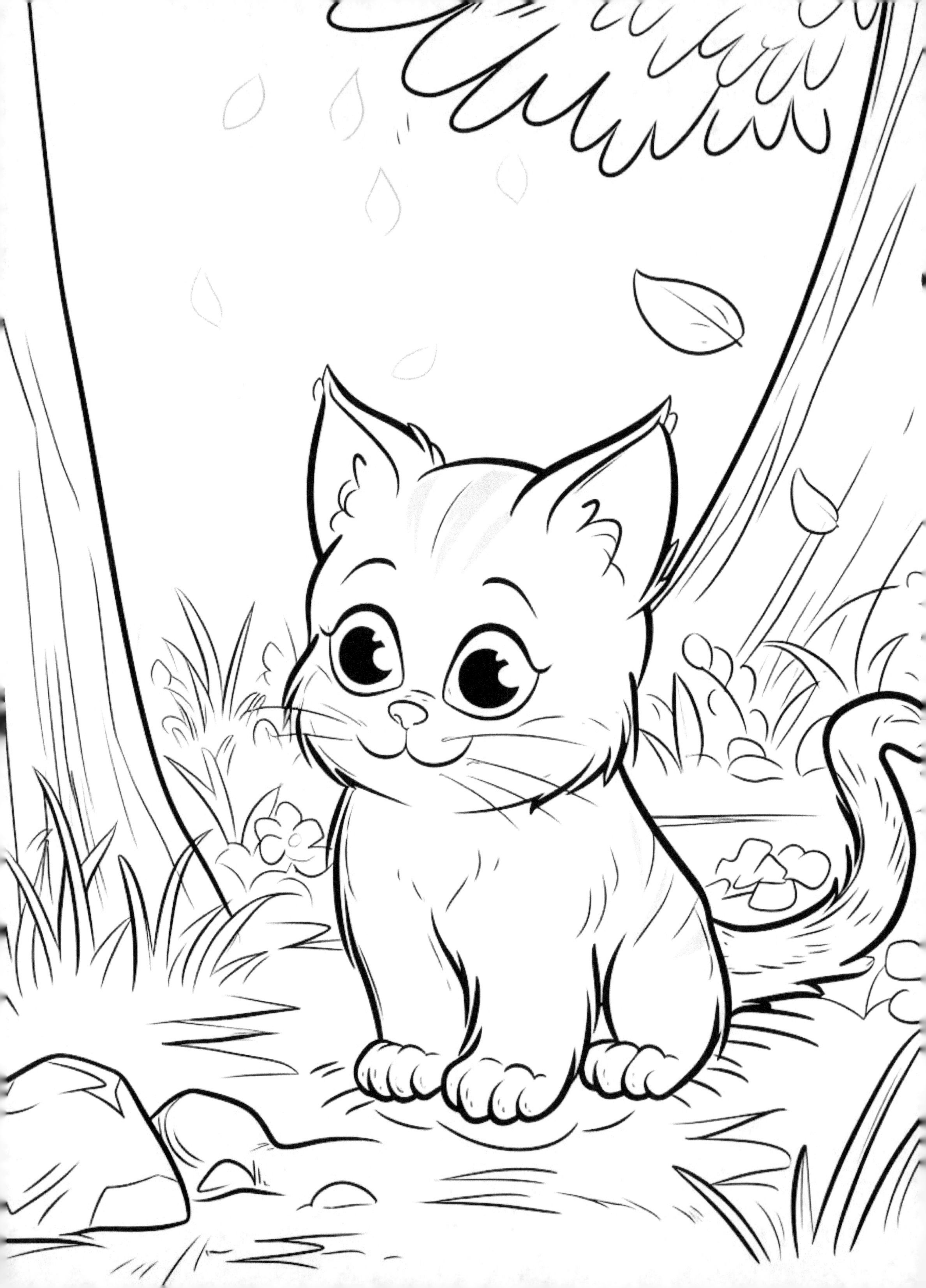

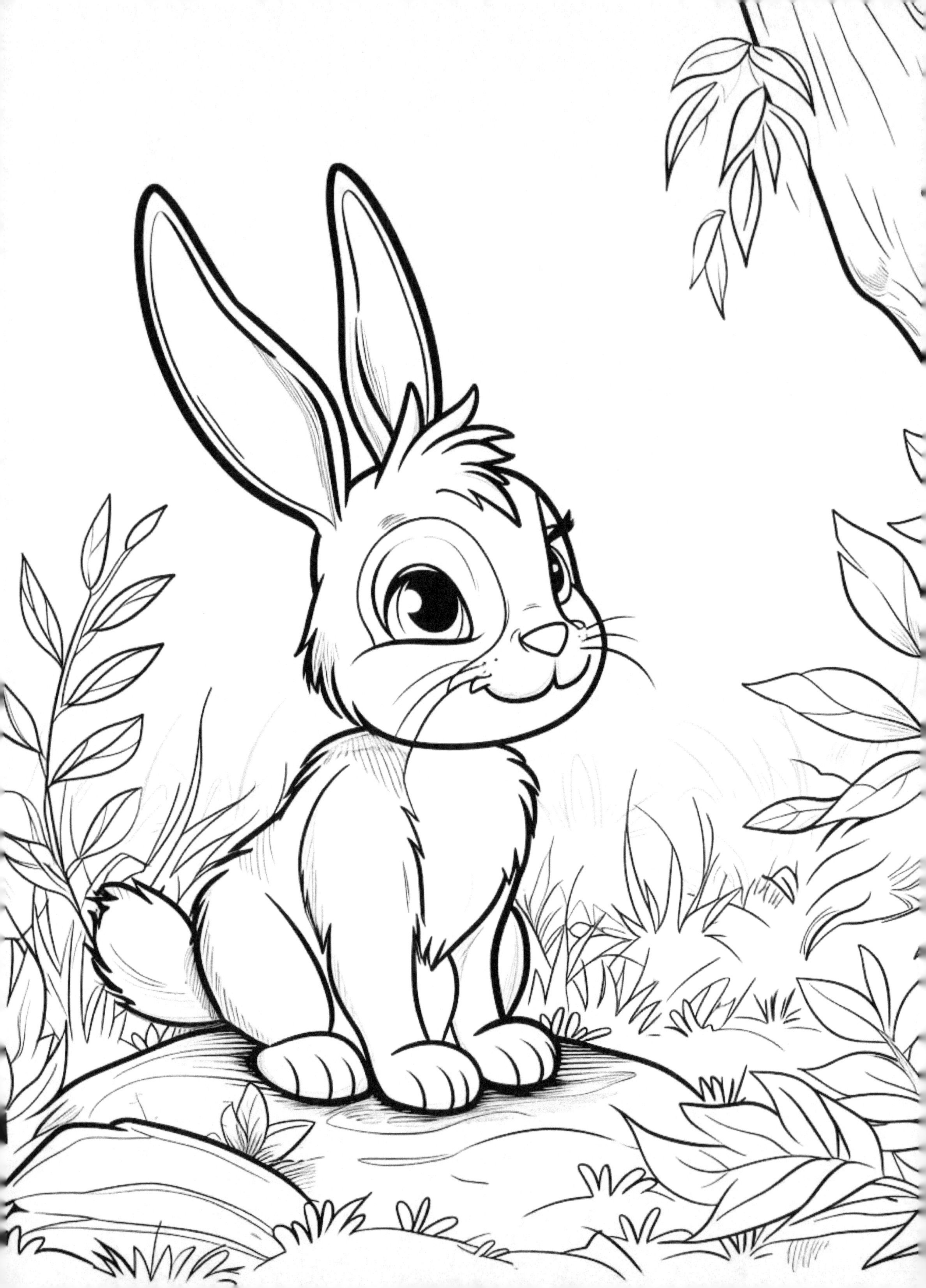

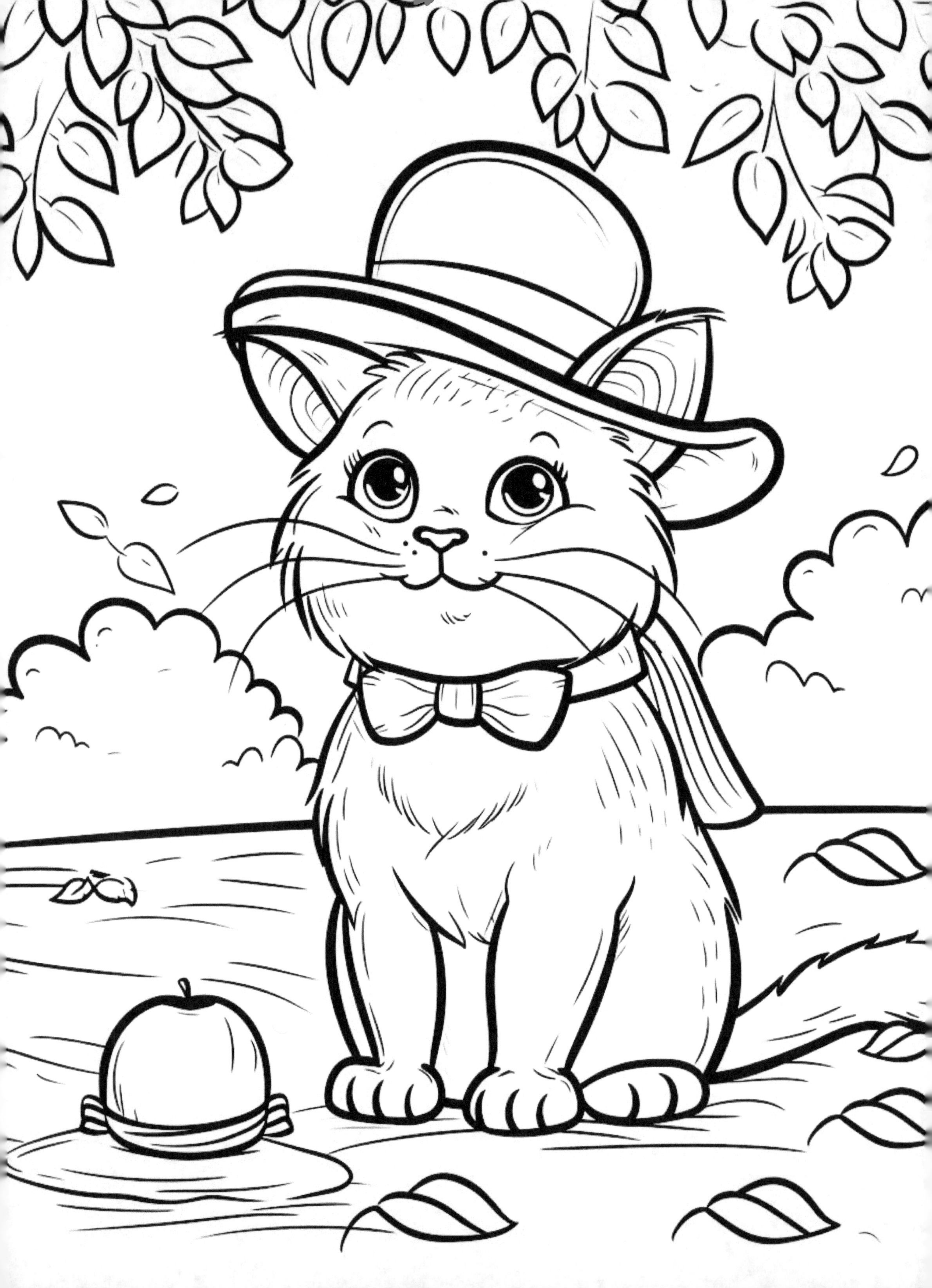

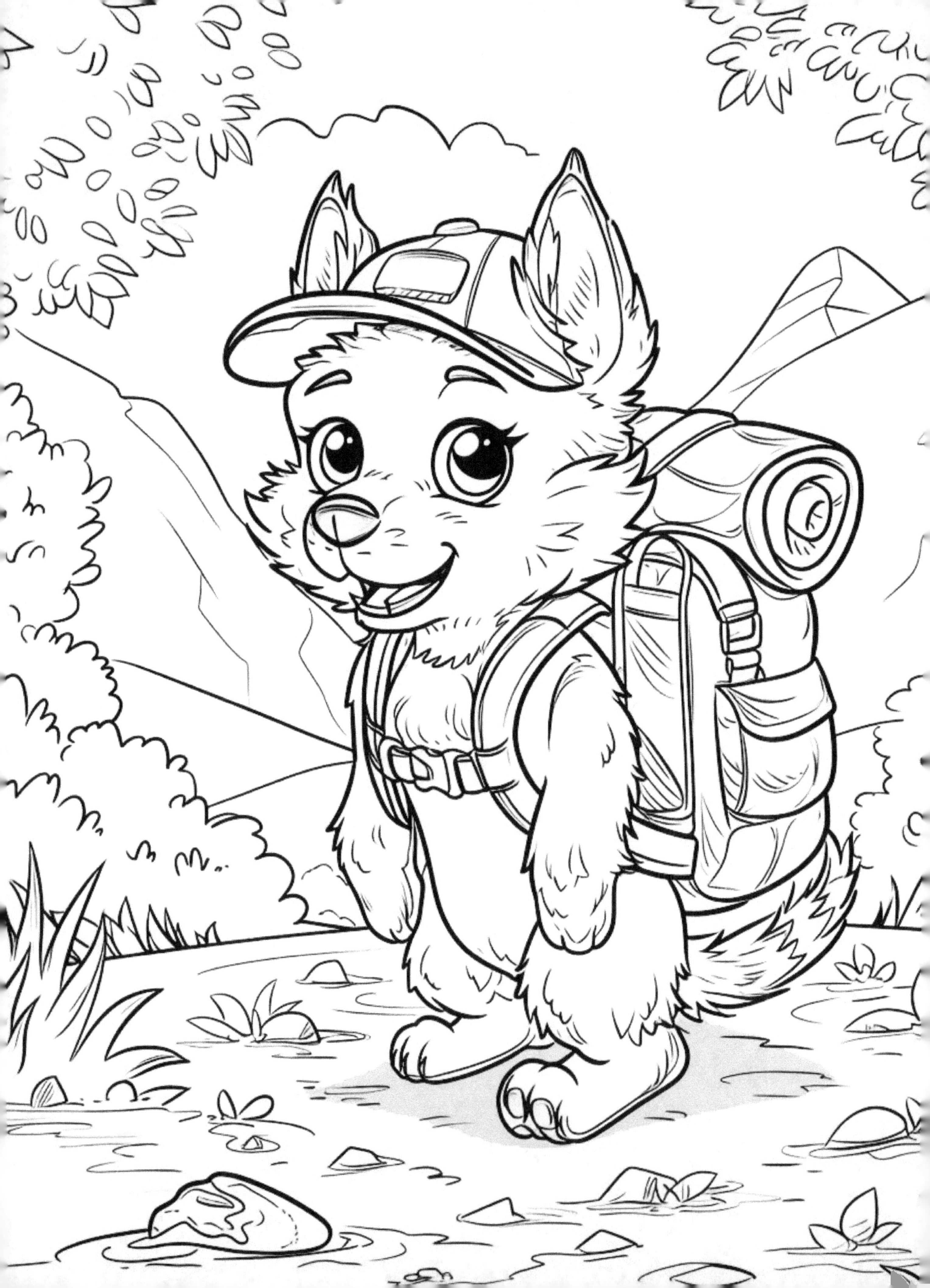

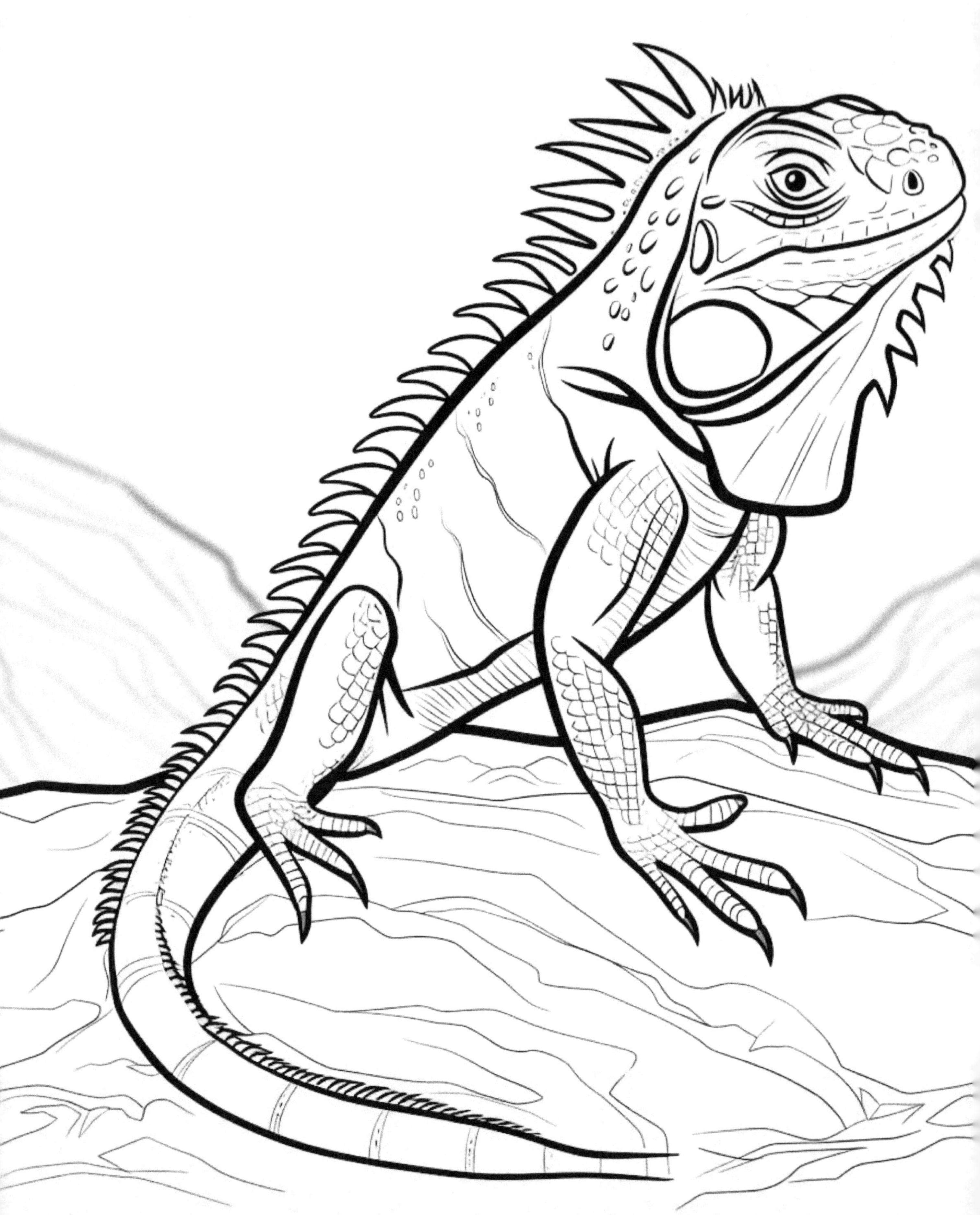

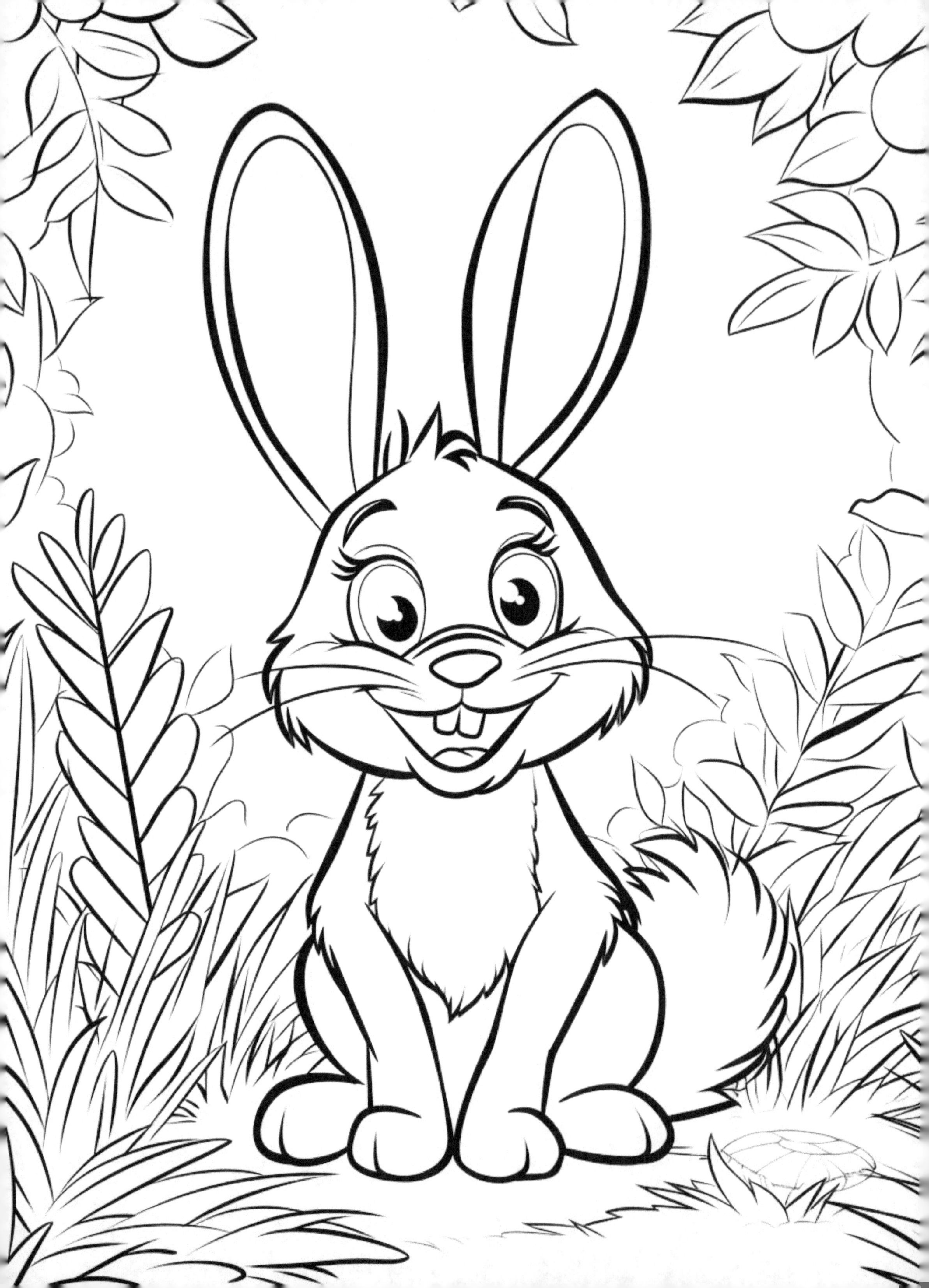

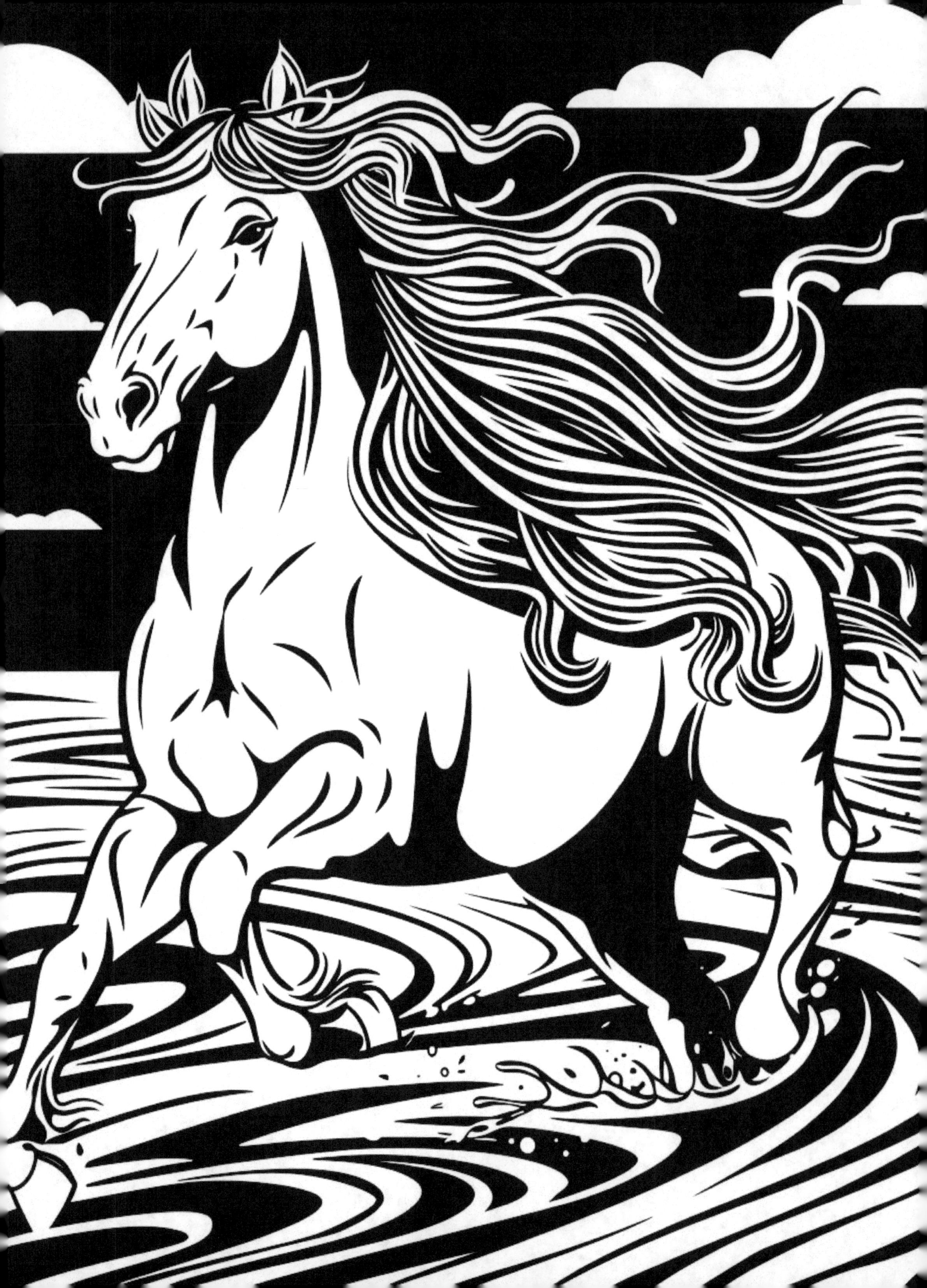

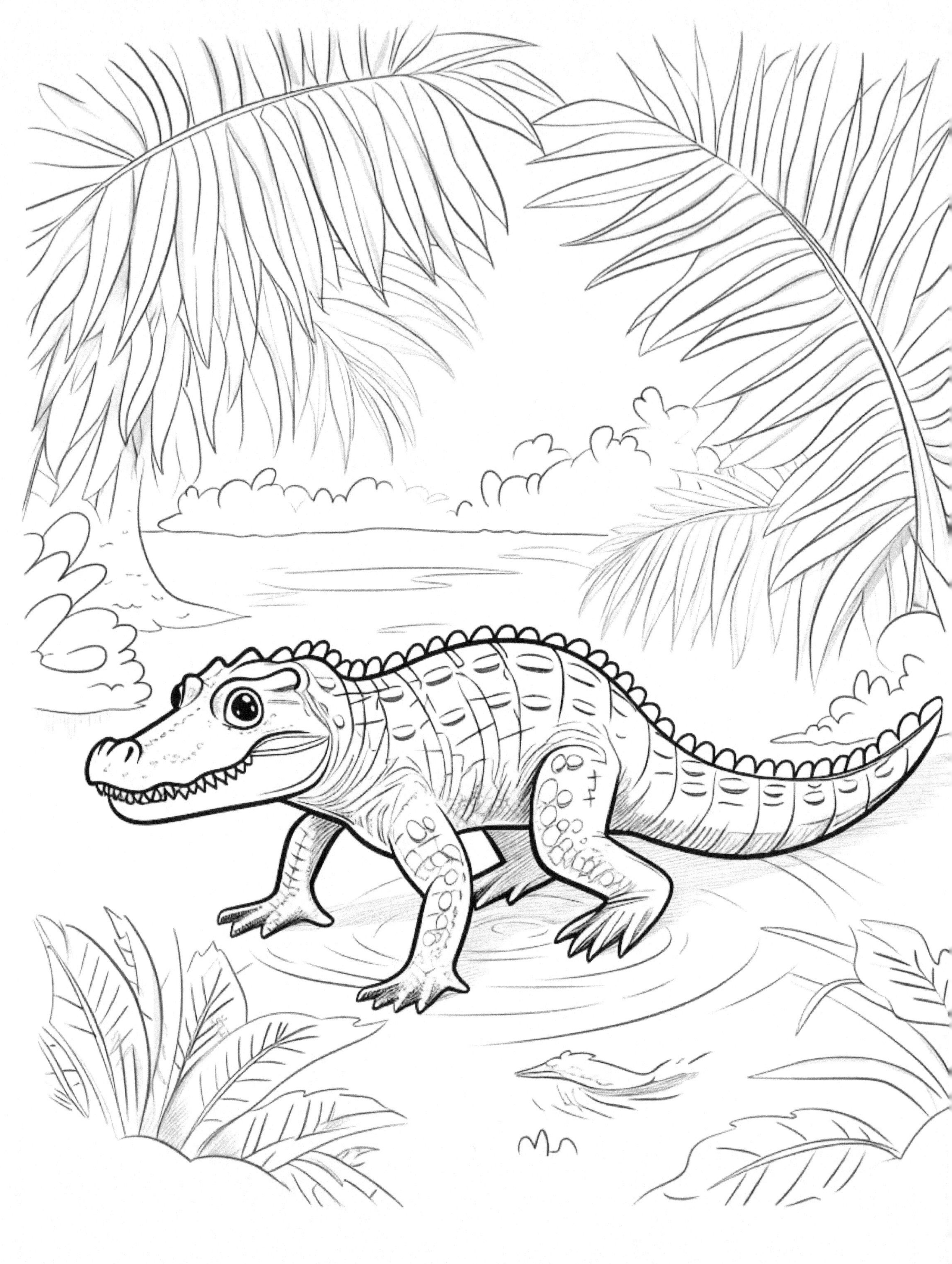

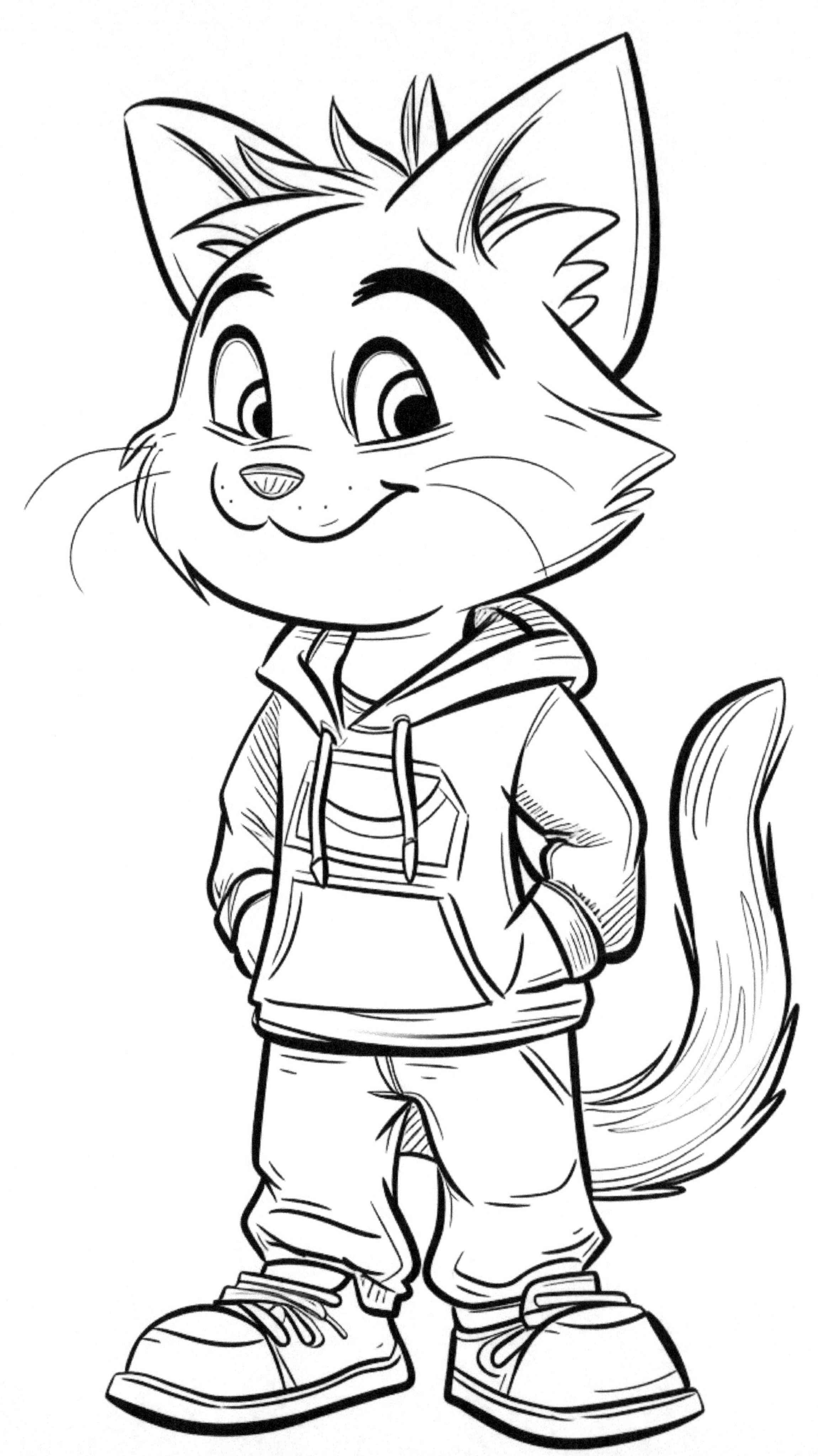

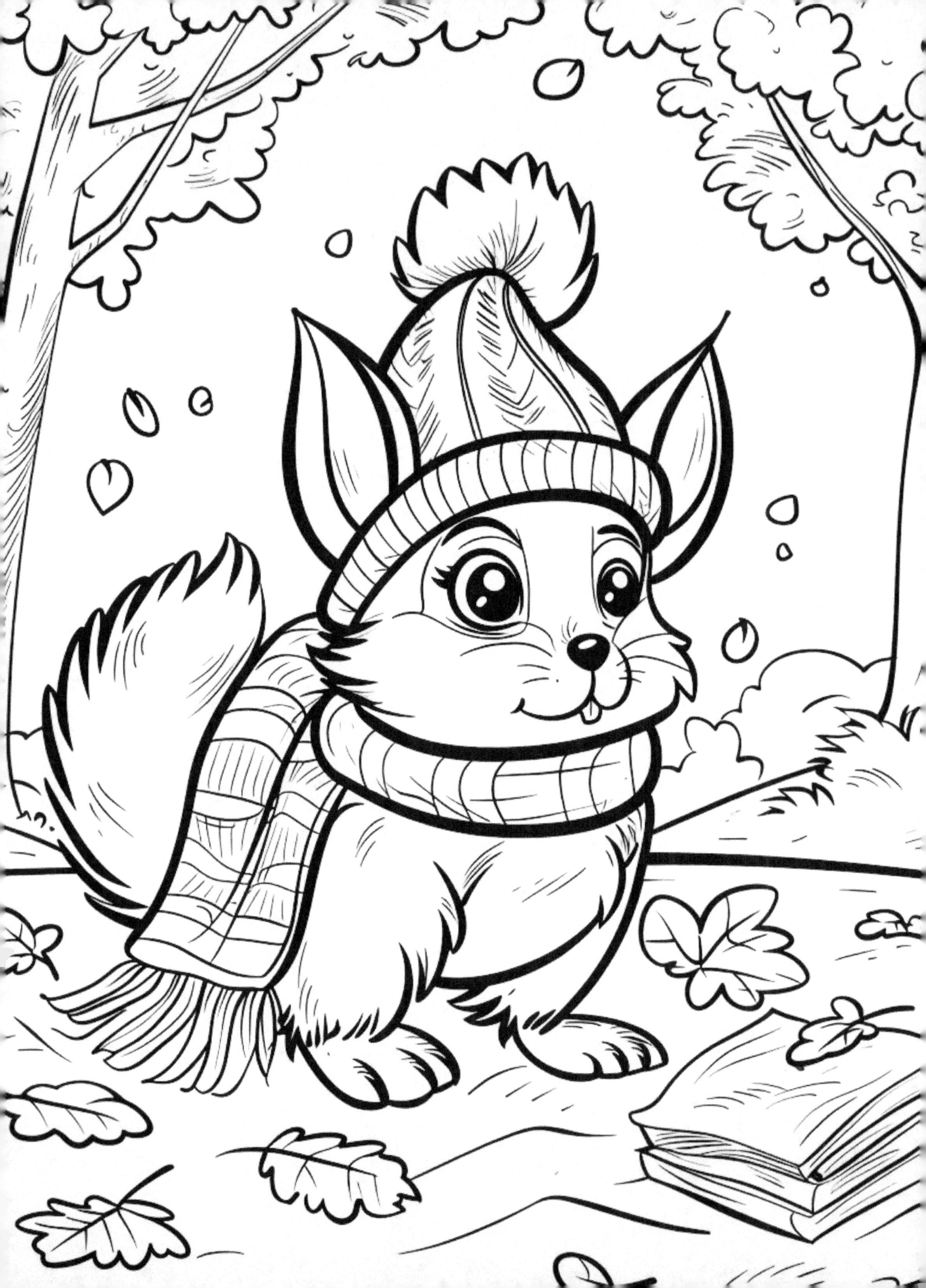

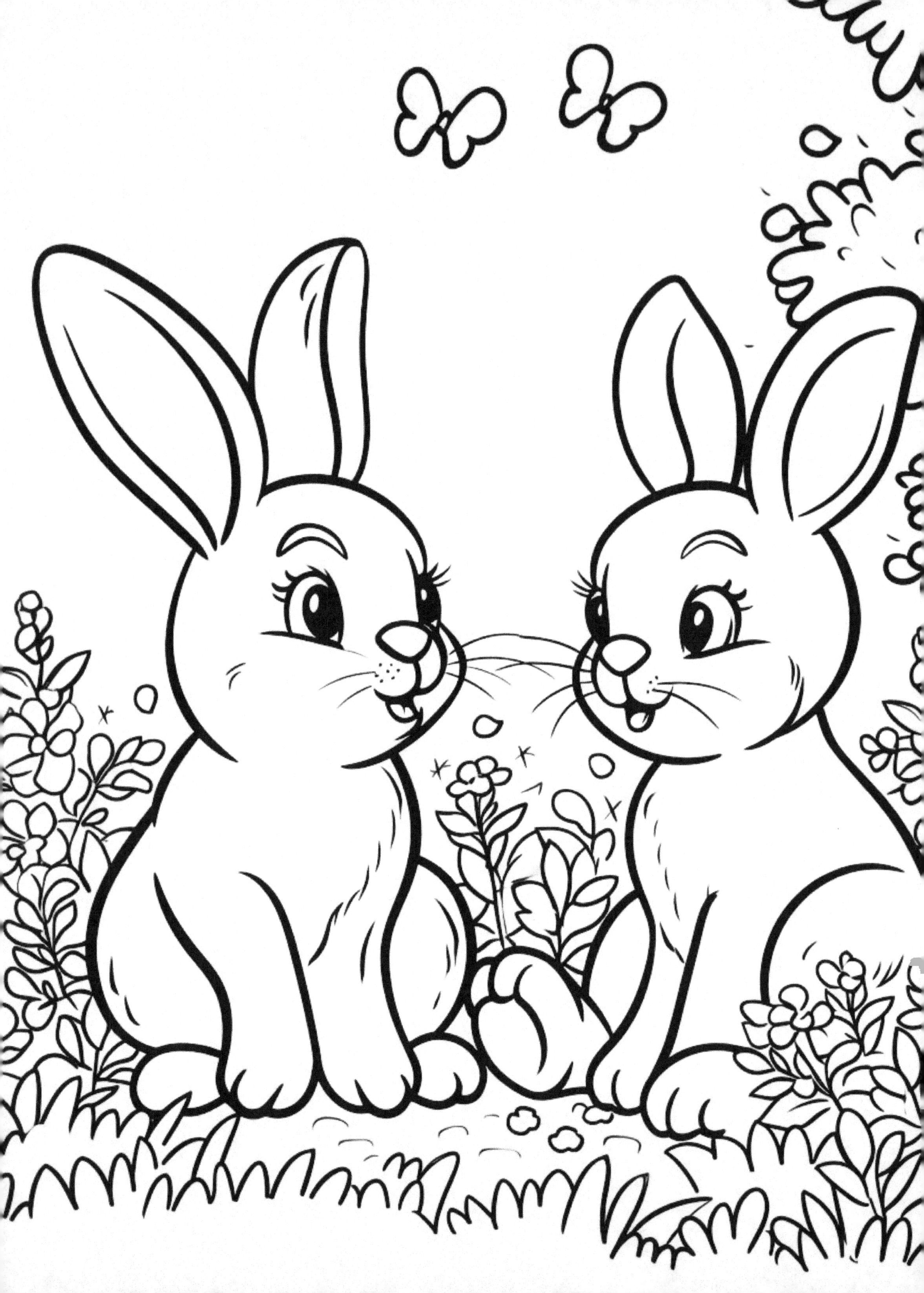

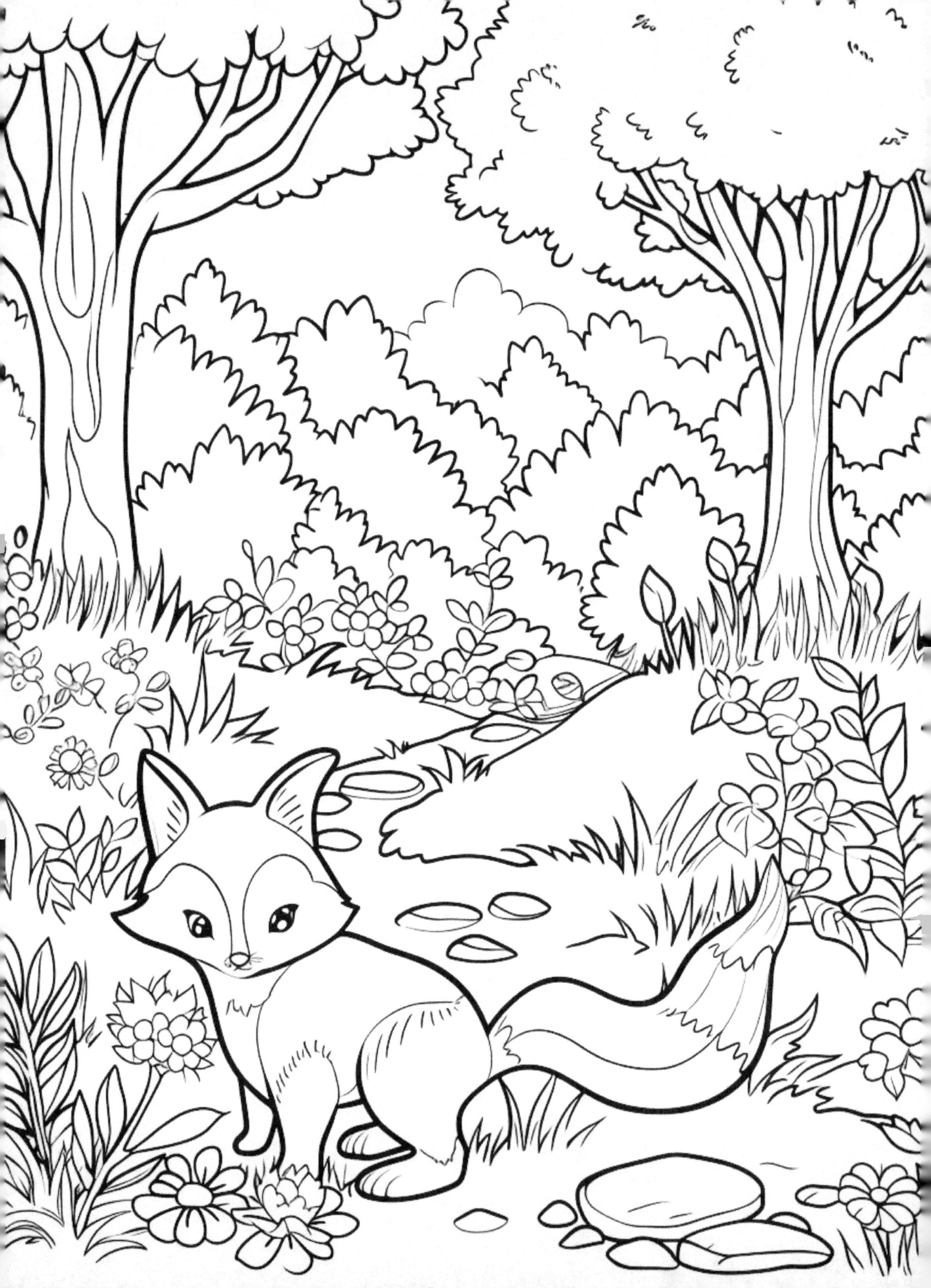

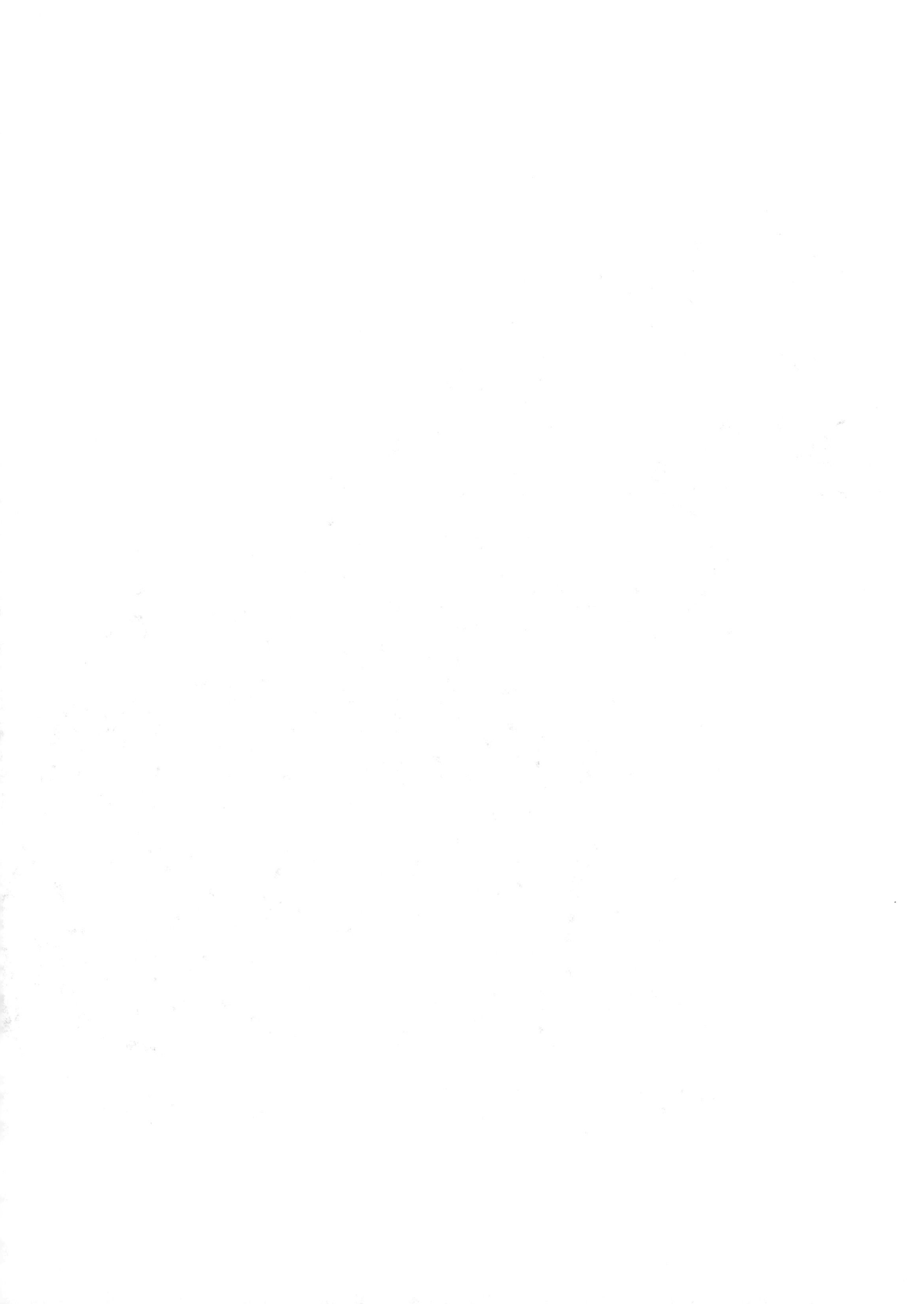

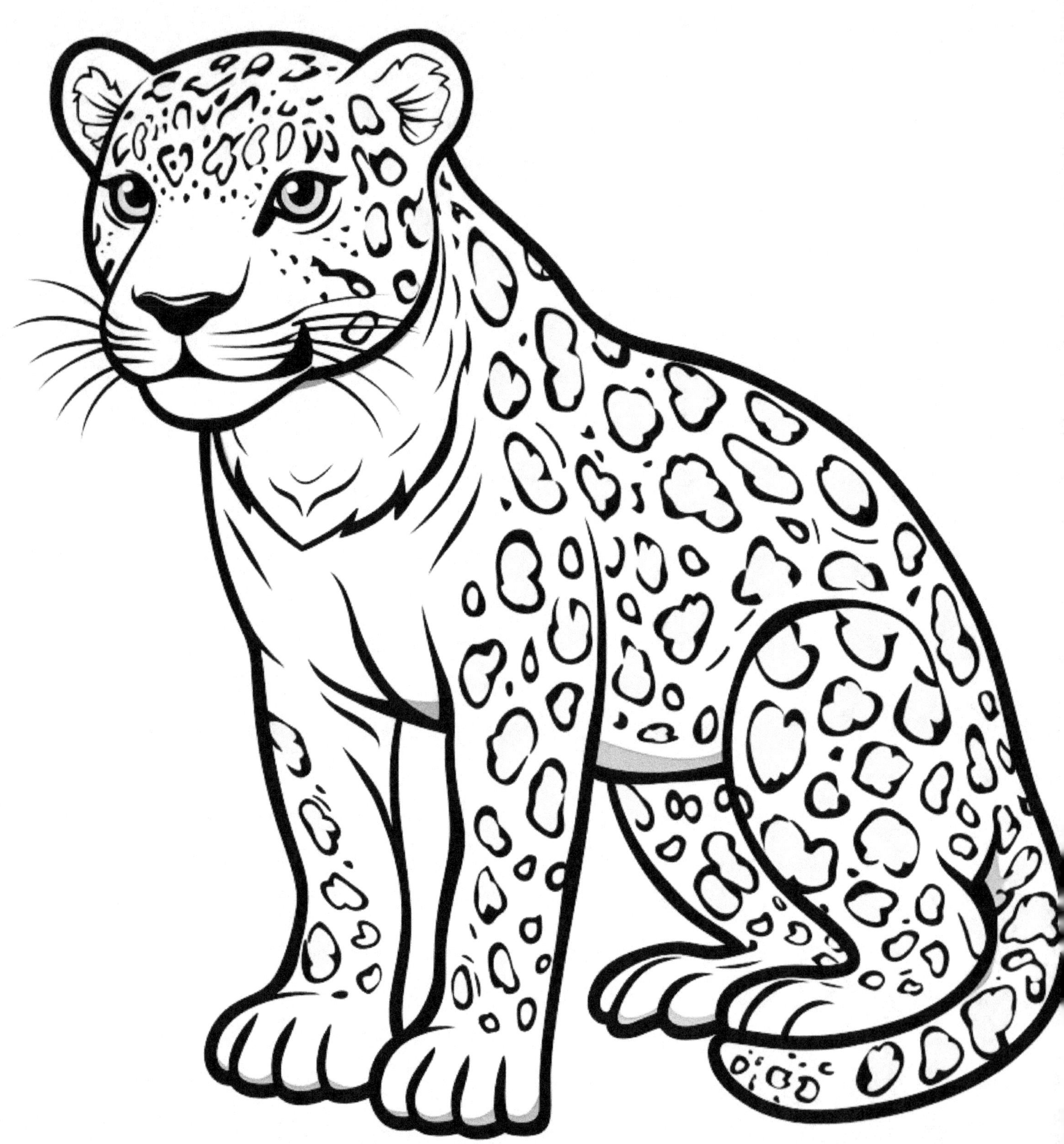

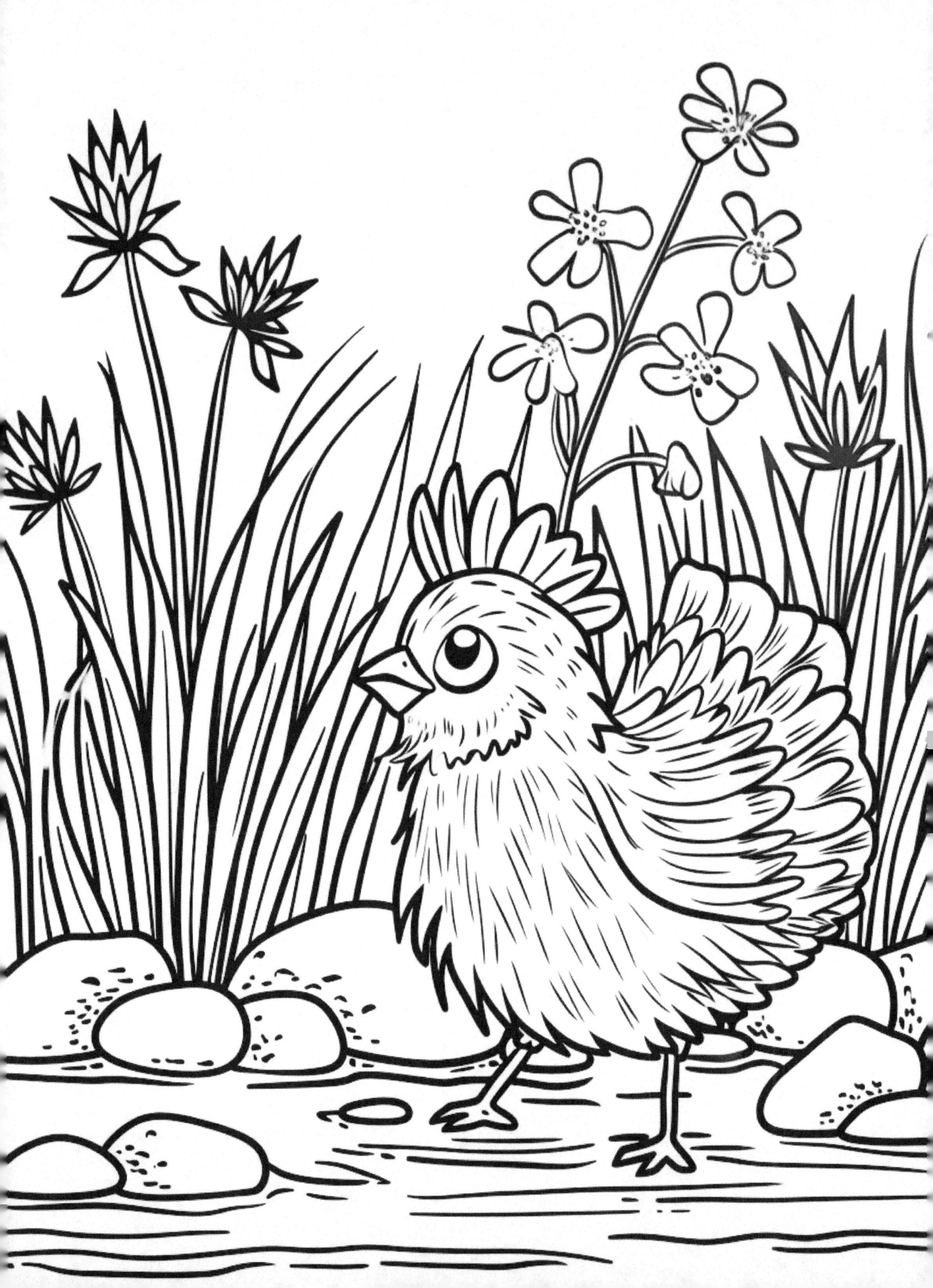

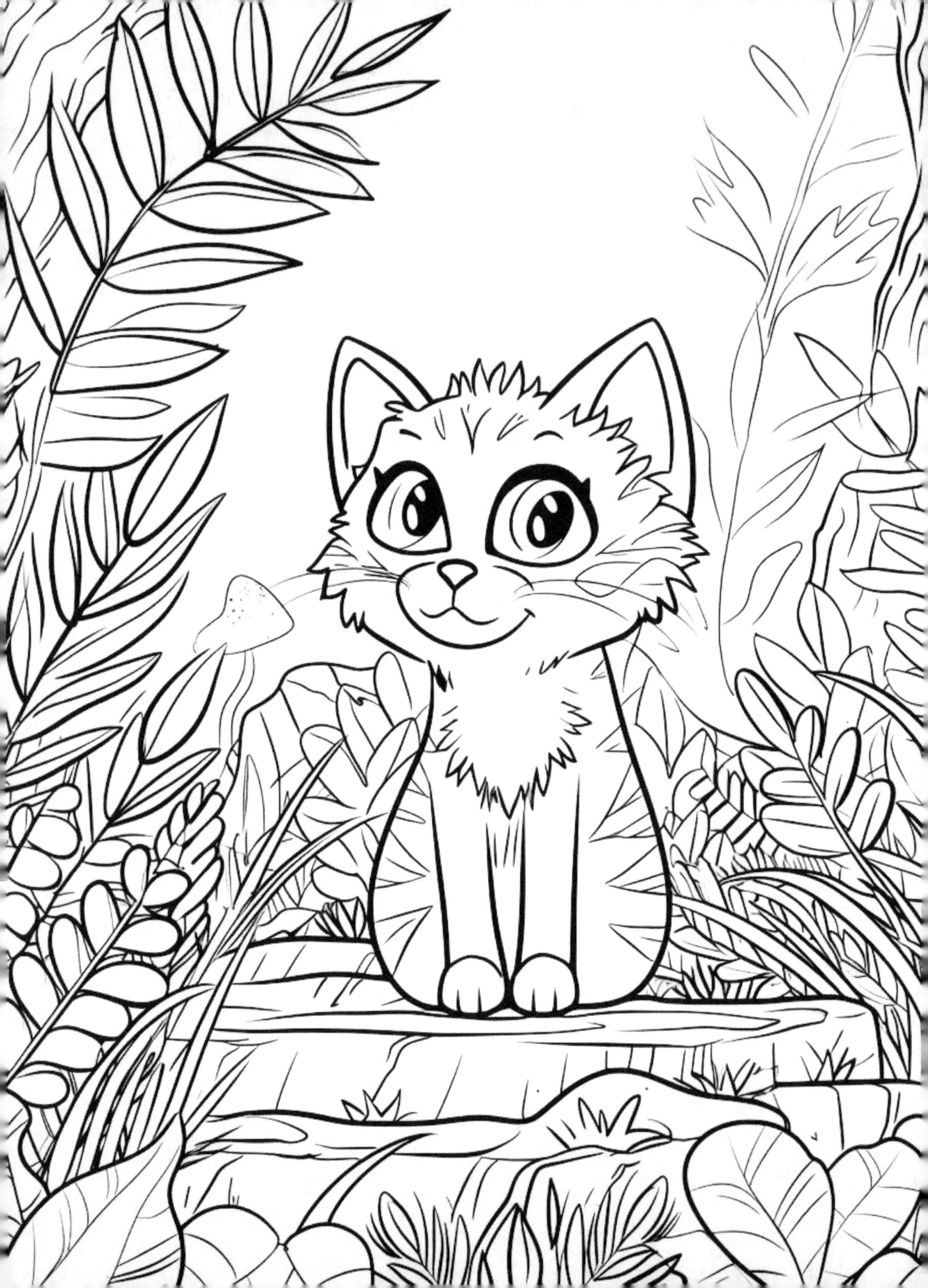

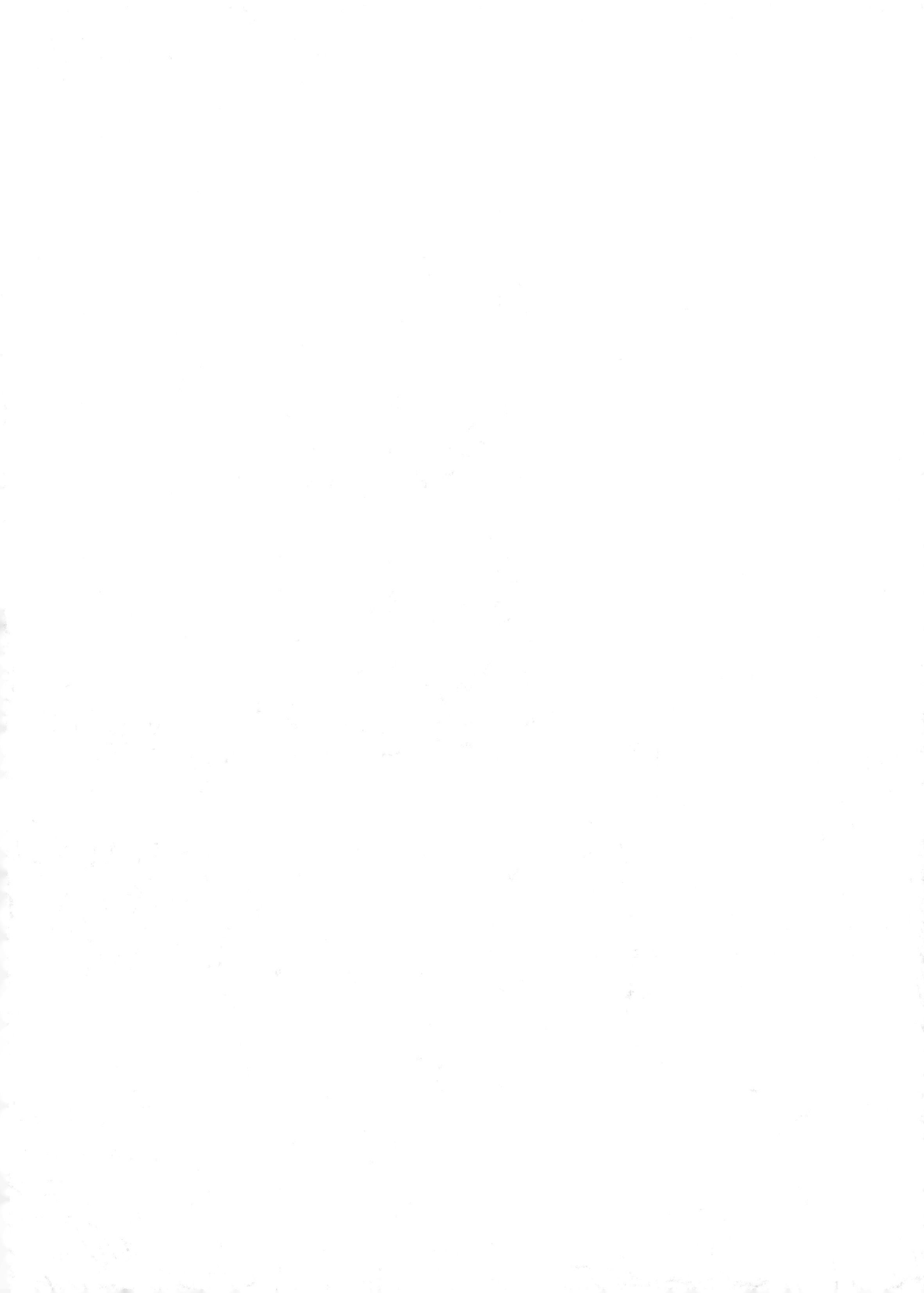

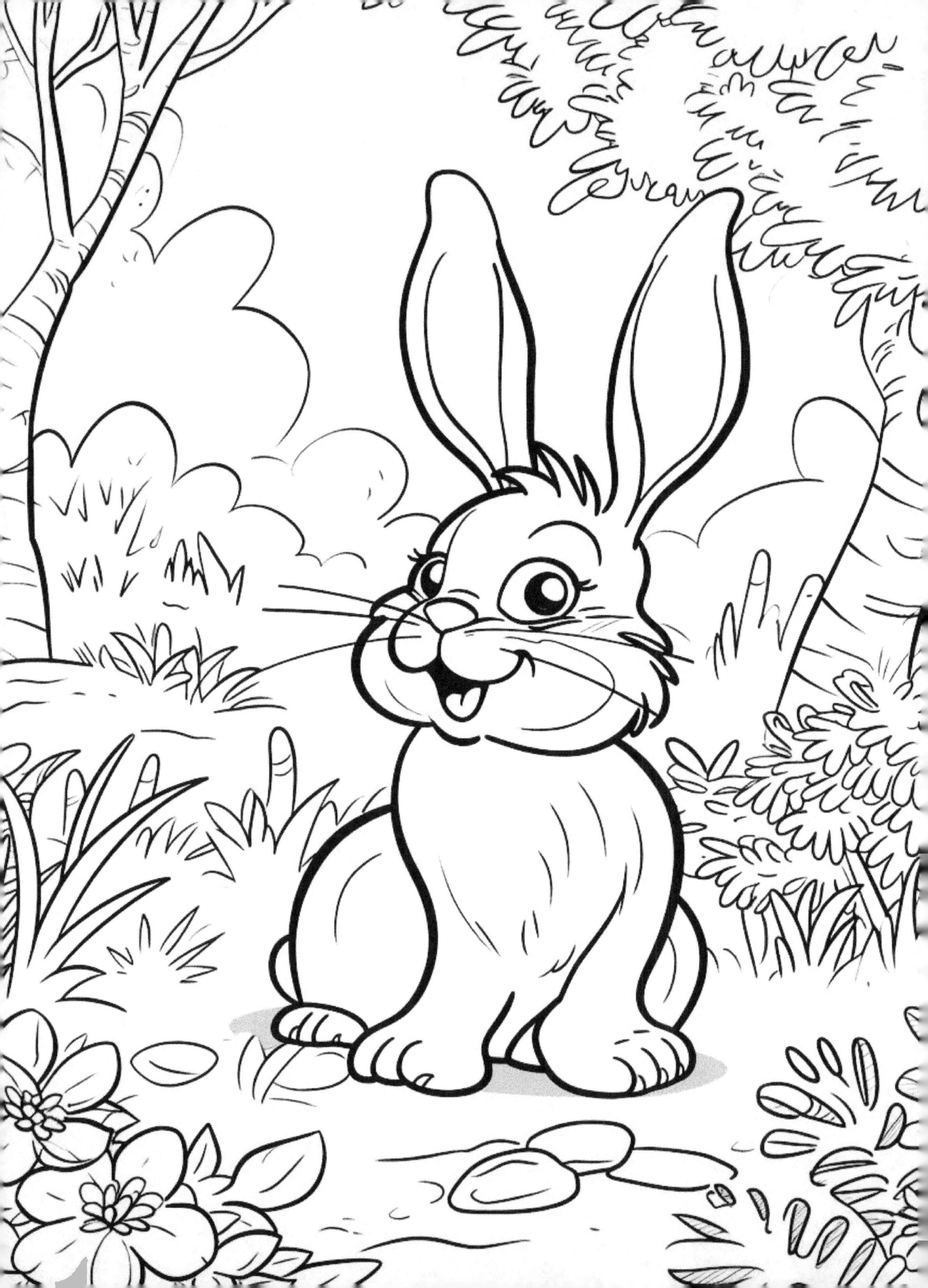

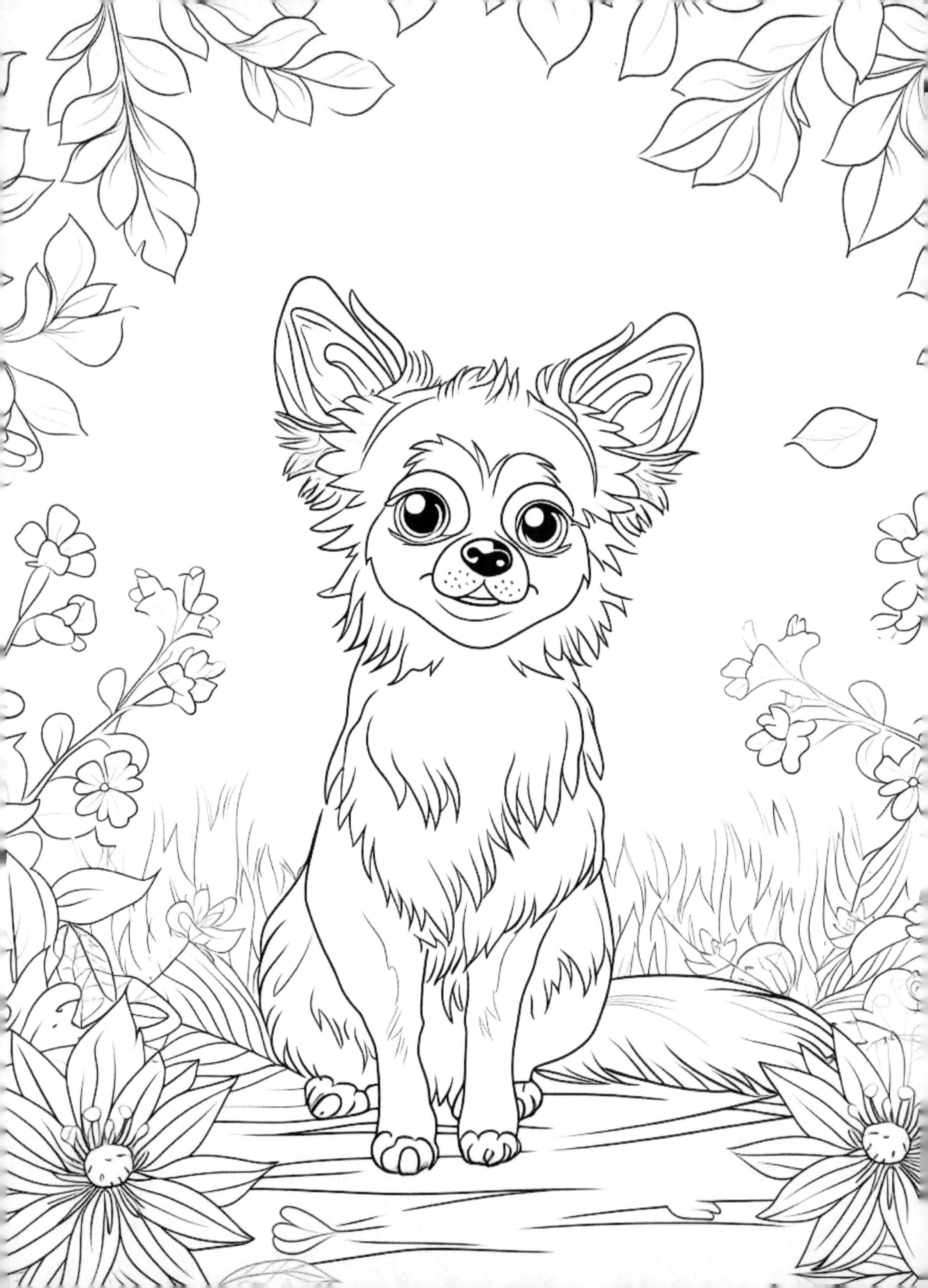

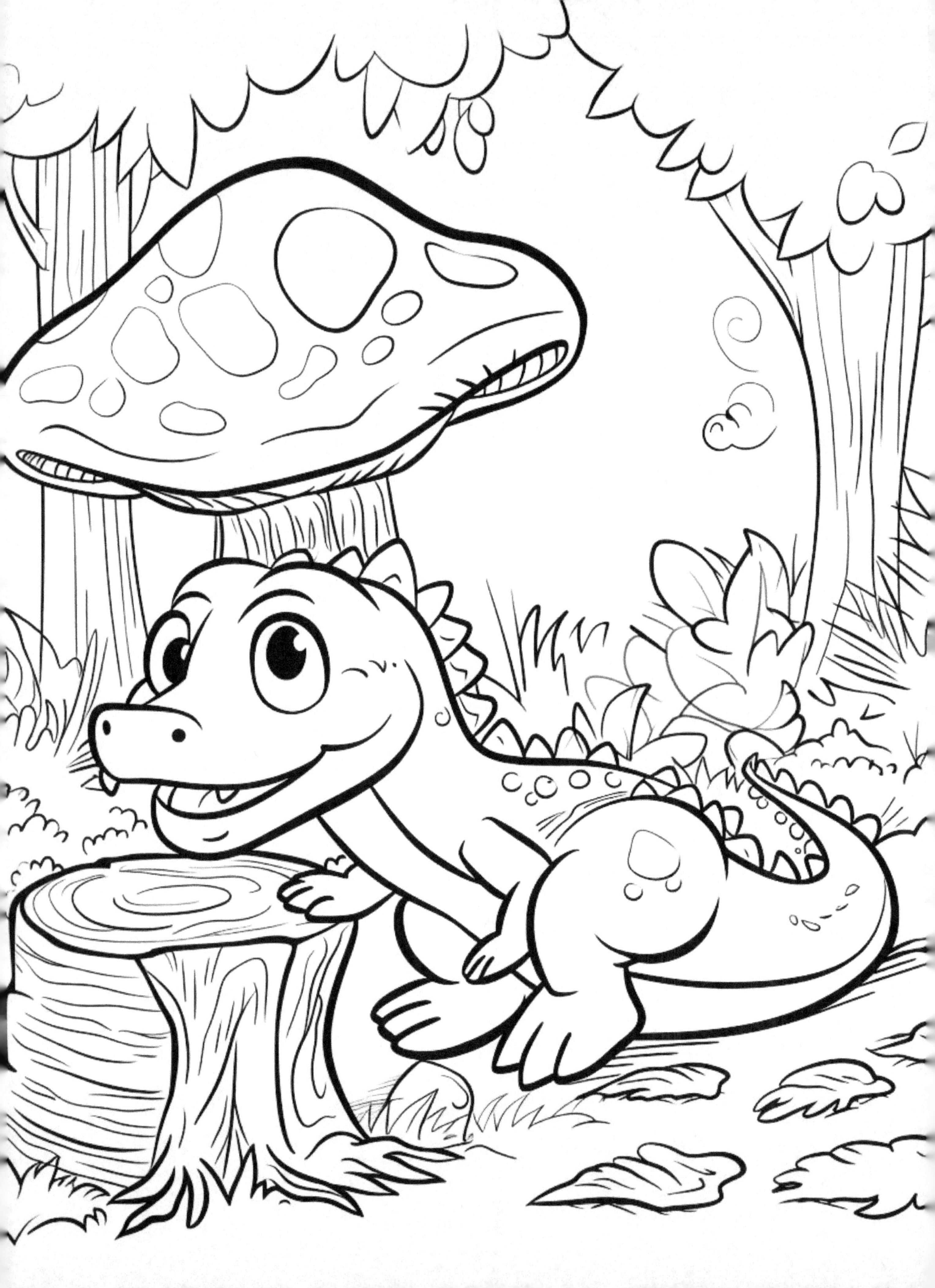

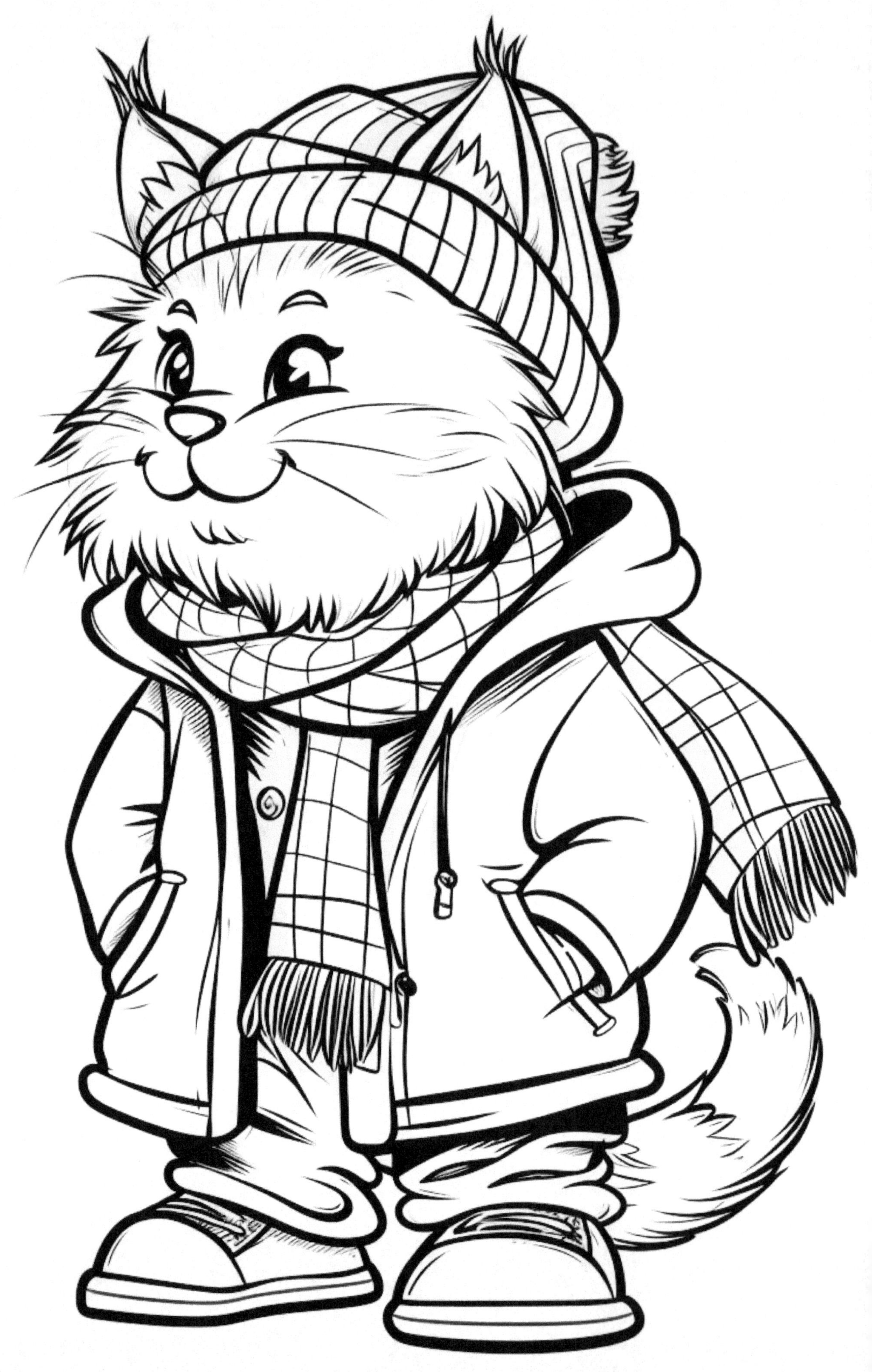

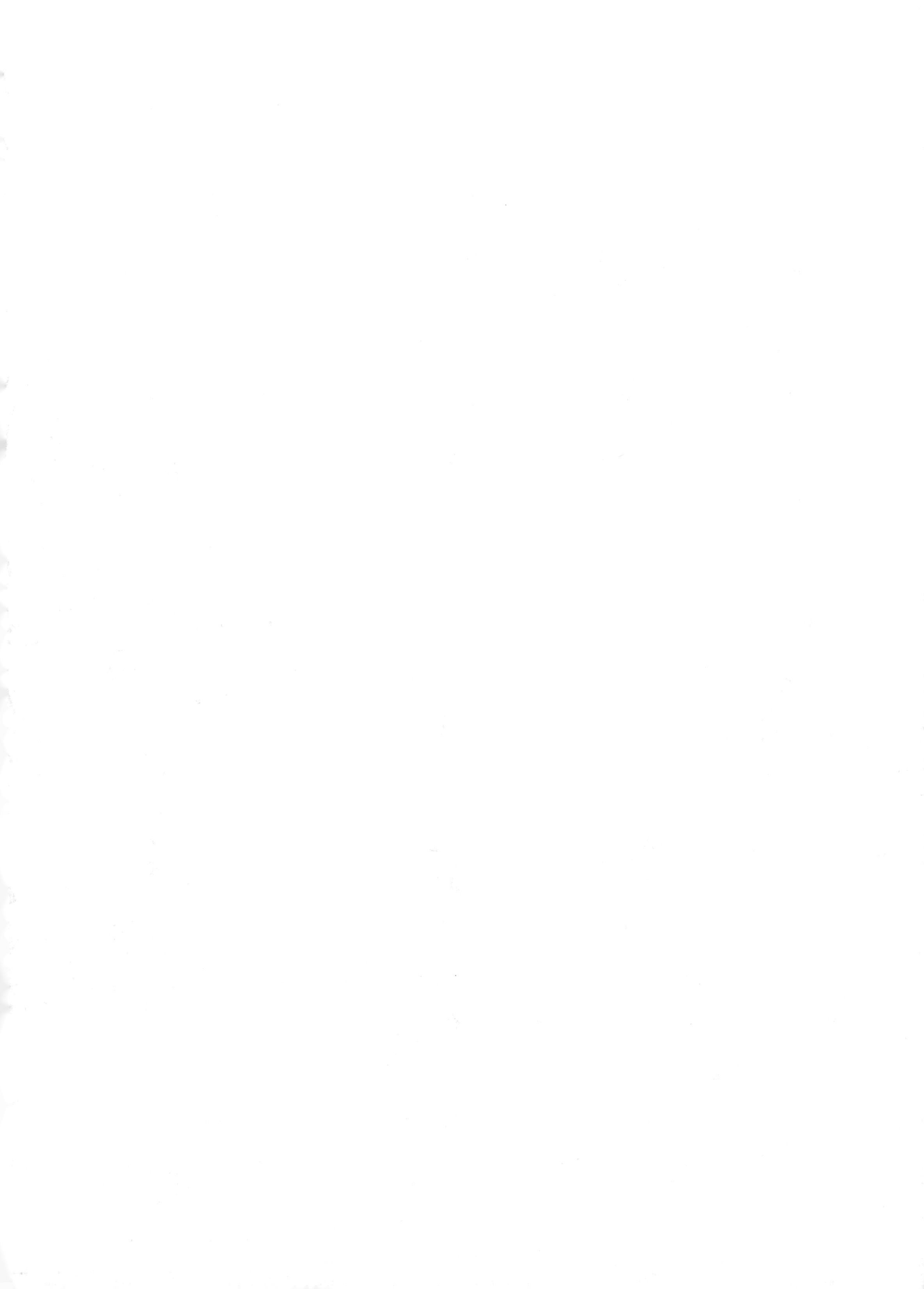

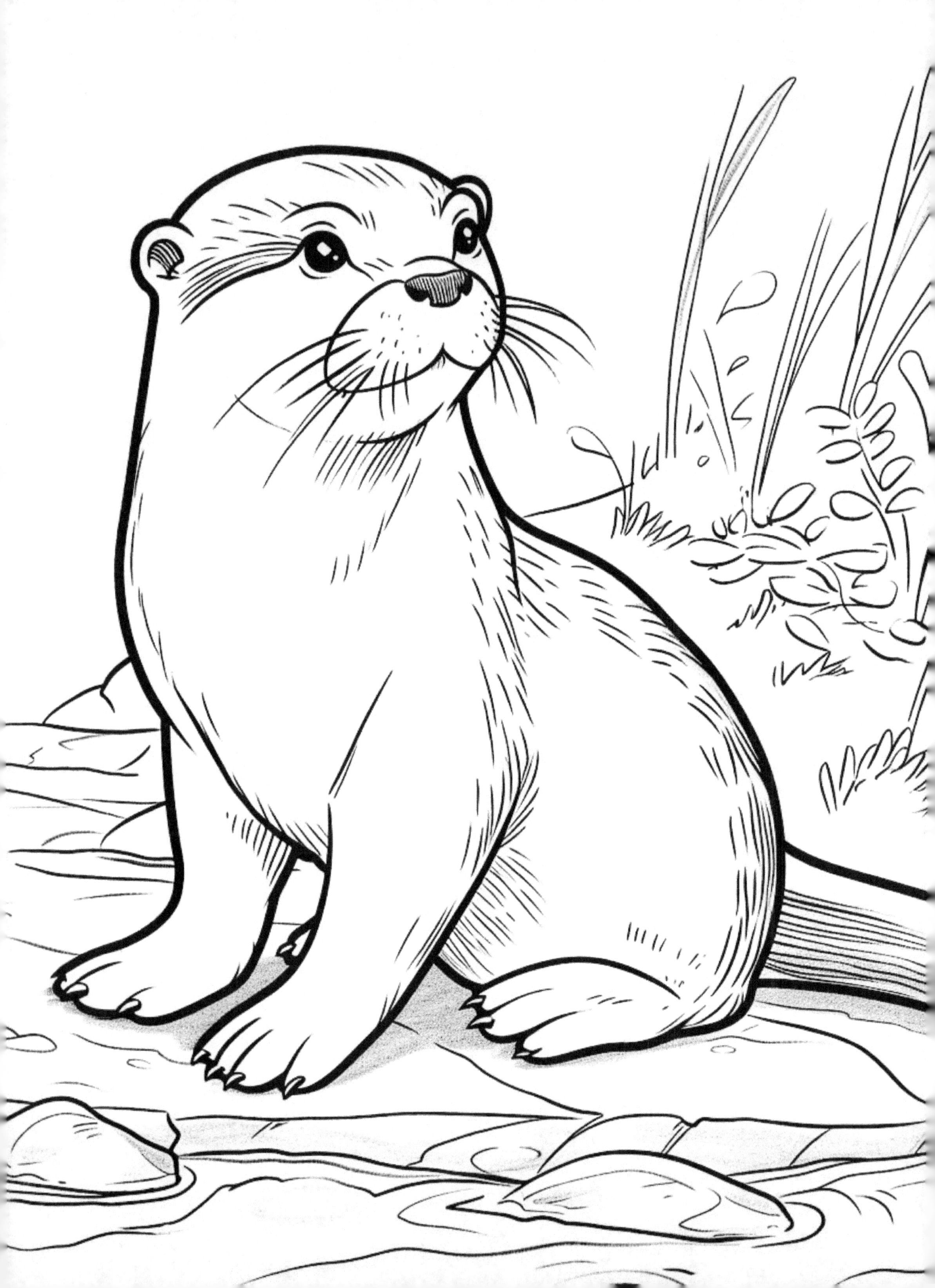

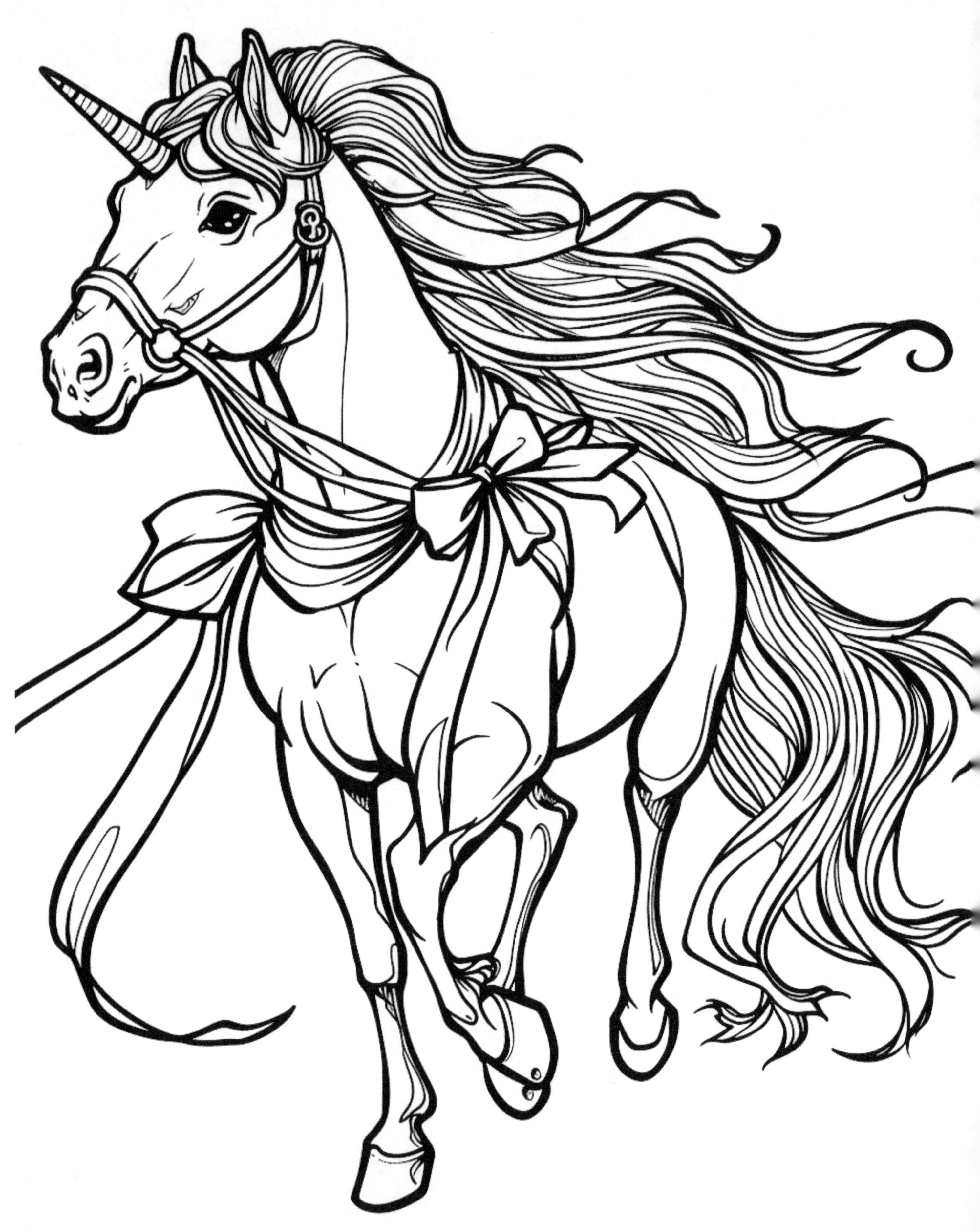

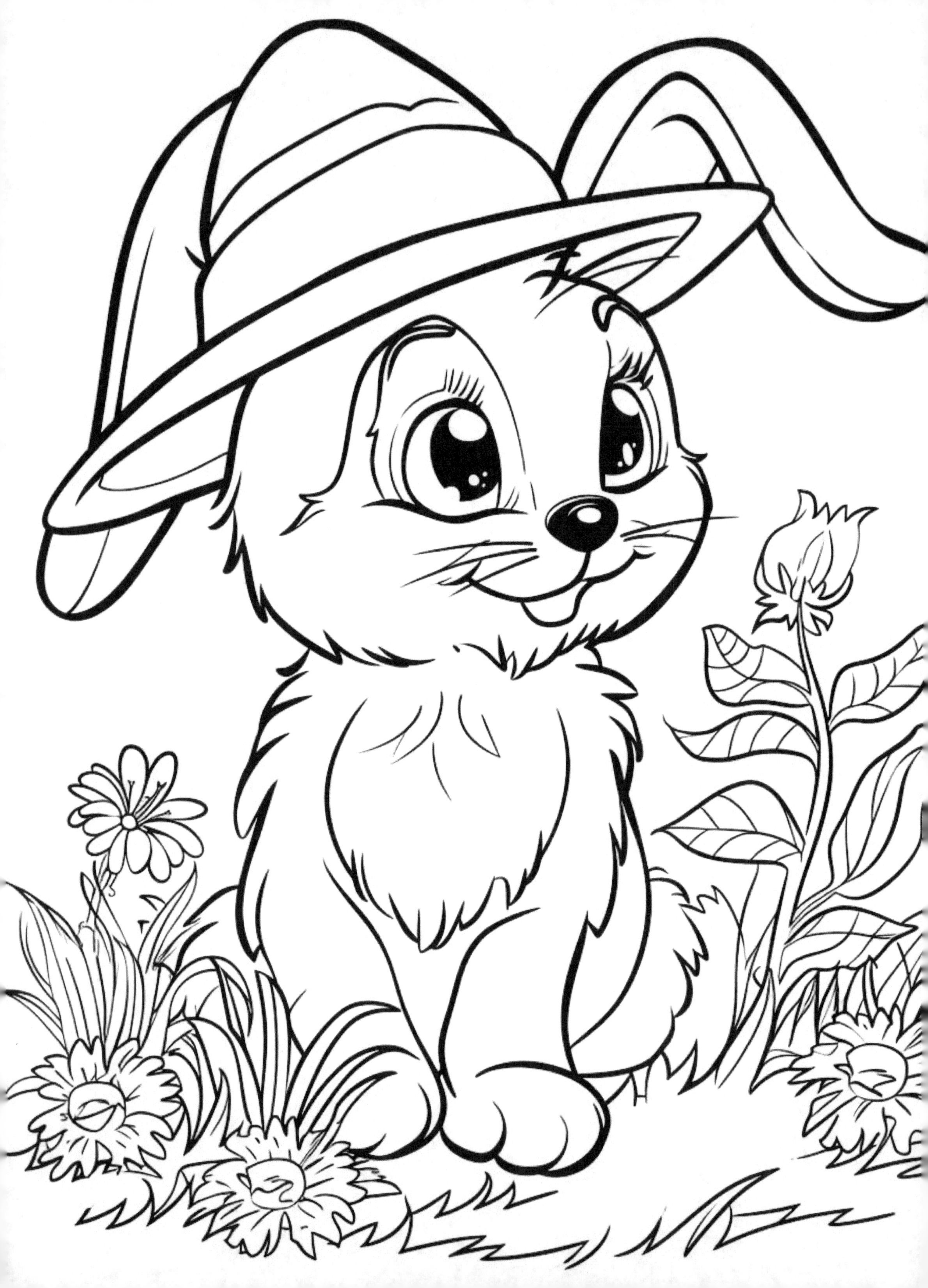

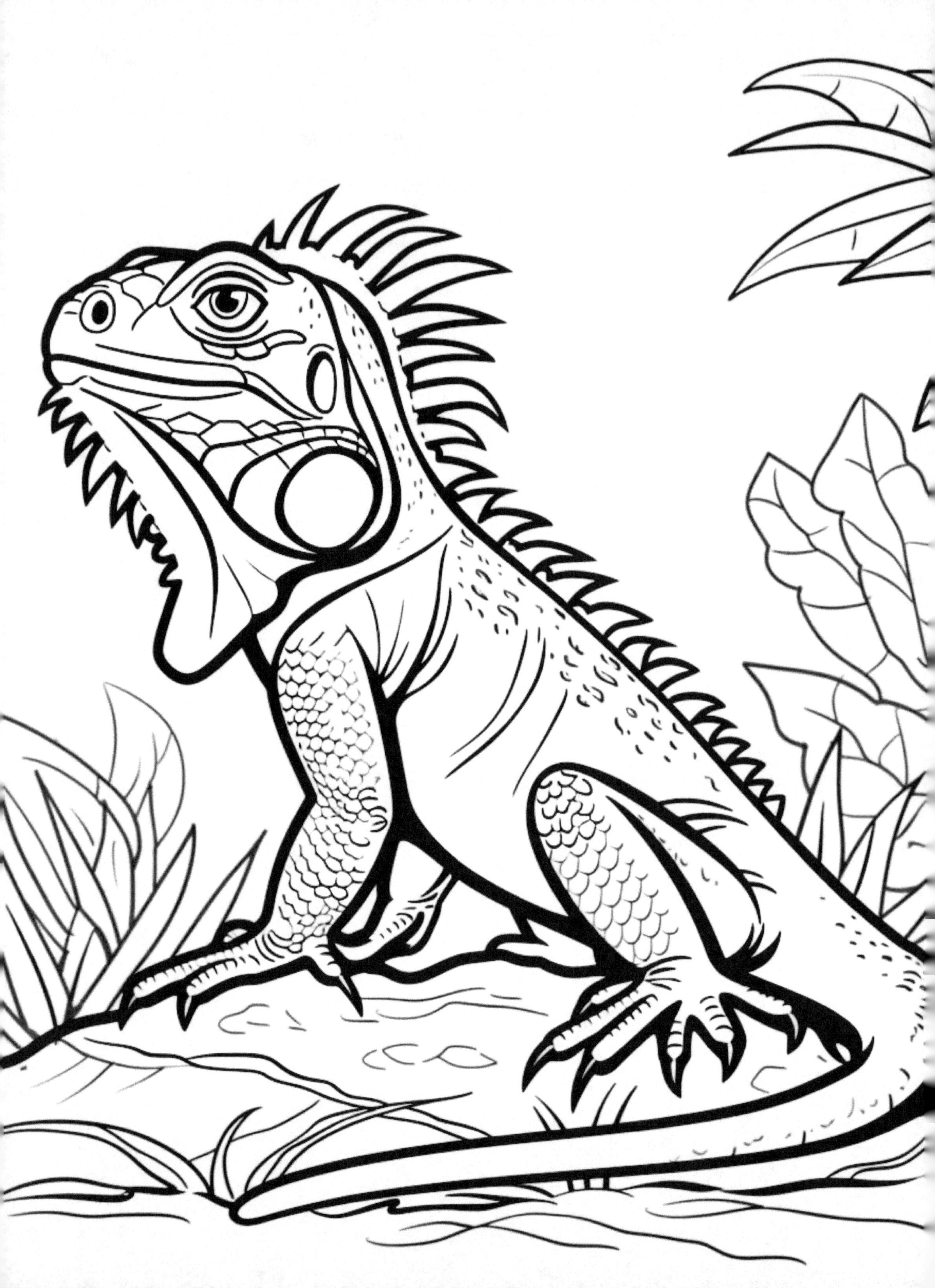

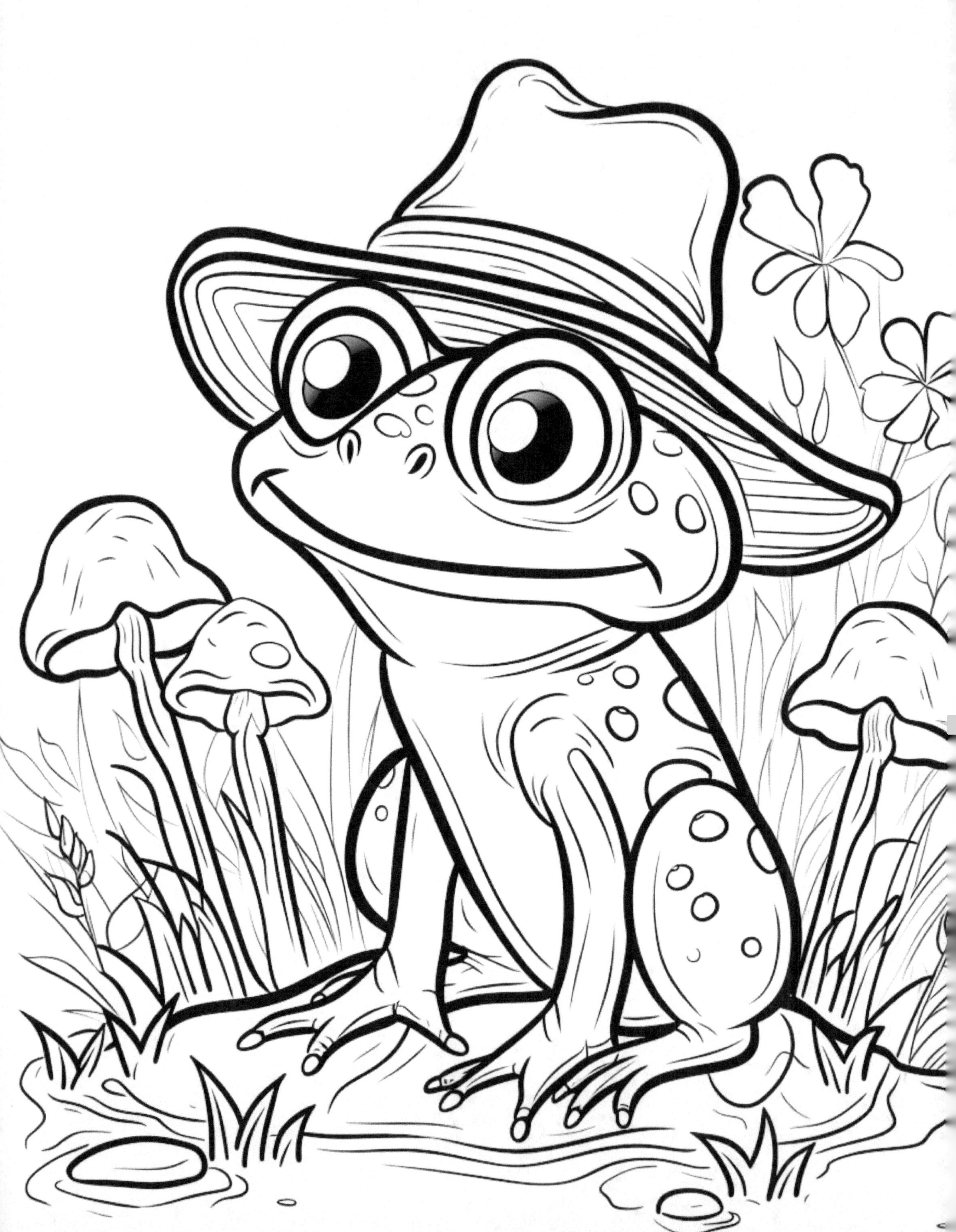

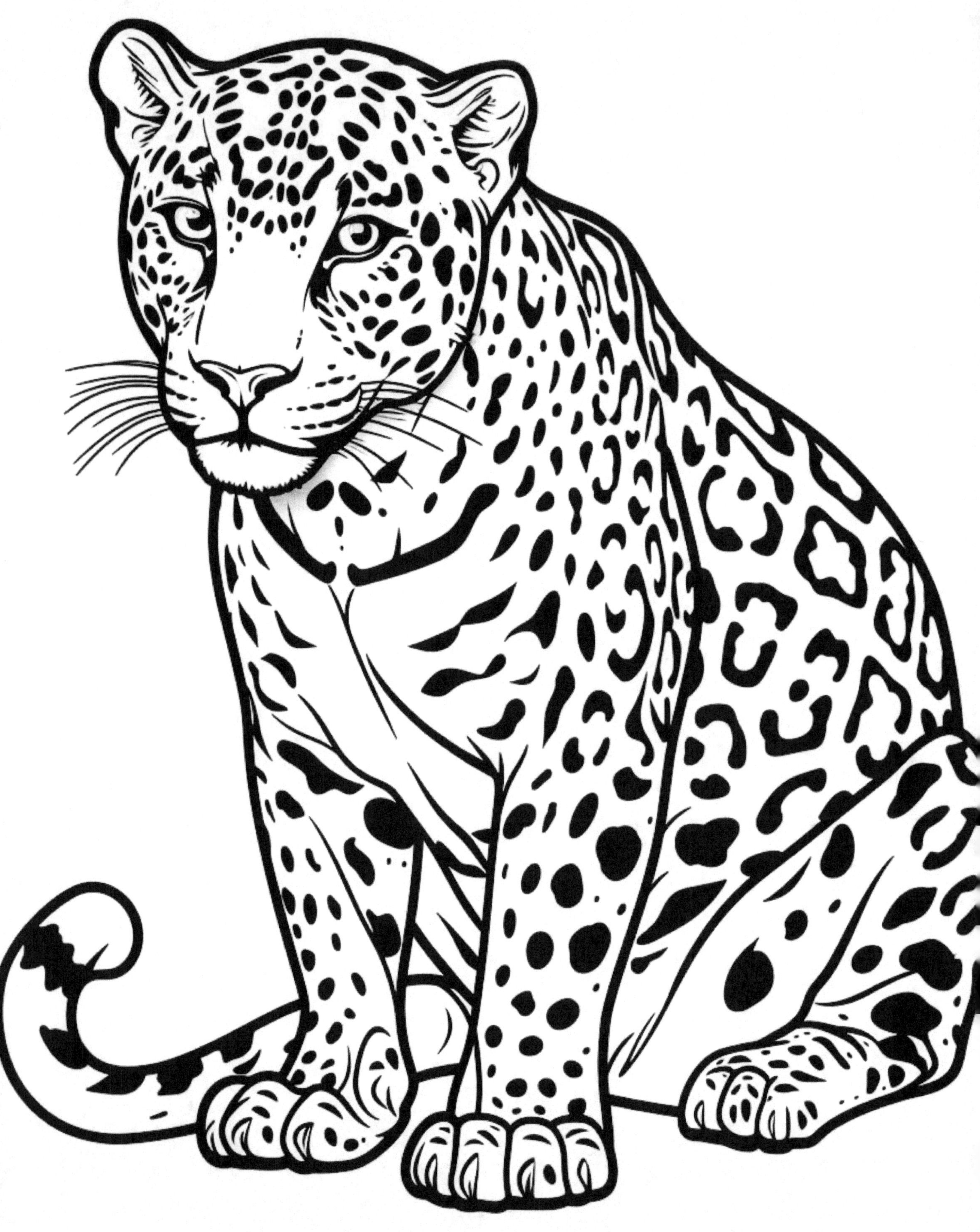

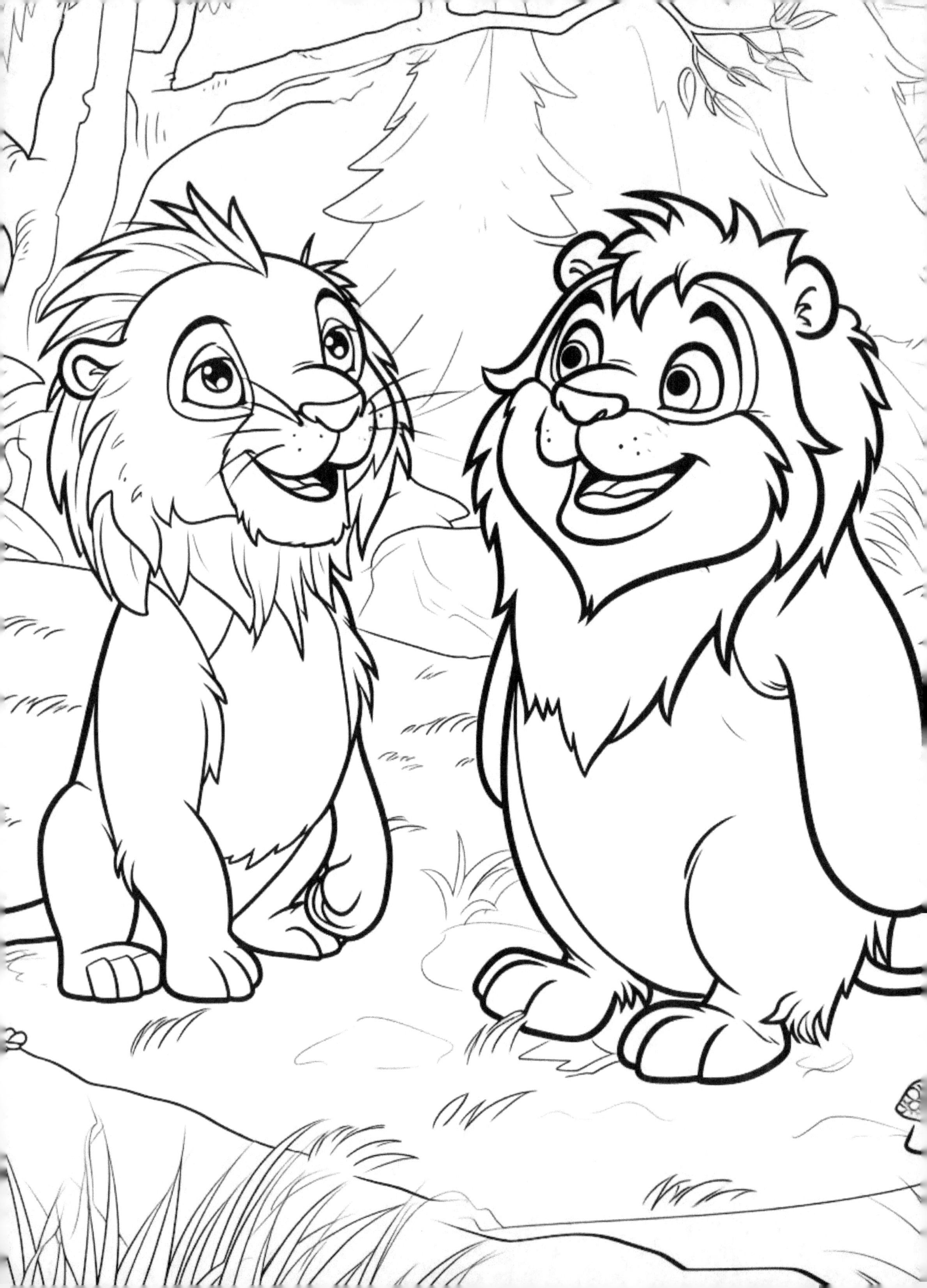

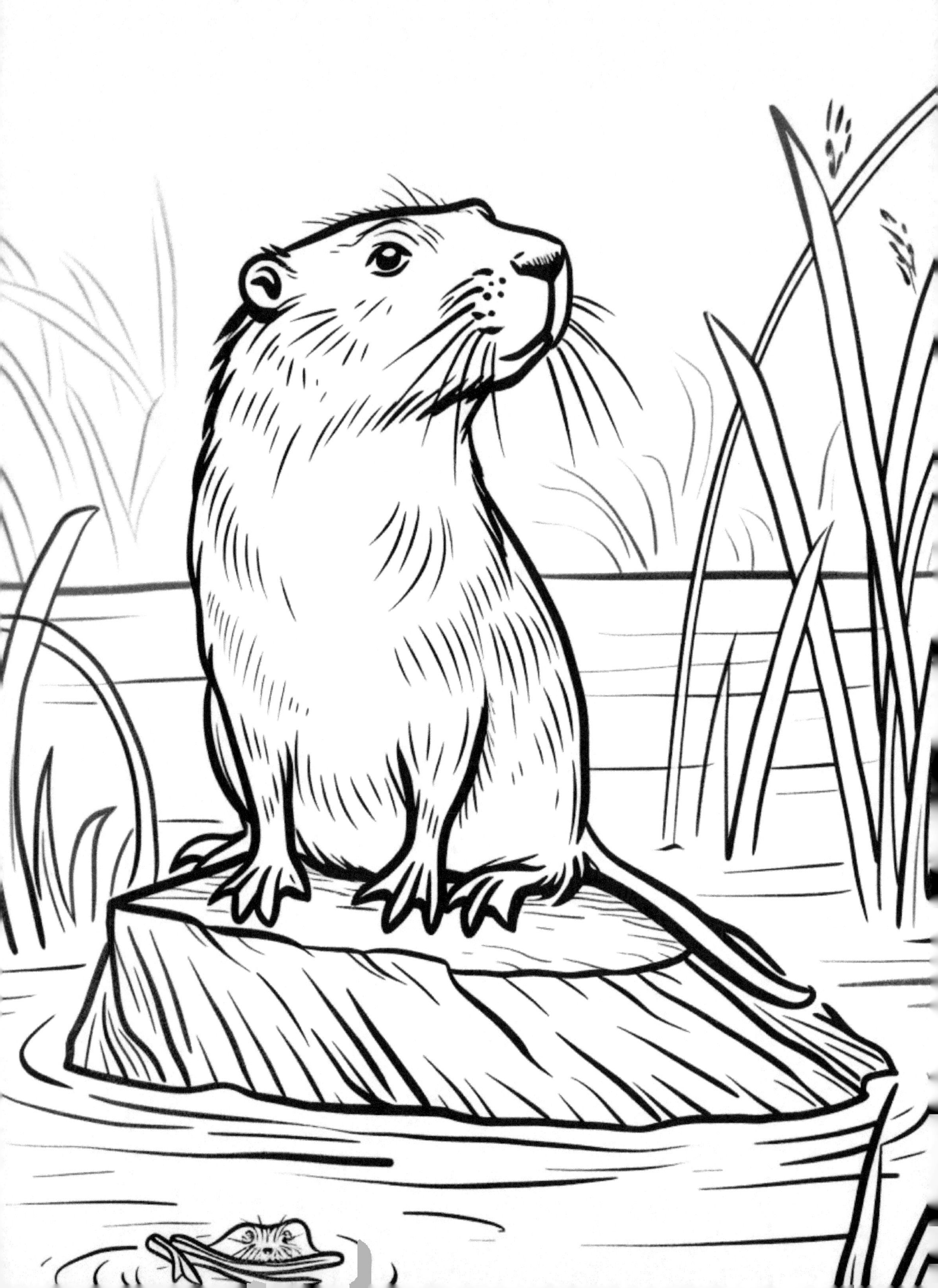

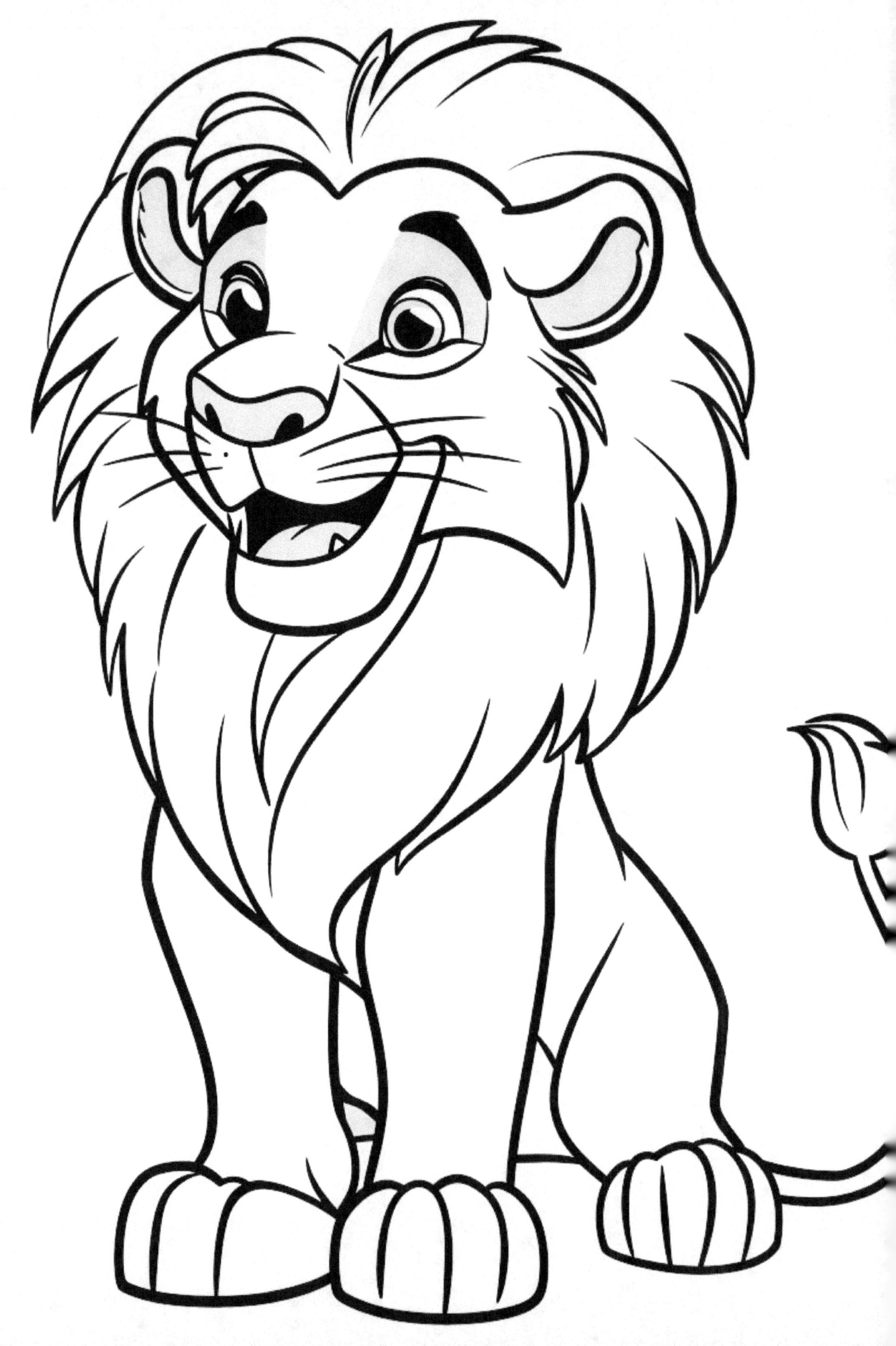

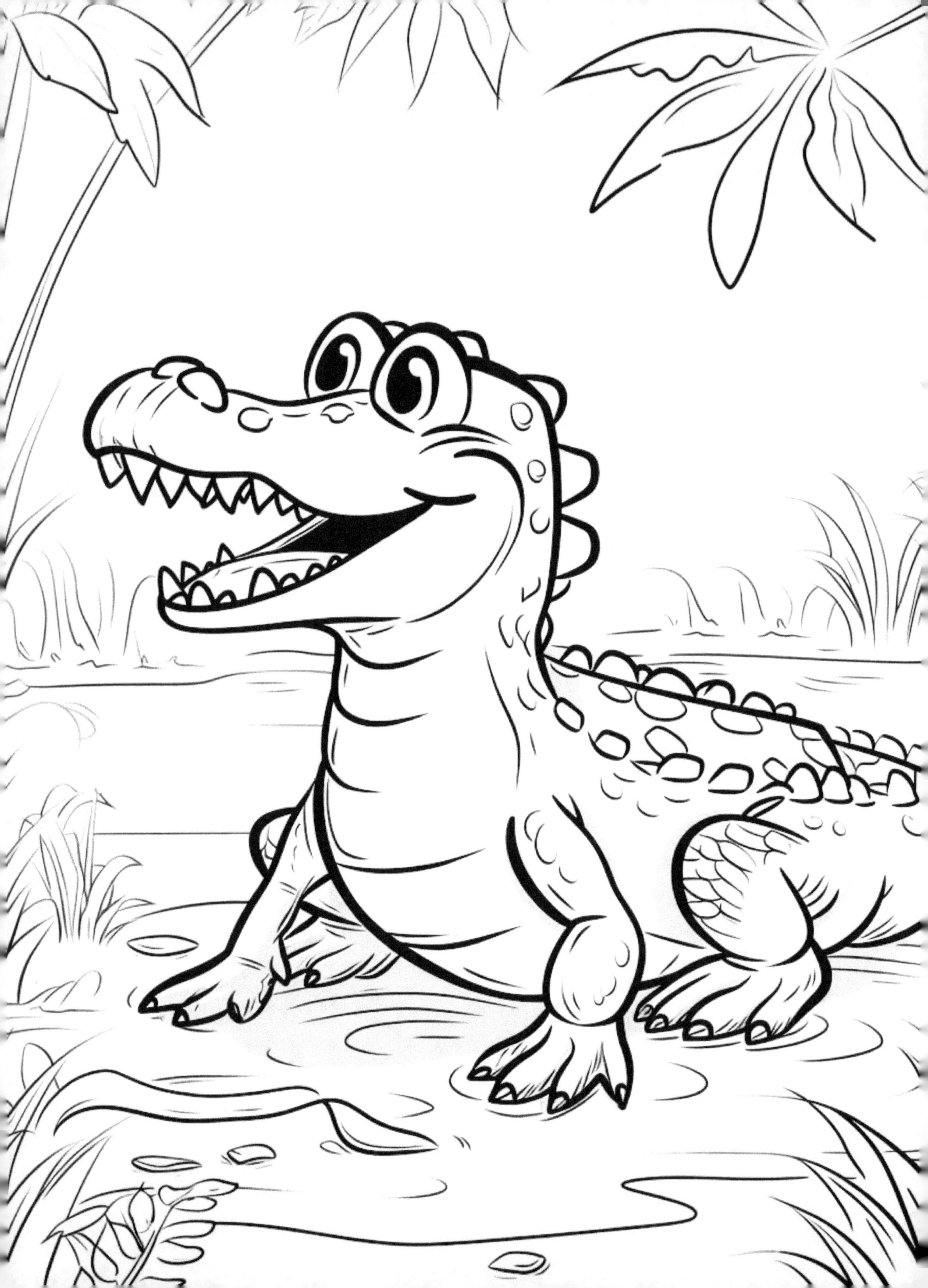

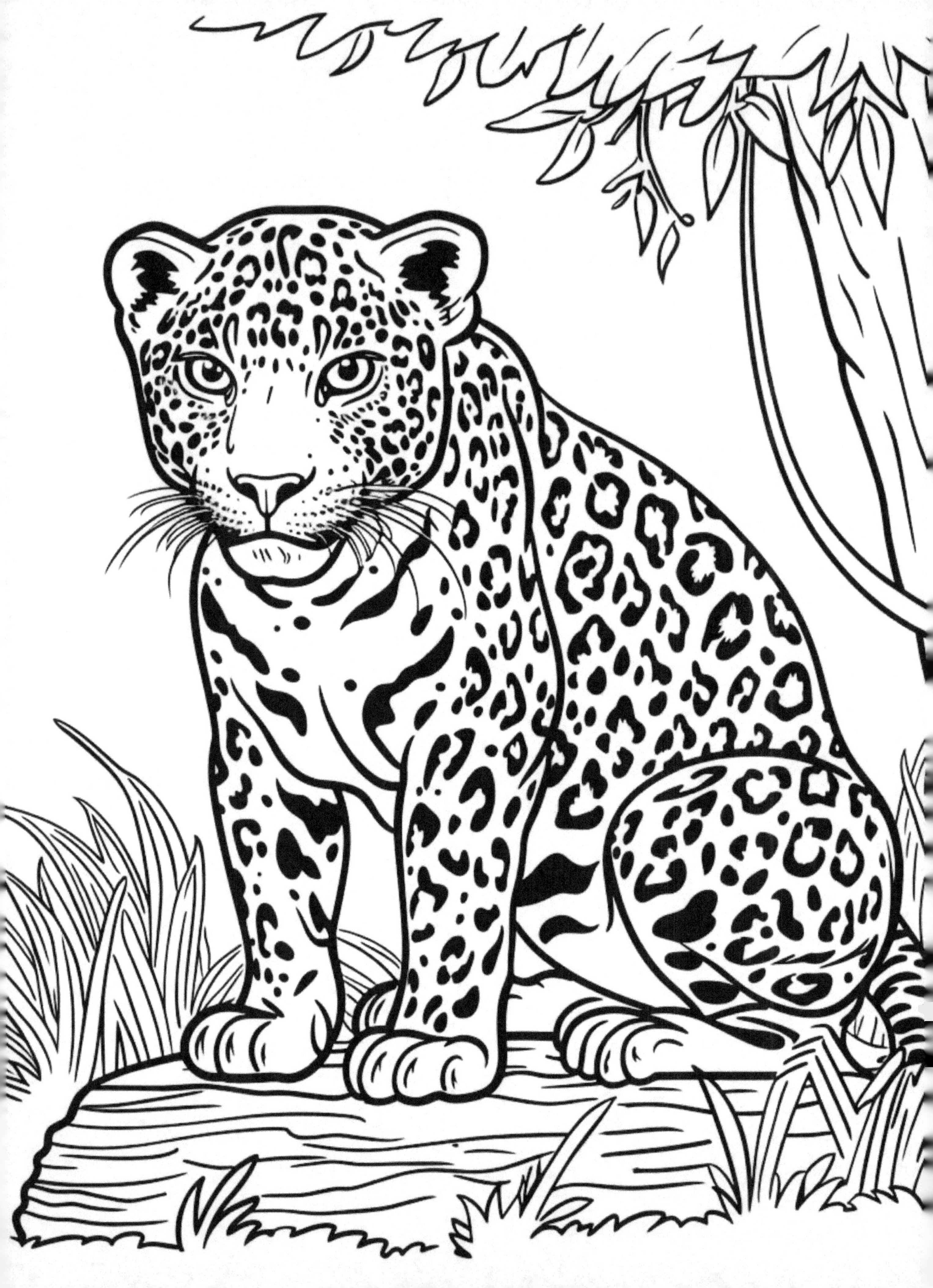

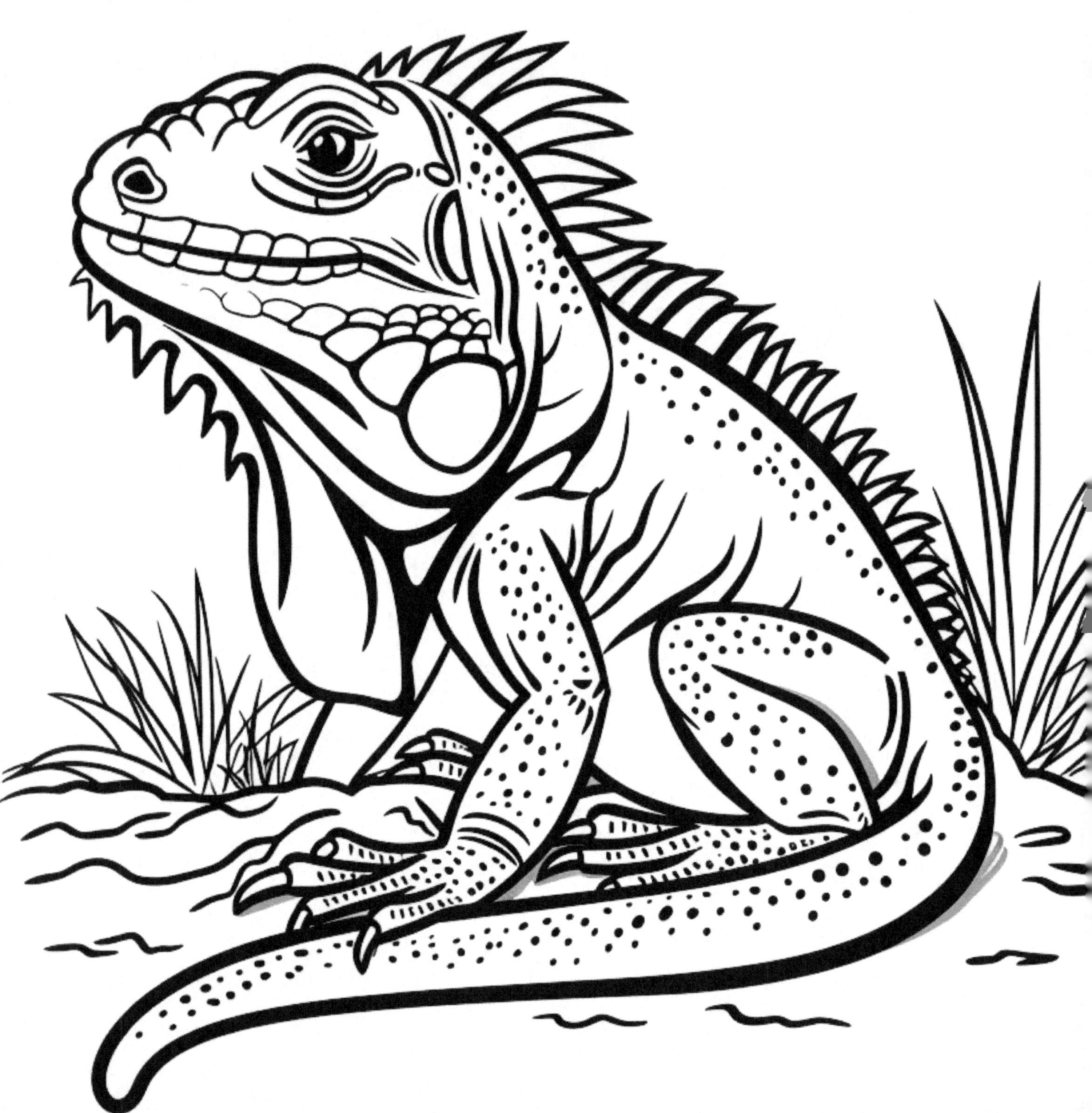

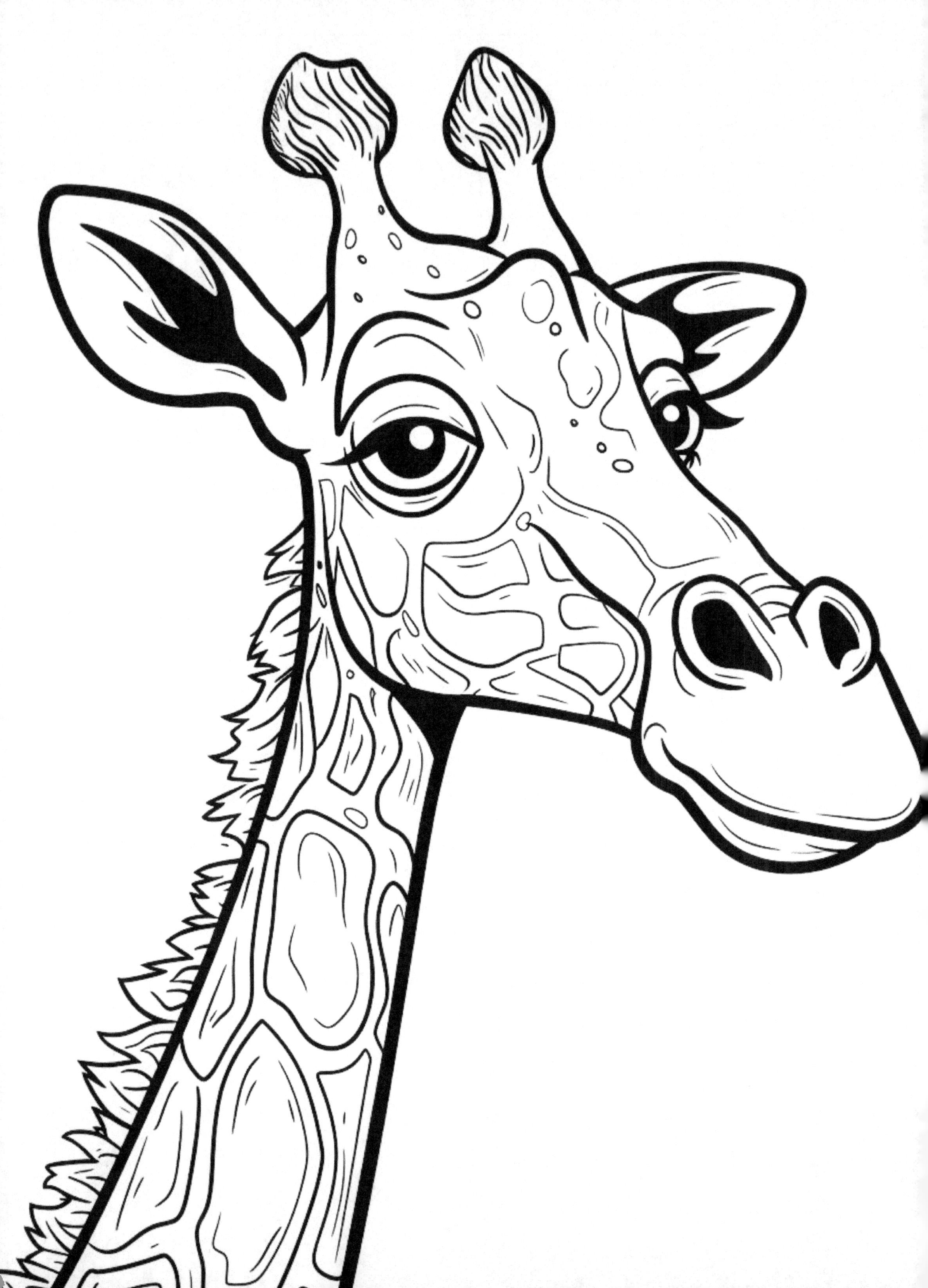

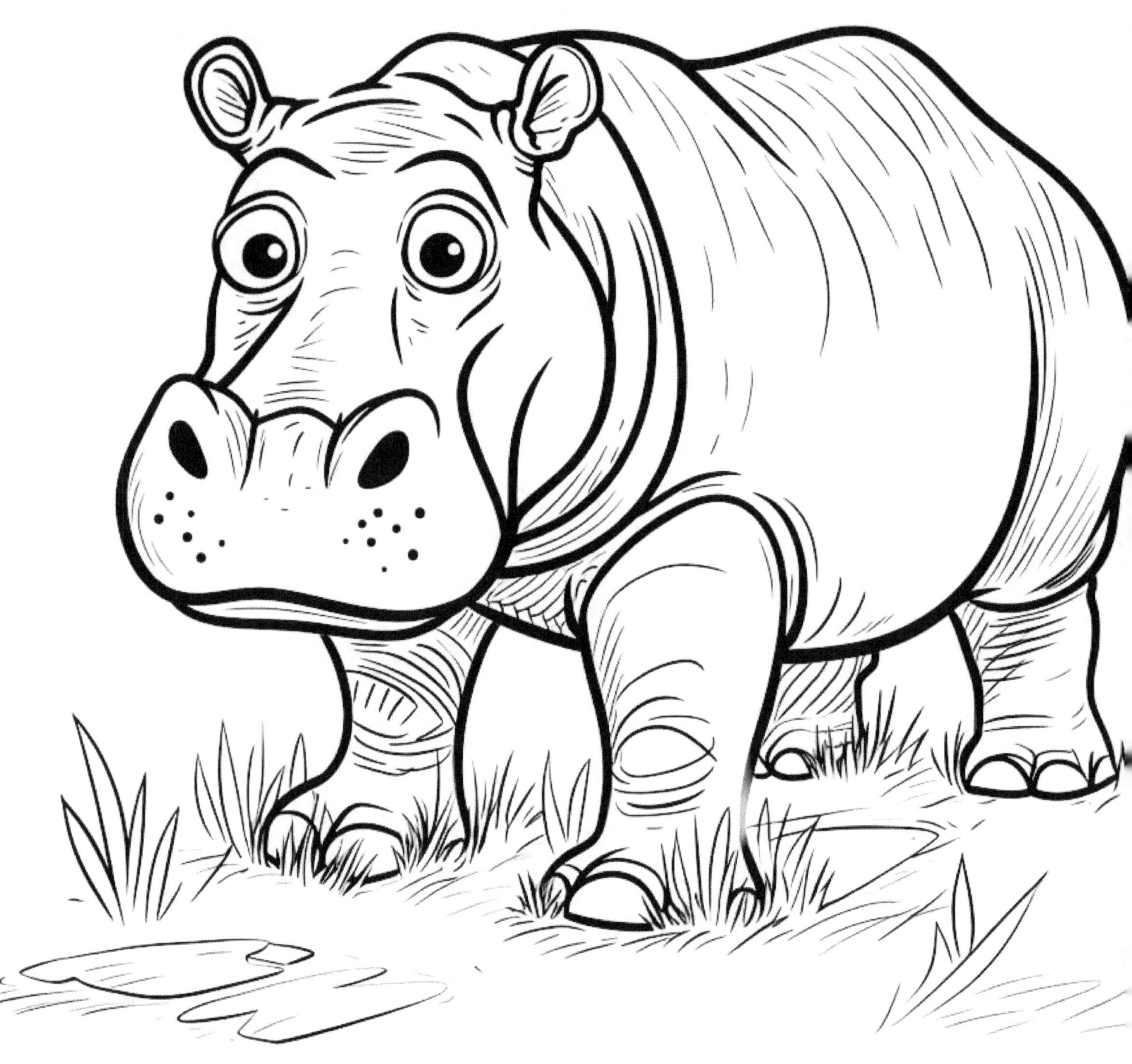

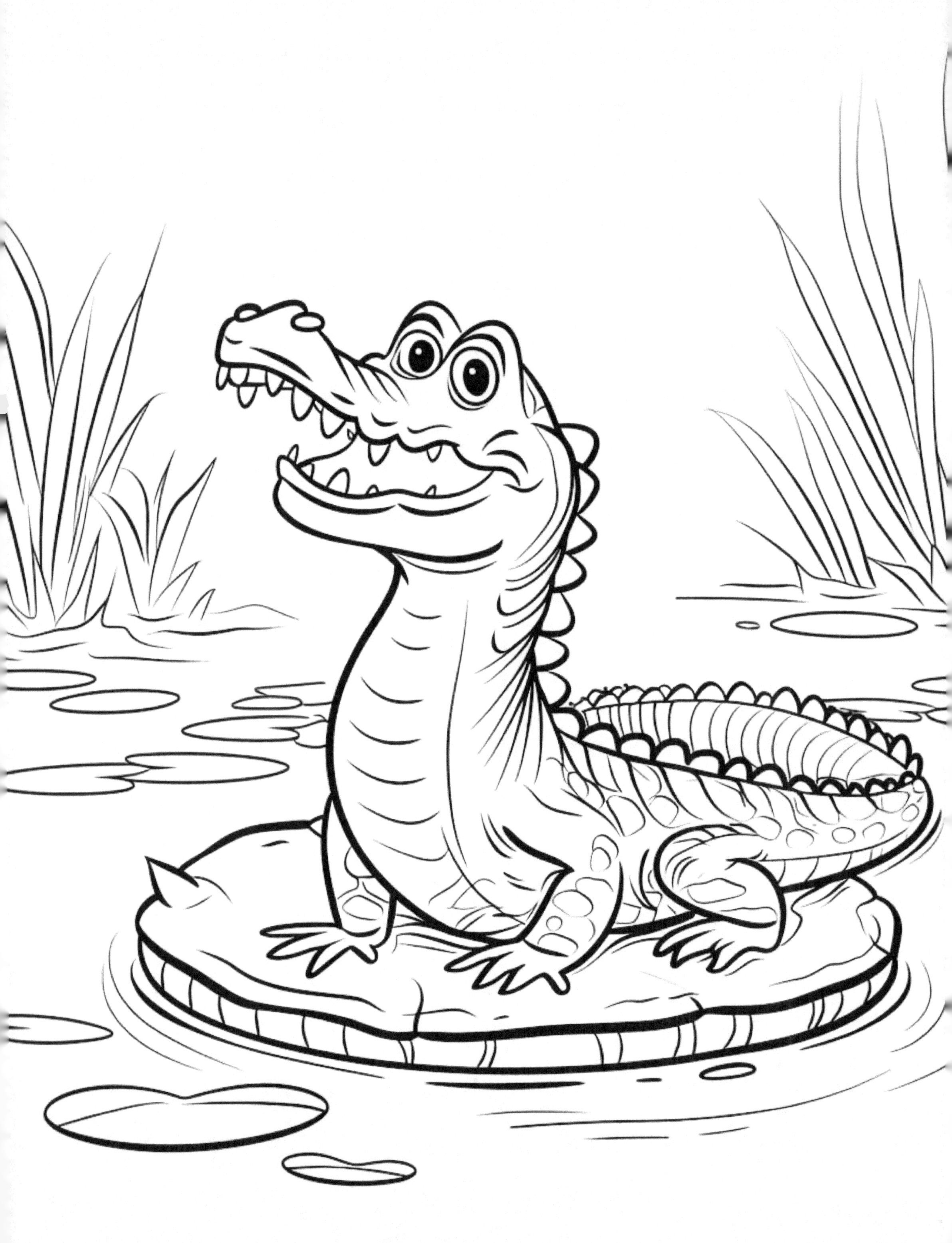

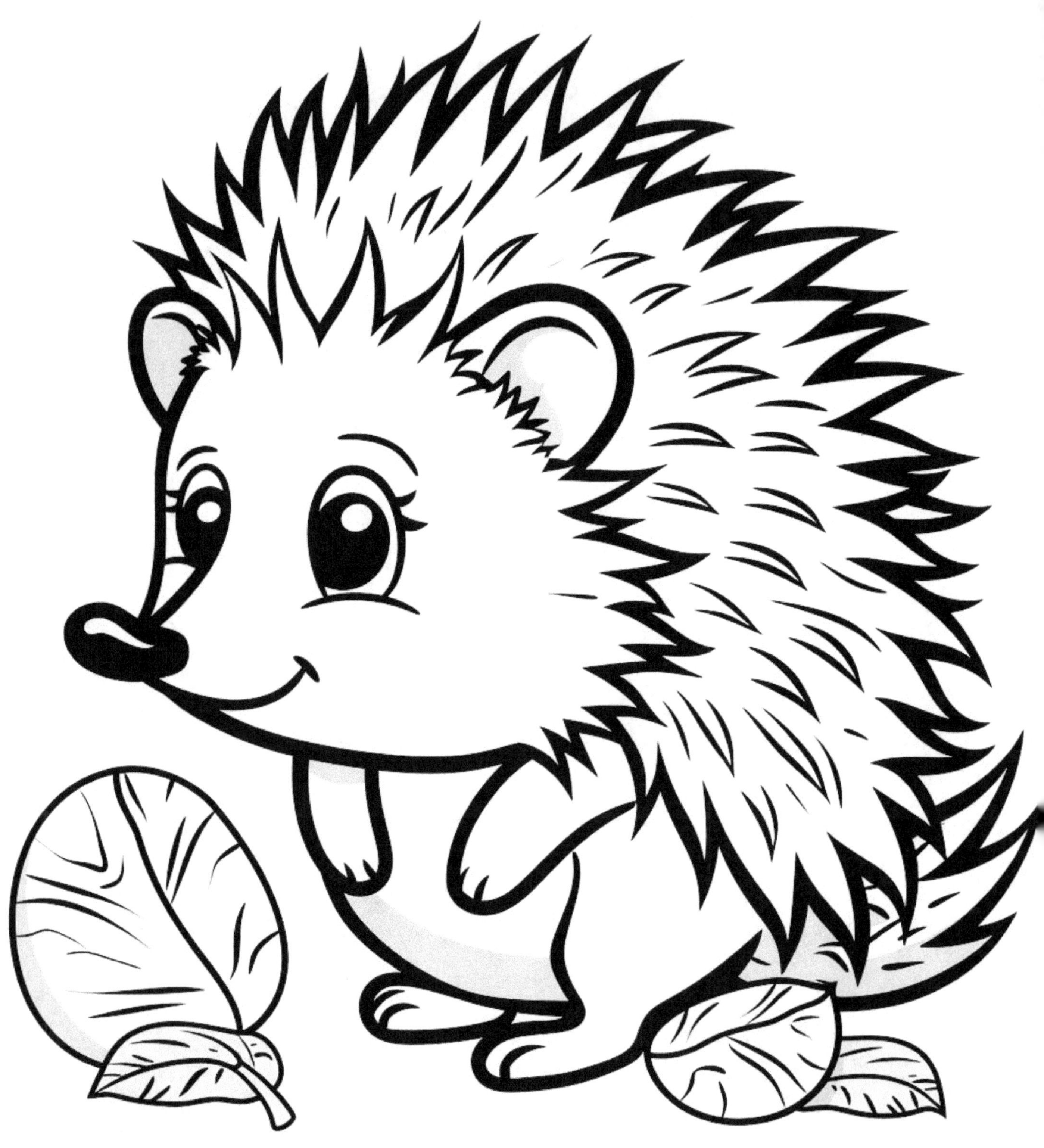

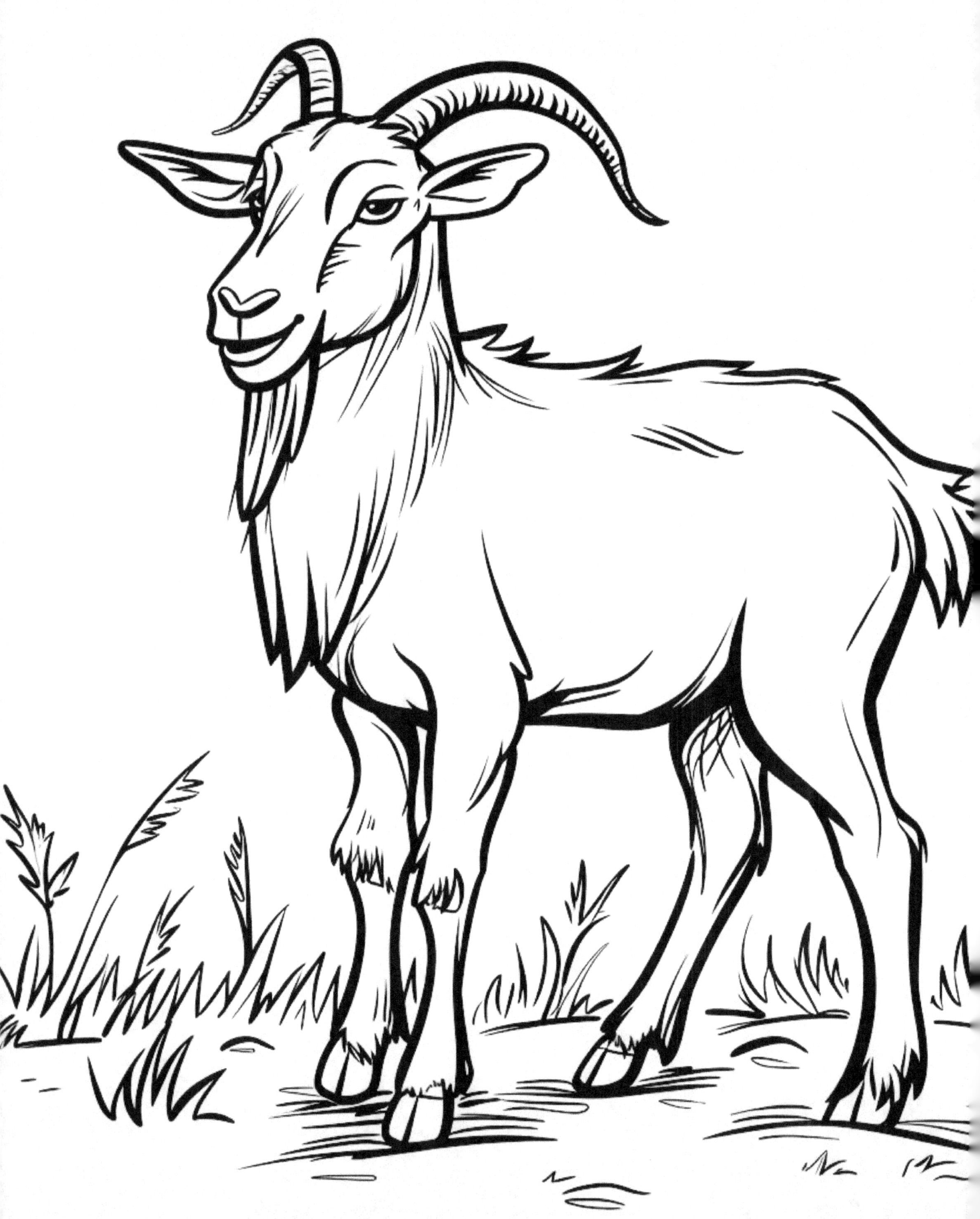

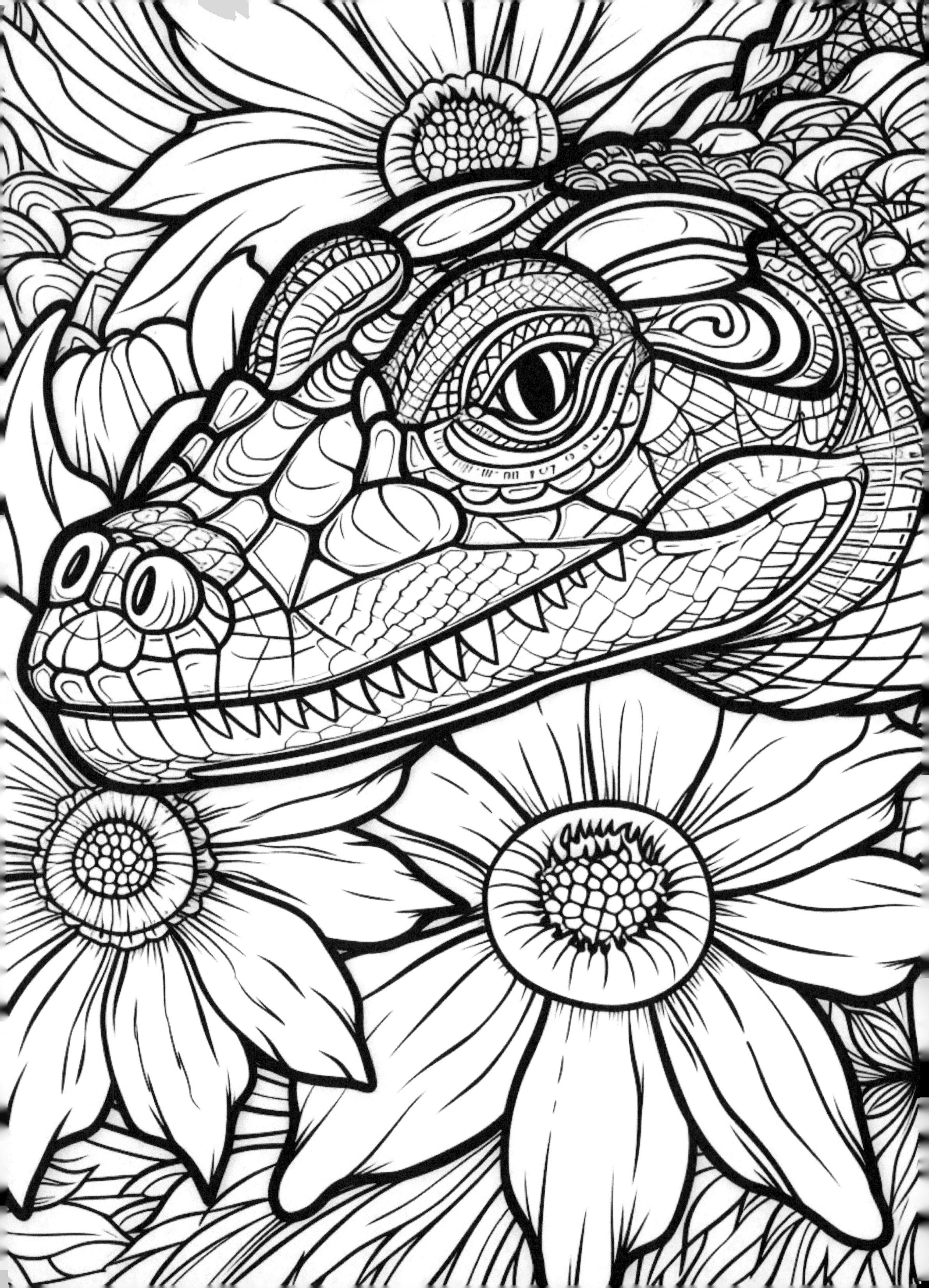

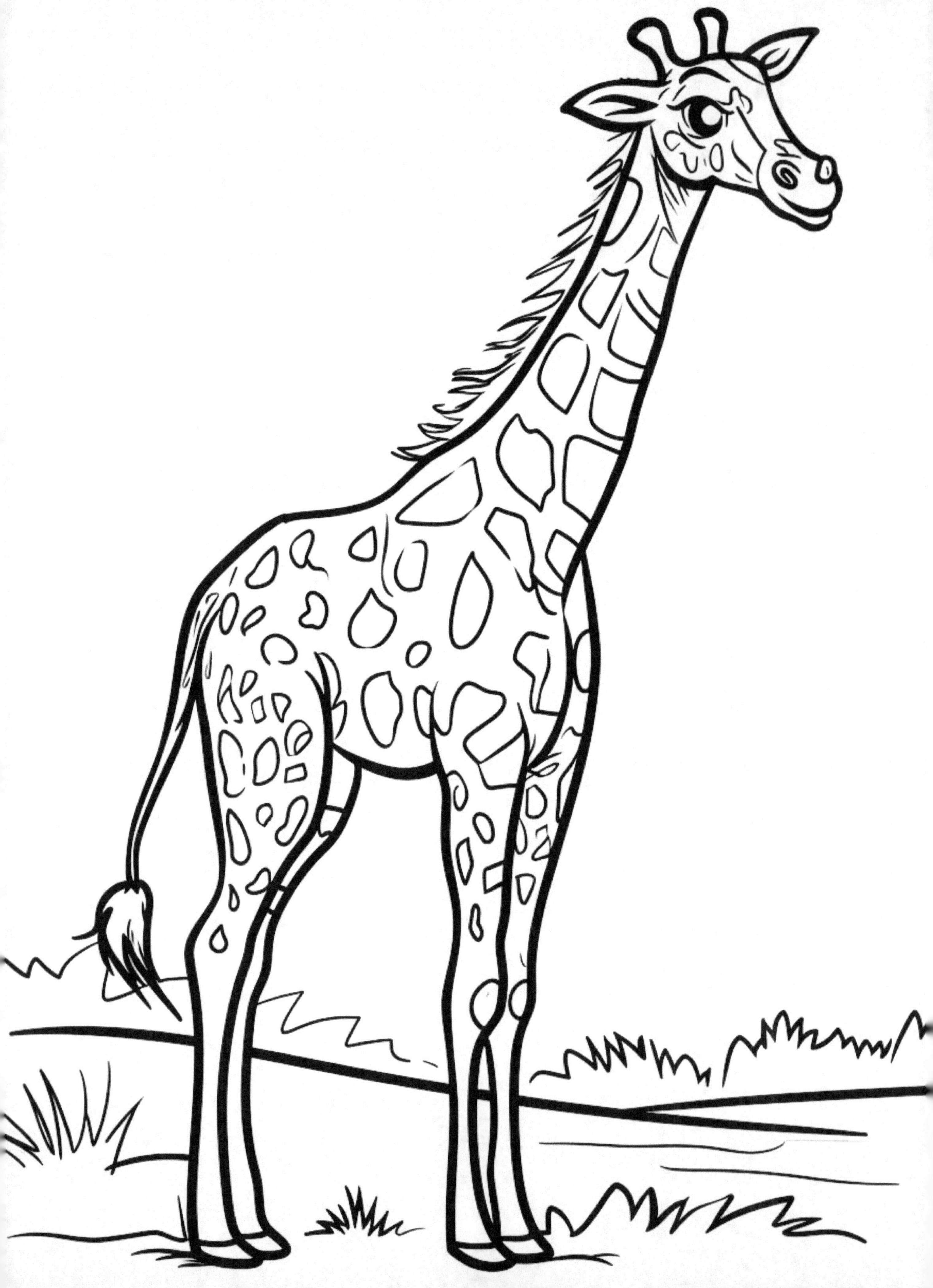

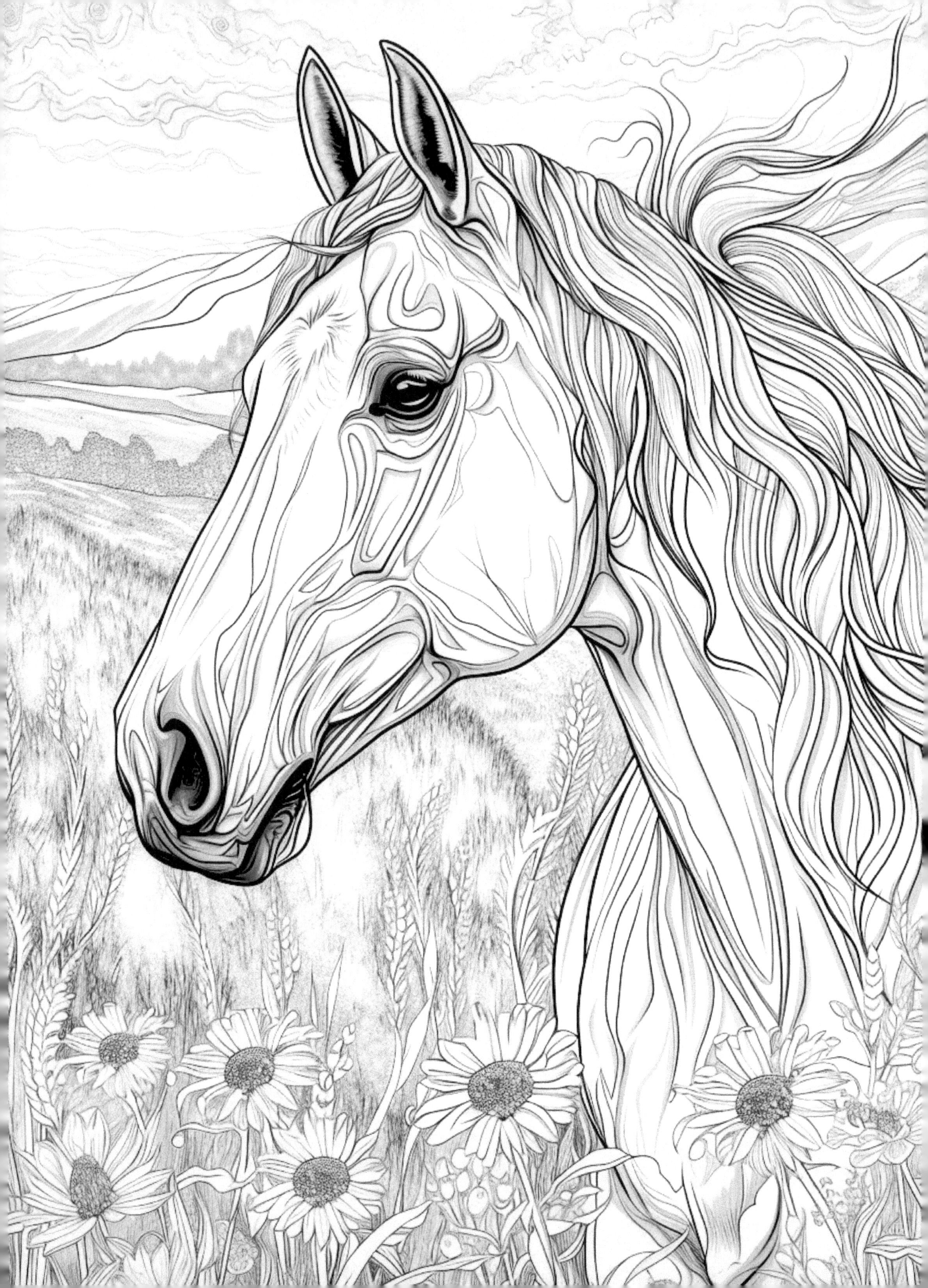

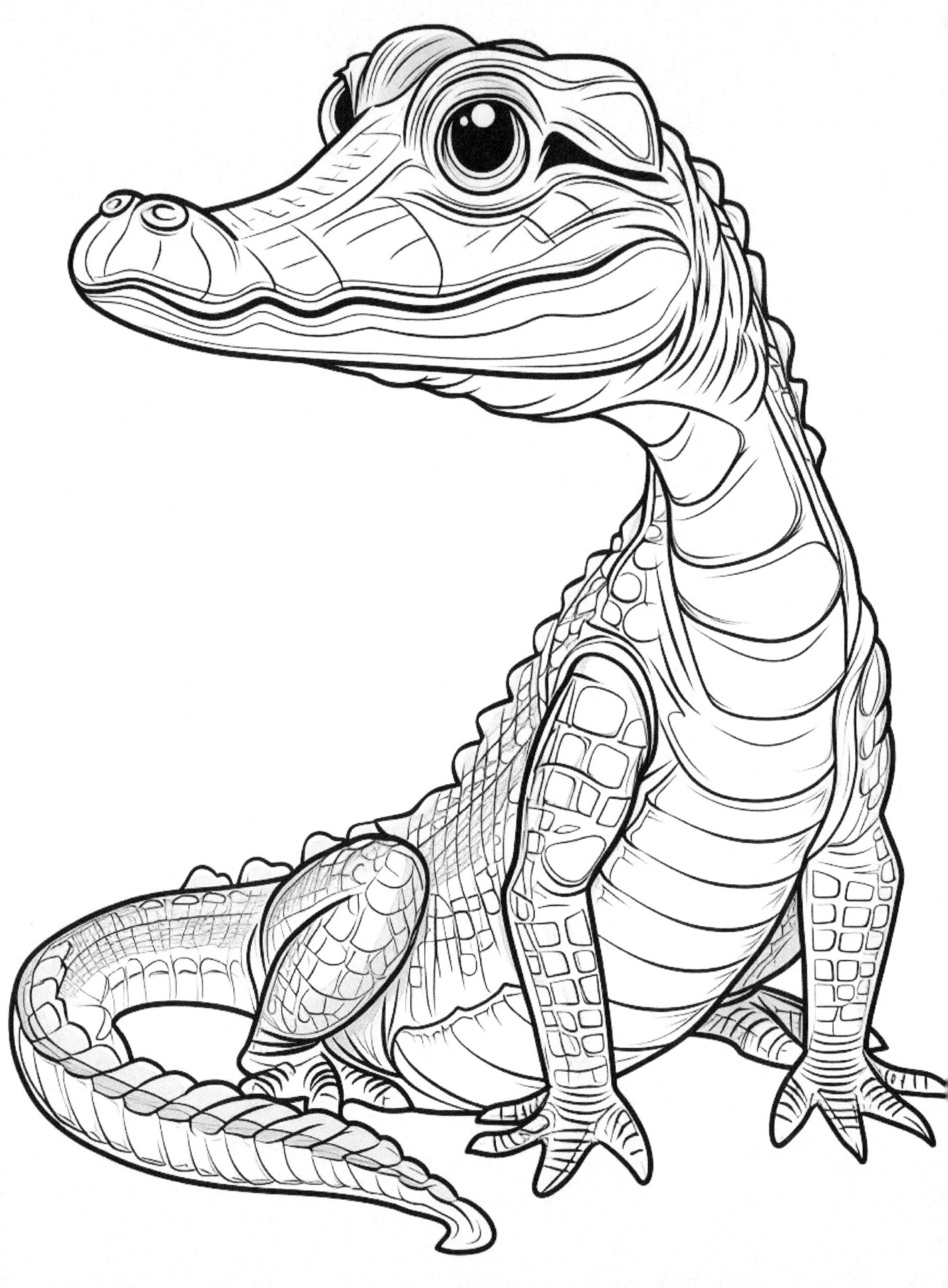

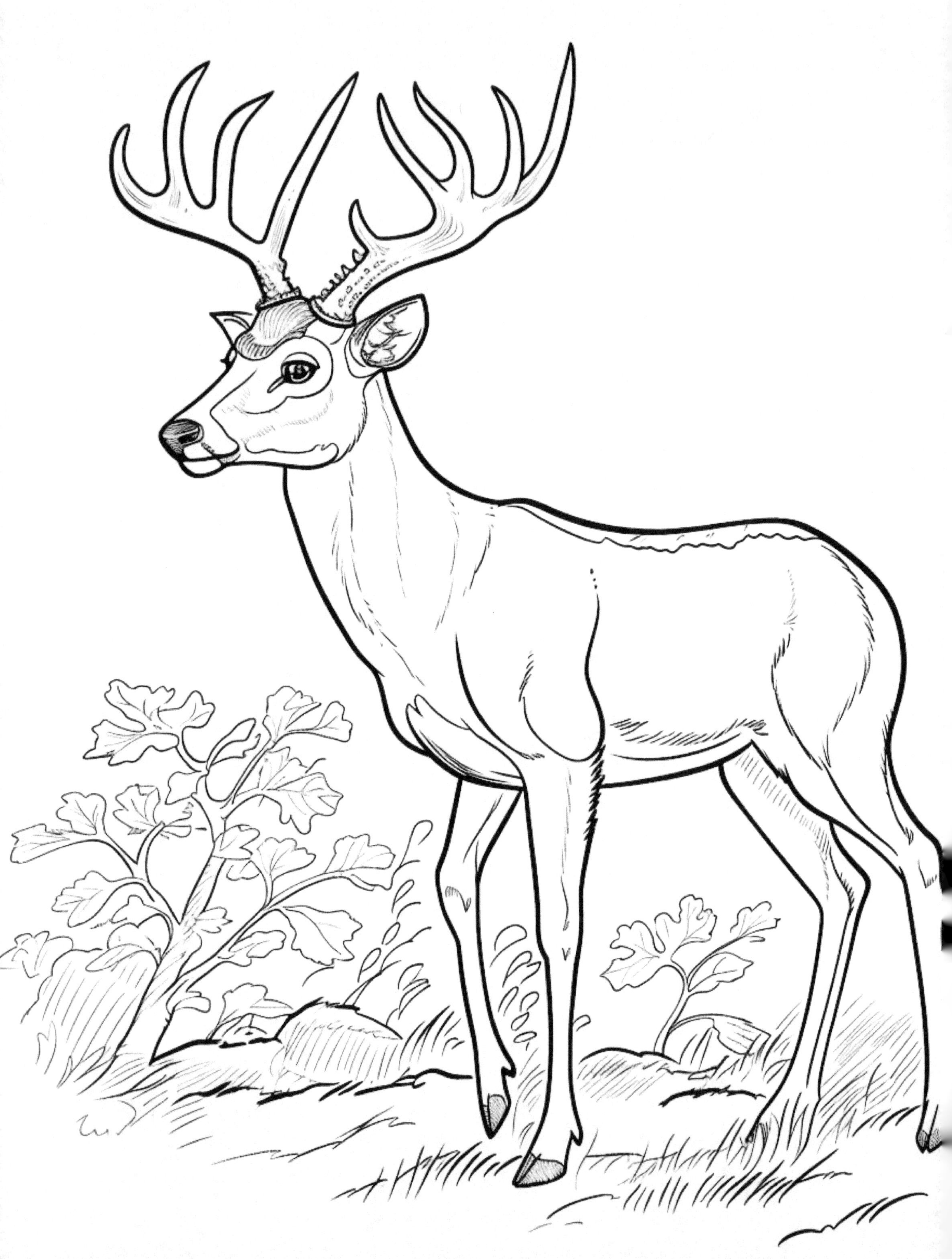

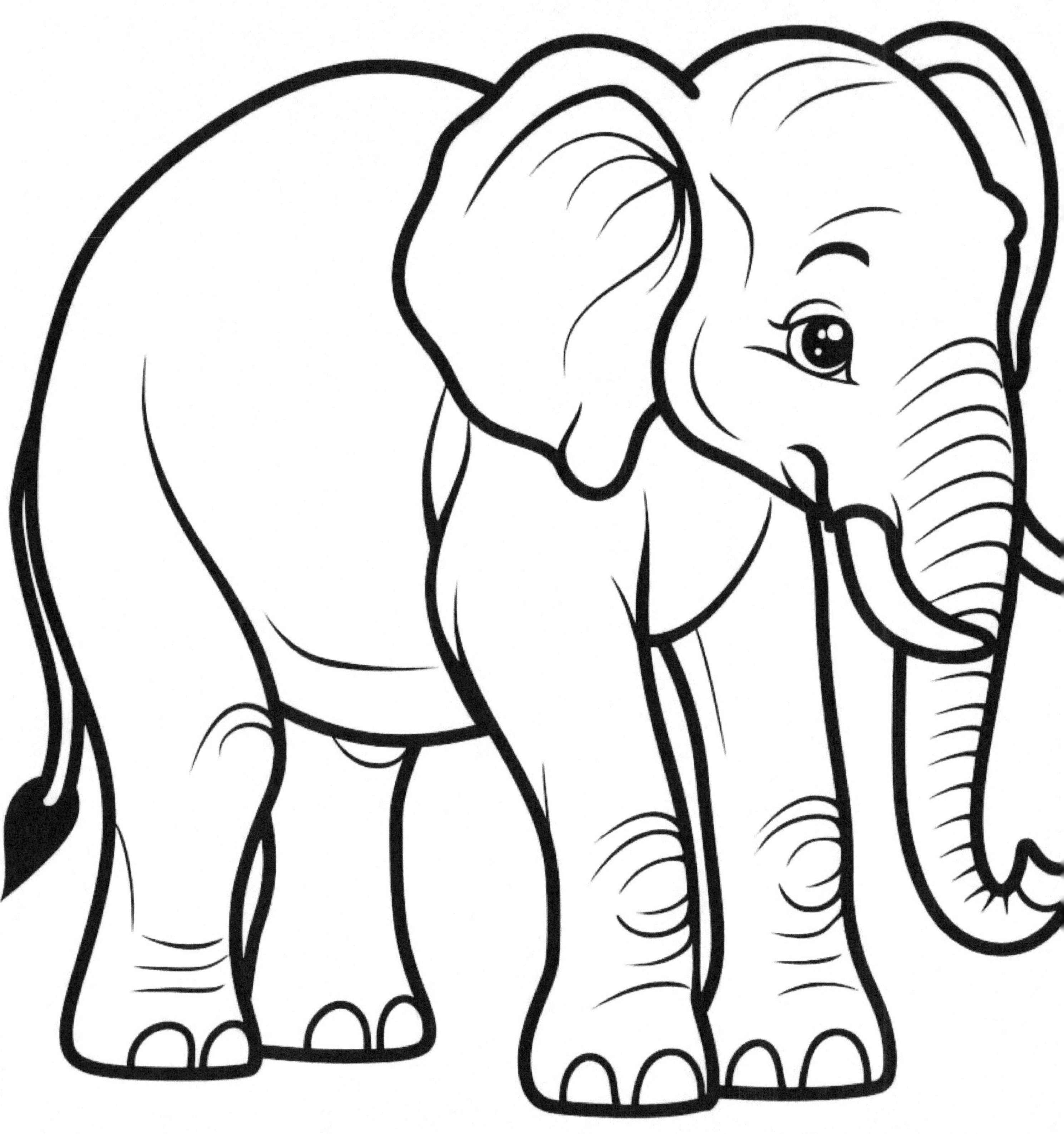

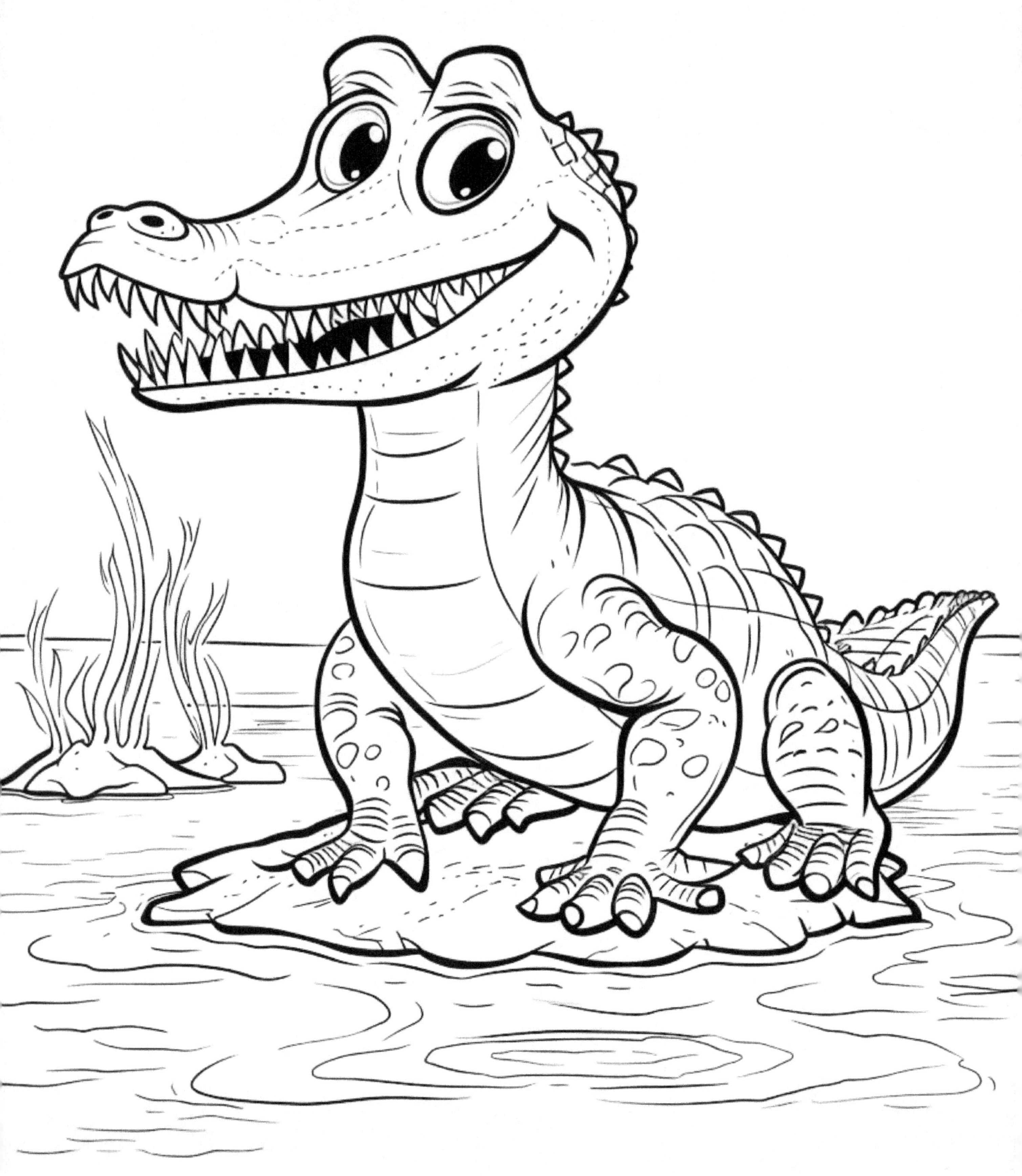

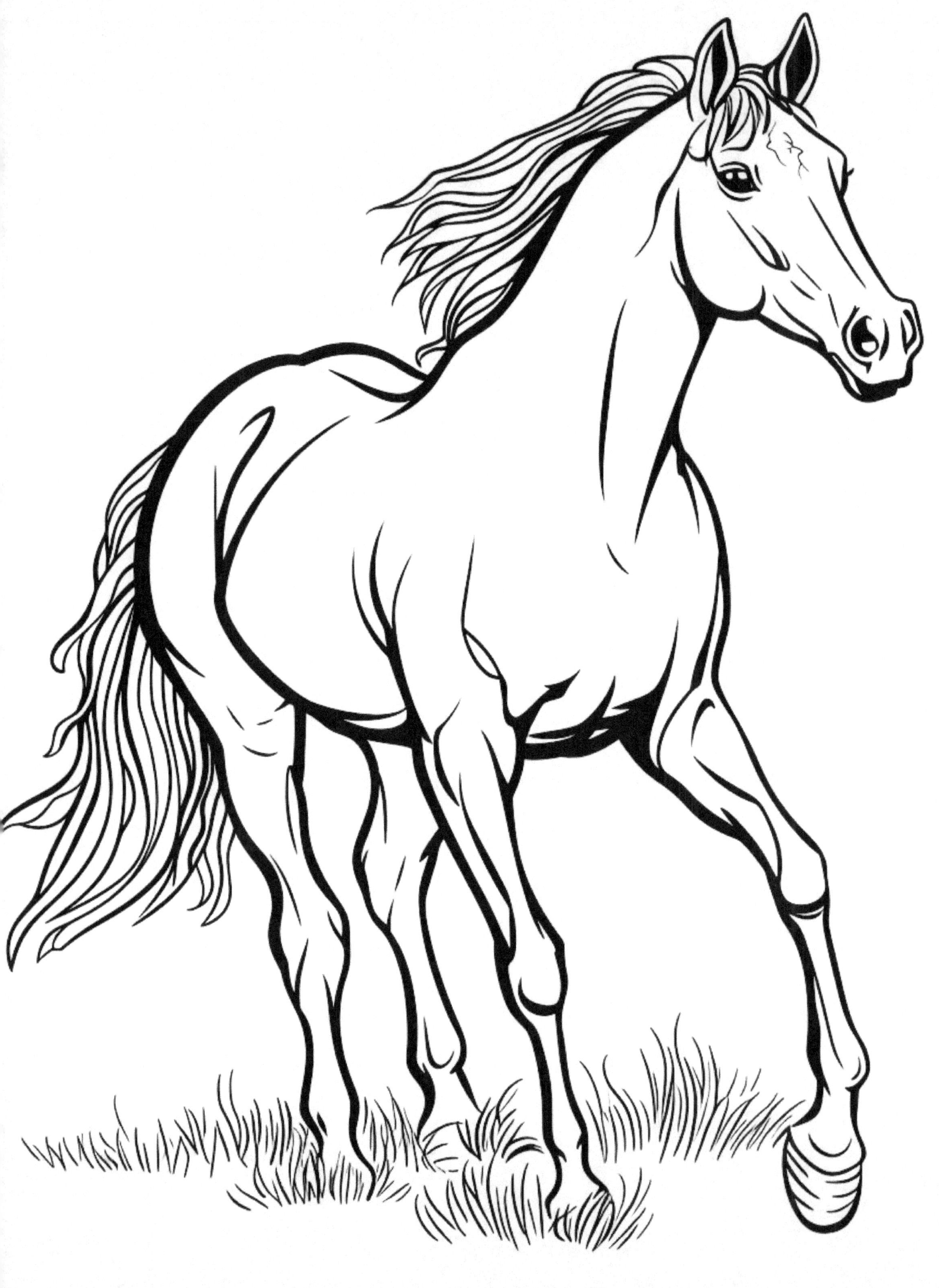

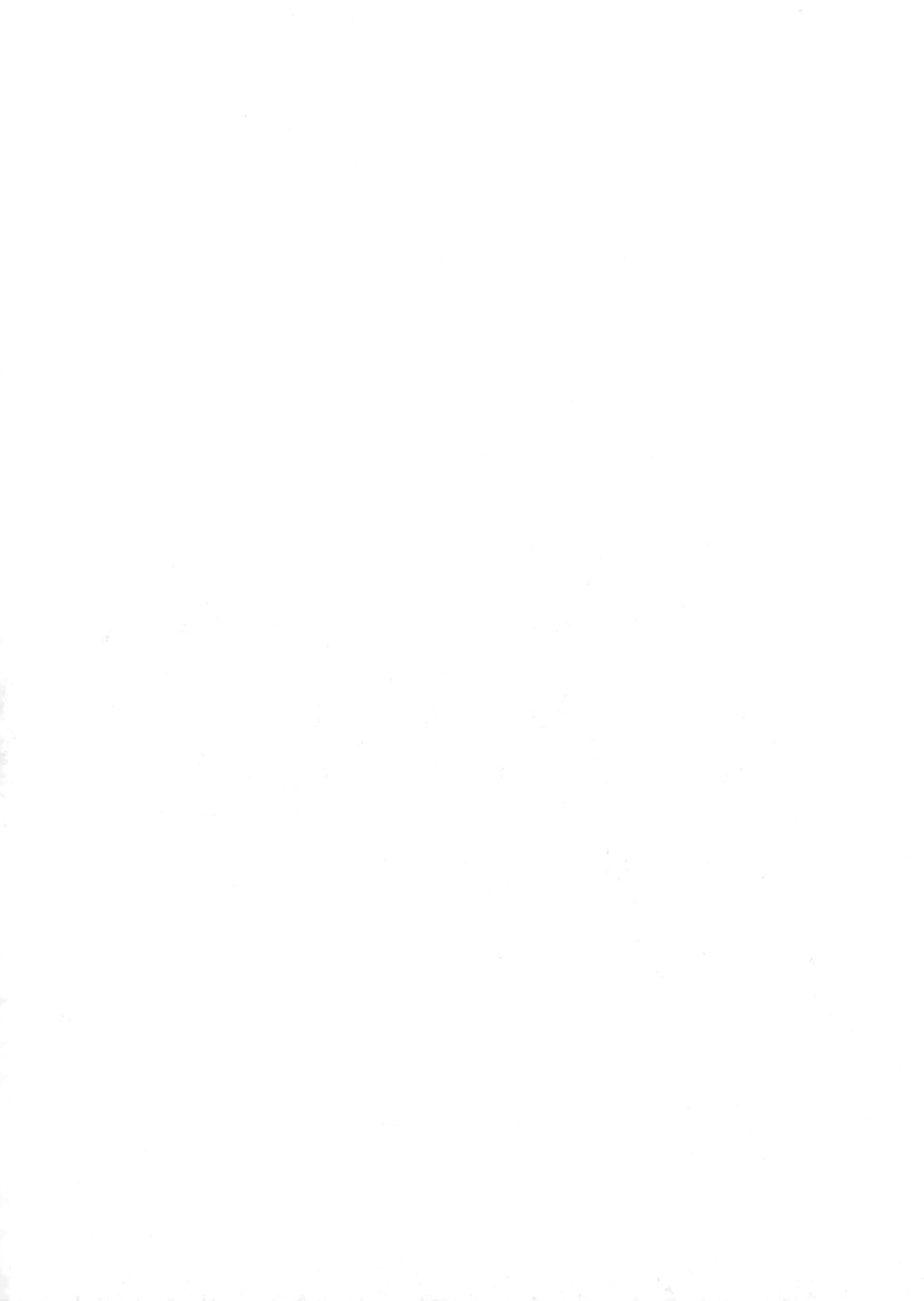

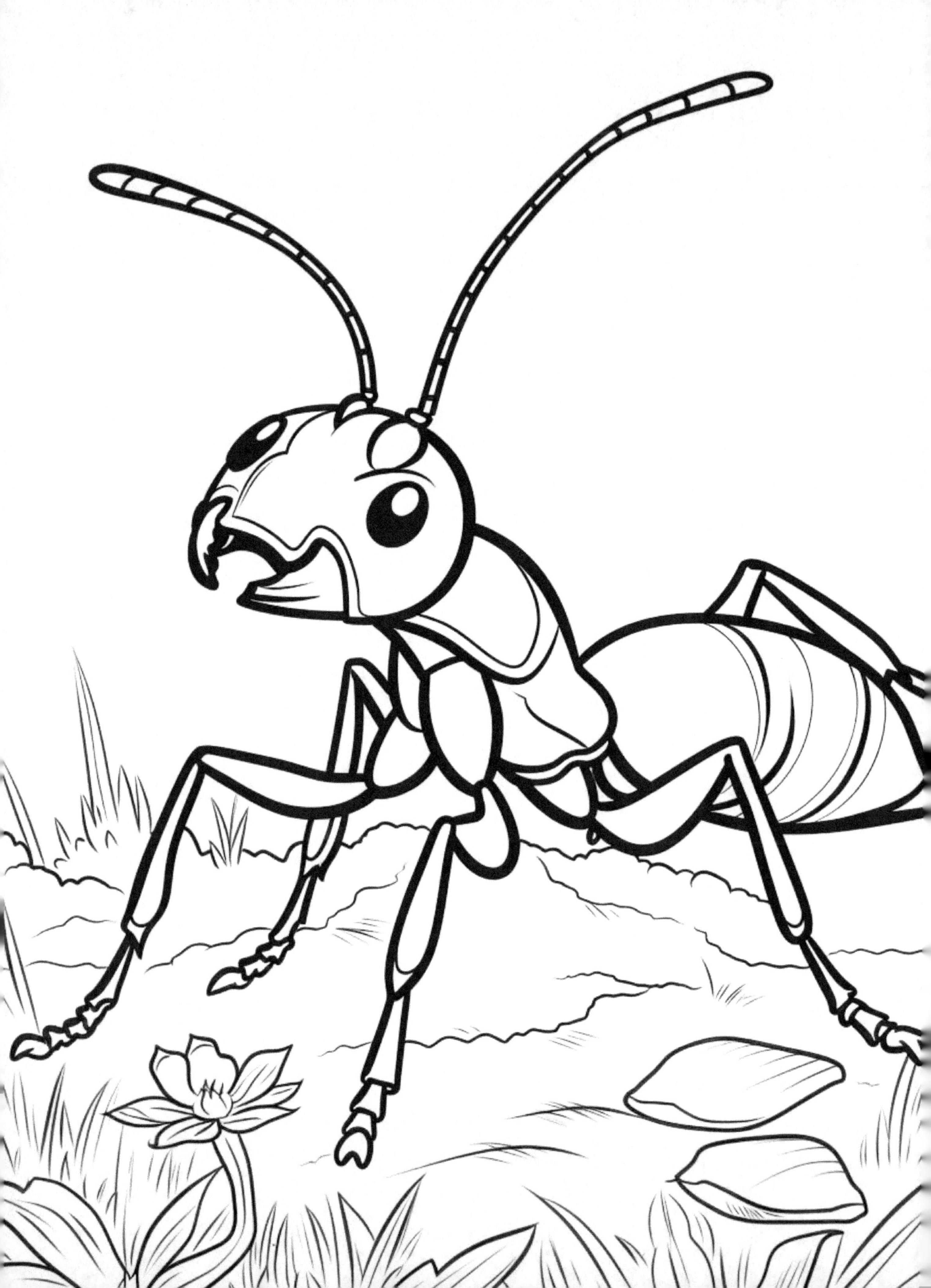

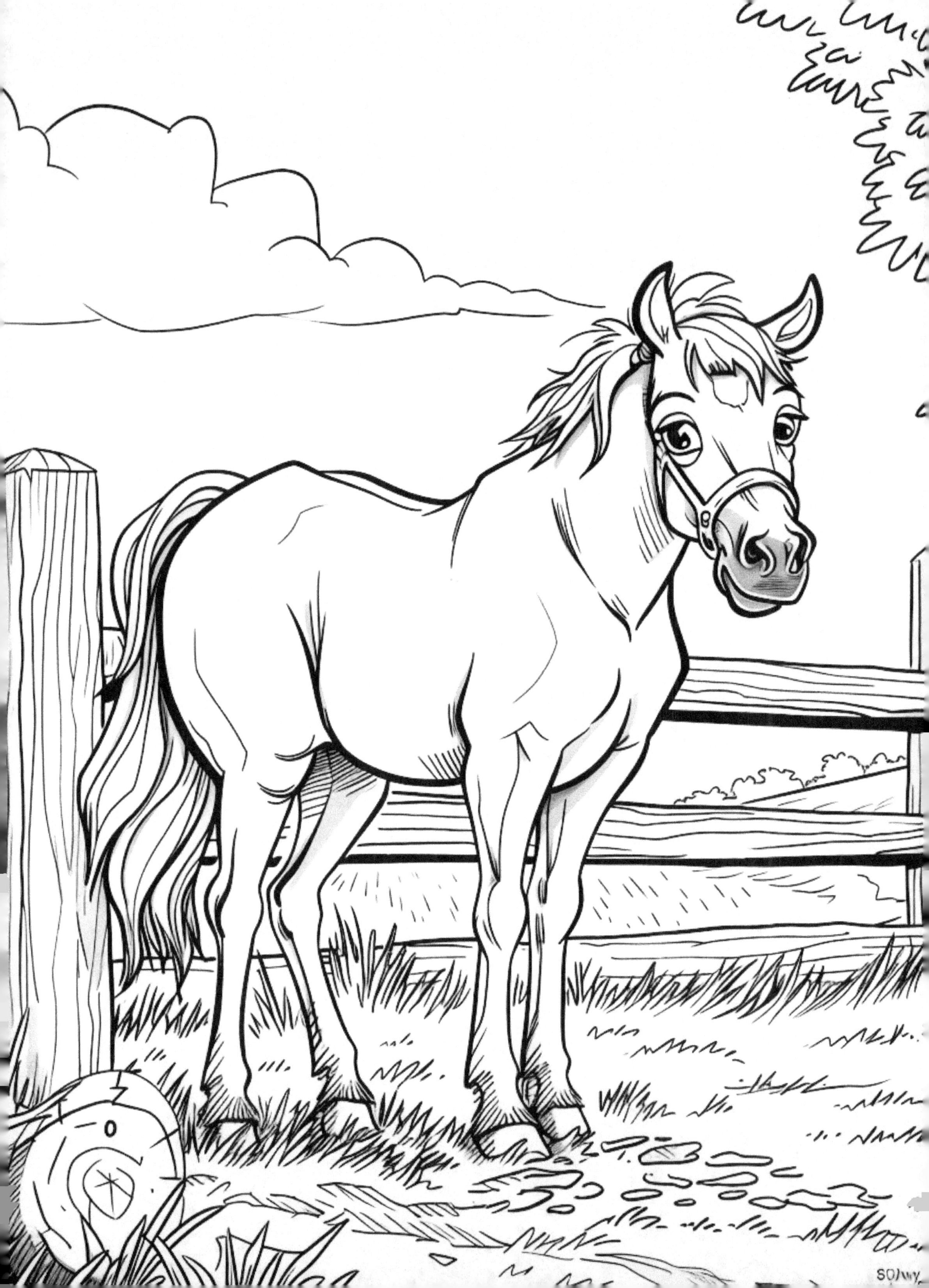

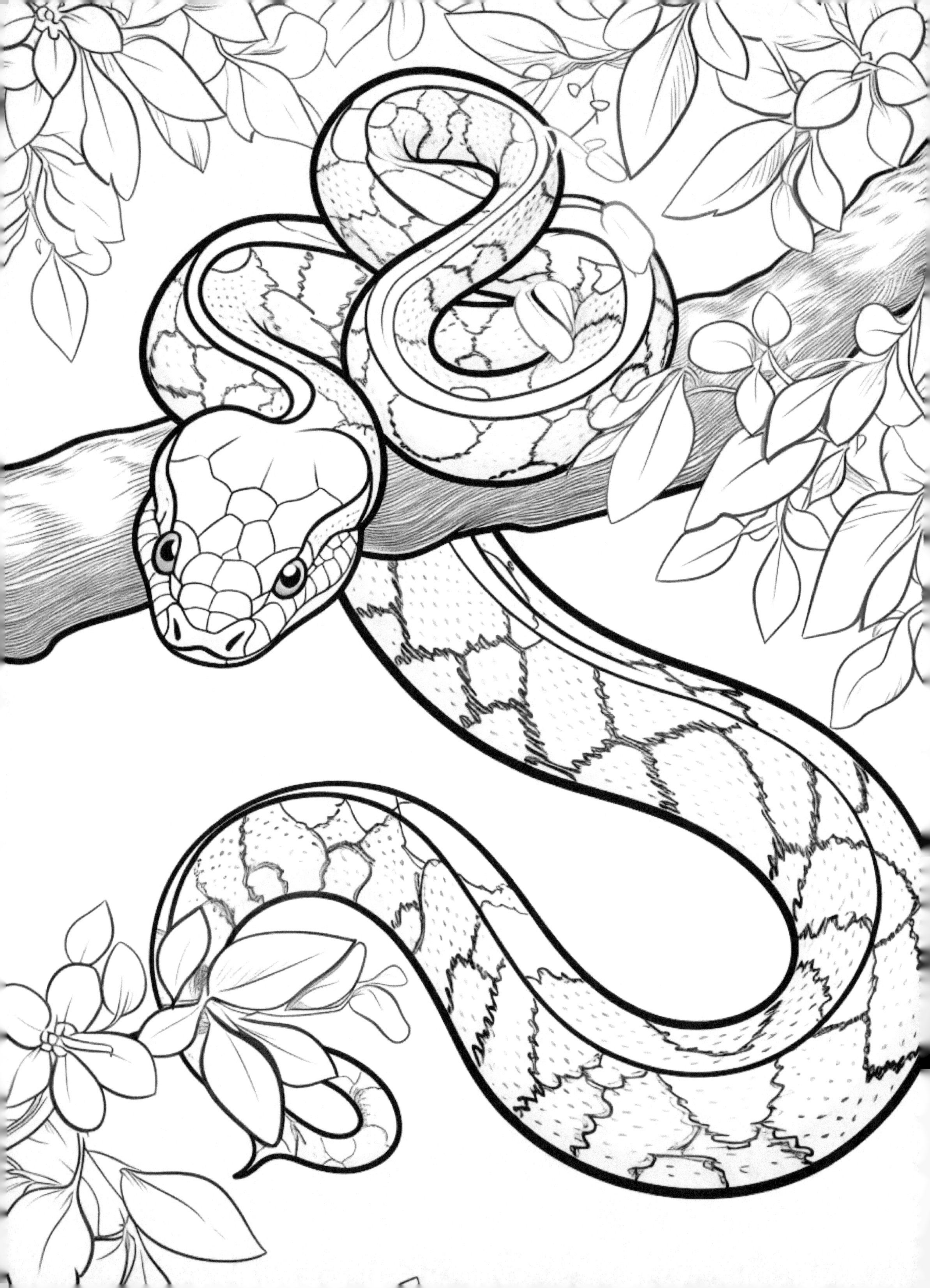

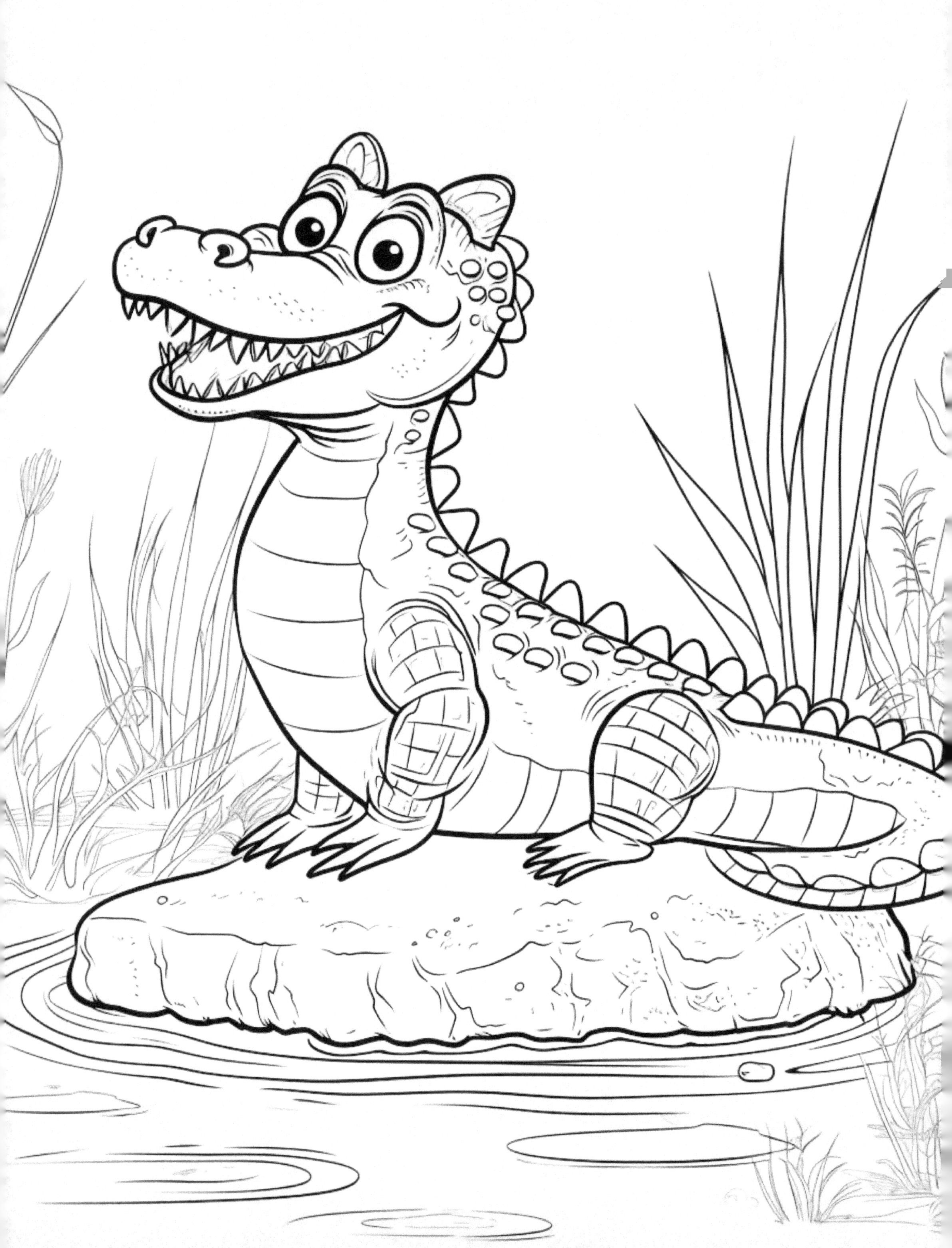

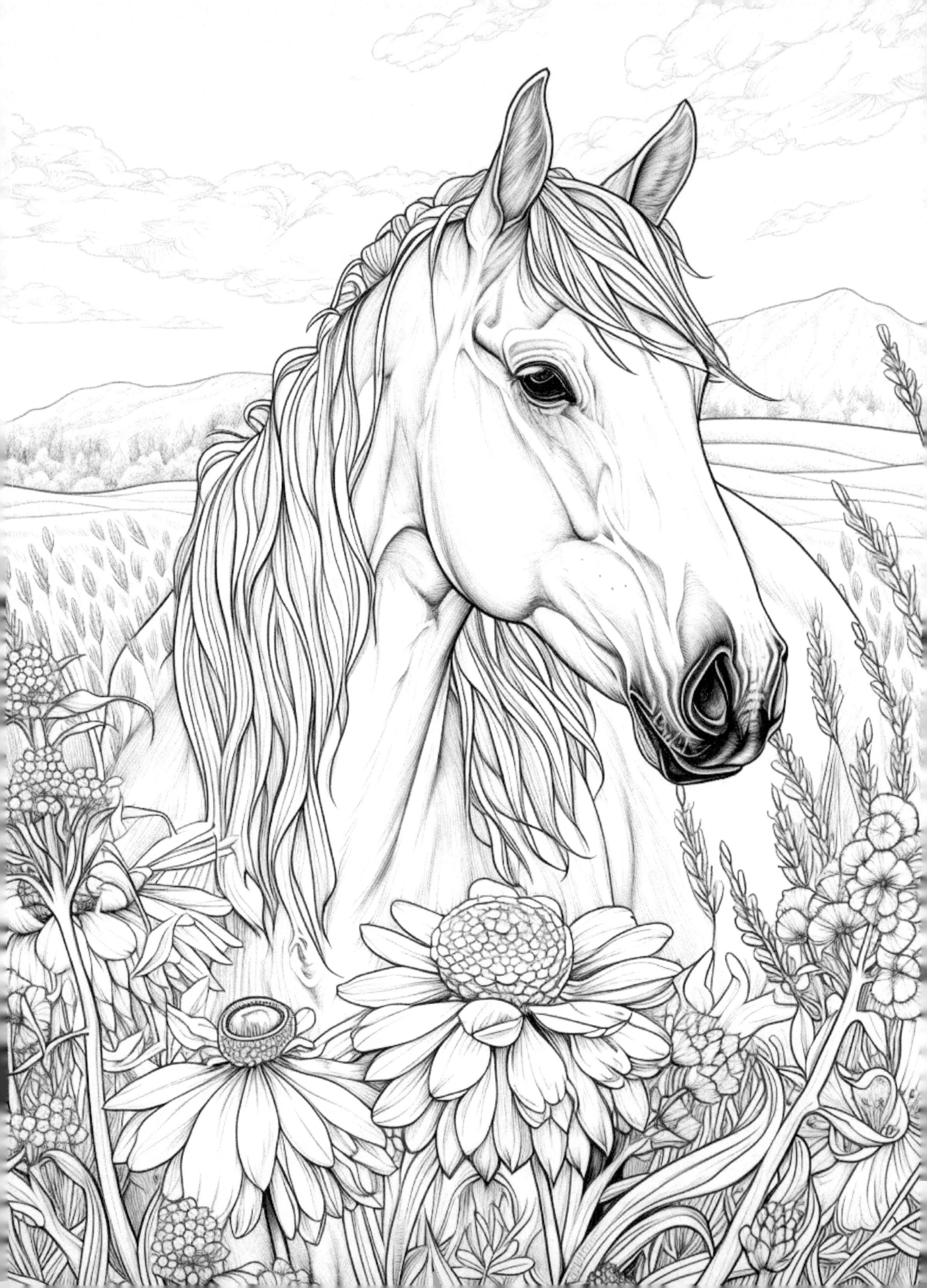

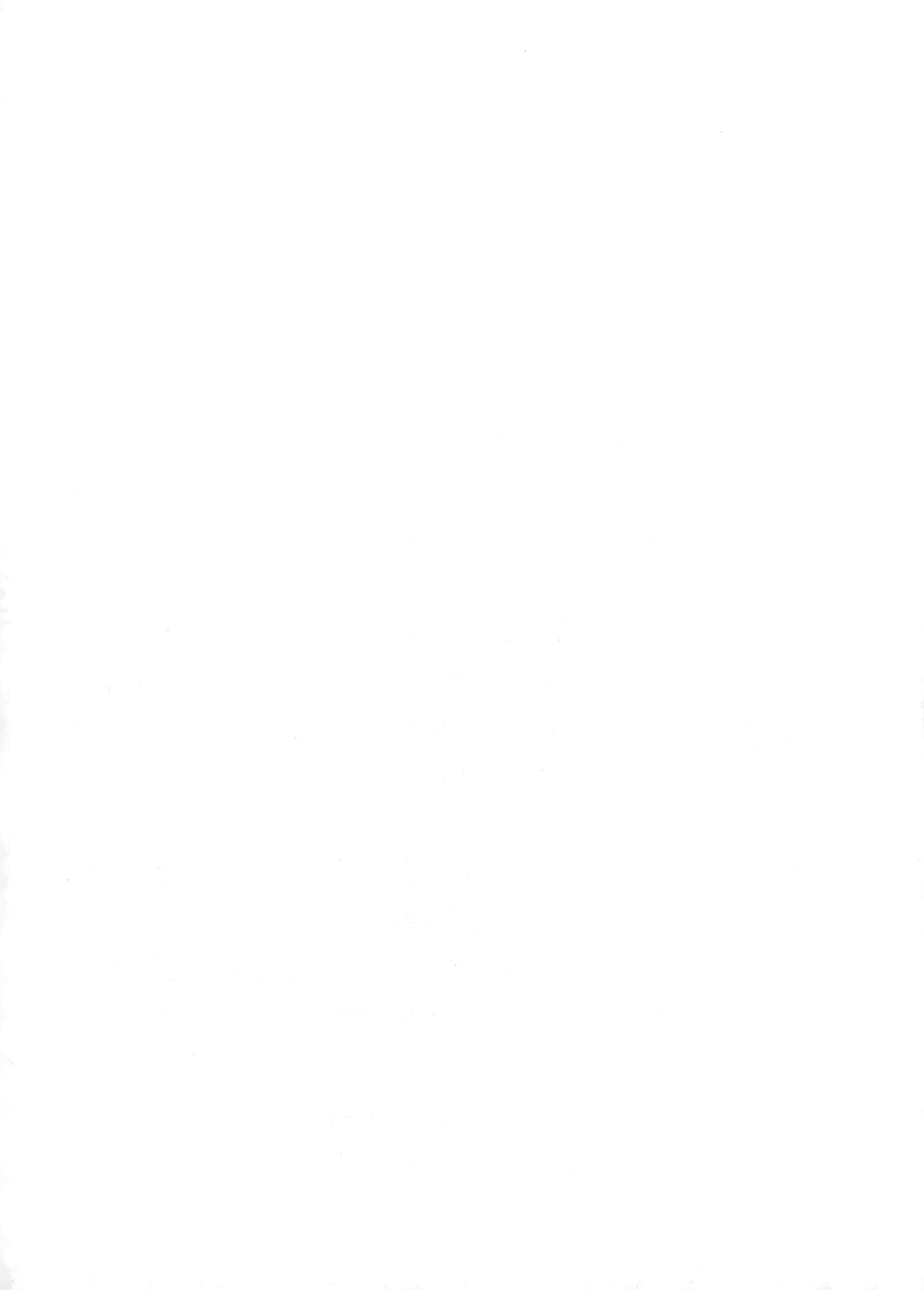

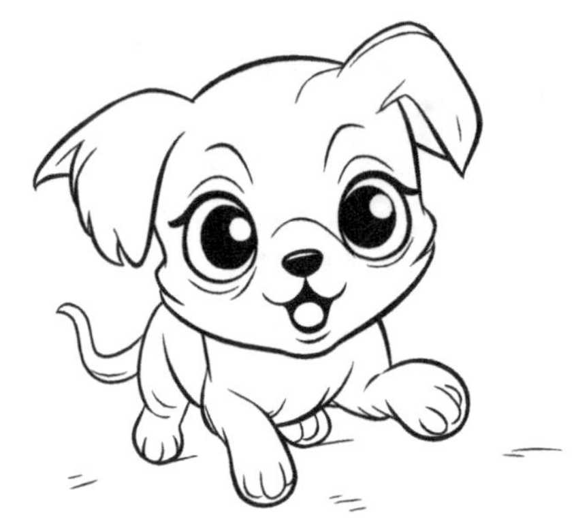

Thank you for joining me on this vibrant journey through the animal kingdom. Your creativity has brought these pages to life, and i hope you found joy, relaxation, and inspiration within them.

Remember, each stroke of your pencil not only adds color to these pages but also brings a bit of magic into the world. I am grateful you chose to embark on this artistic adventure with me.

May your days be filled with color and your heart with the wild spirit of nature. Until our next adventure, keep creating, keep dreaming, and keep exploring the beauty that surrounds us.

With heartfelt thanks,
Artur Sobolevskij

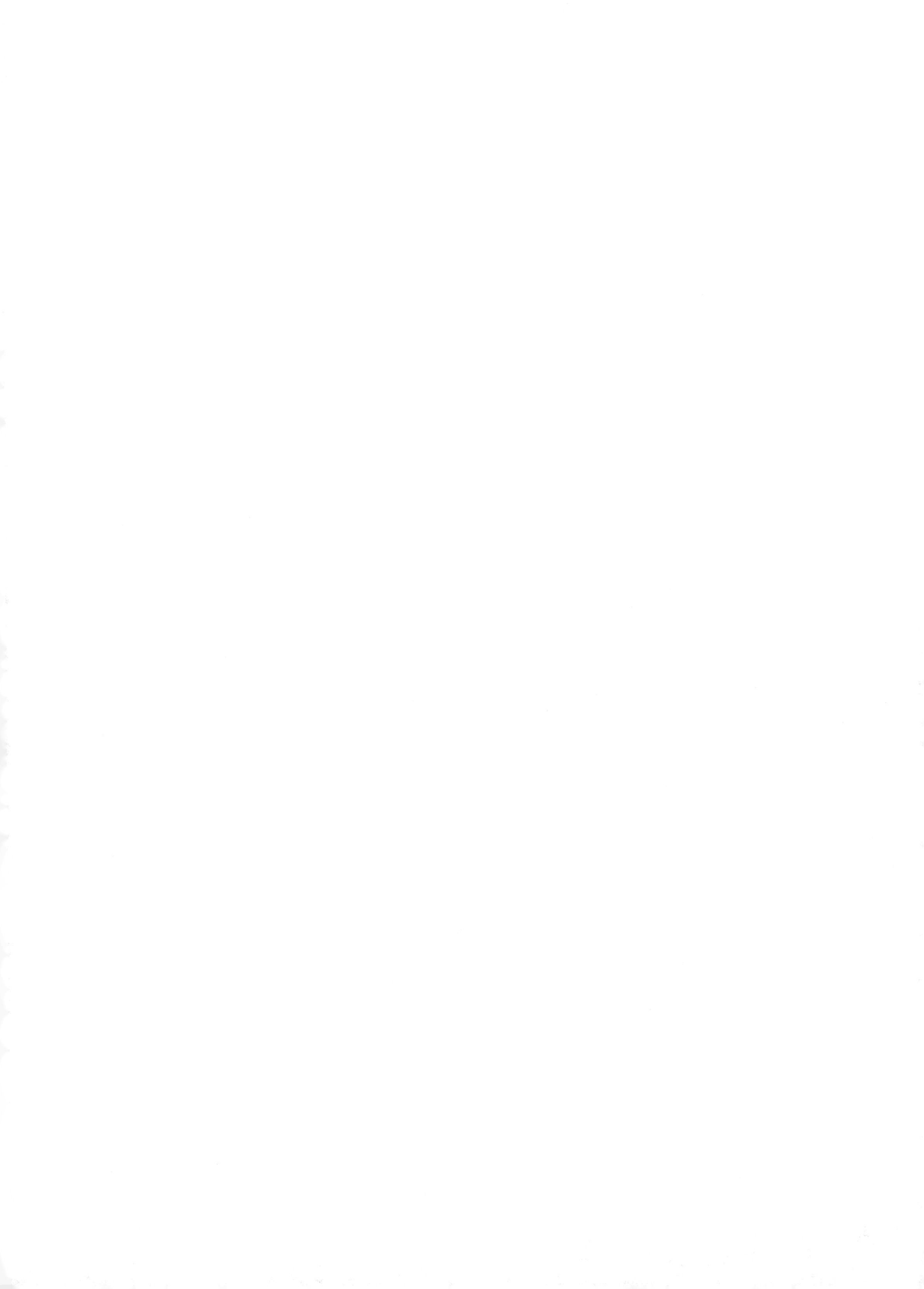